Business Ethics

Business Ethics

A European Approach

Edited by

Brian Harvey
Manchester Business School

Prentice Hall
New York   London   Toronto   Sydney   Tokyo   Singapore

First published 1994 by
Prentice Hall International (UK) Limited
Campus 400, Maylands Avenue
Hemel Hempstead
Hertfordshire, HP2 7EZ
A division of
Simon & Schuster International Group

Typeset in 10/12pt Sabon and Rockwell
by Hands Fotoset, Leicester

Printed and bound in Great Britain by
Redwood Books, Trowbridge, Wiltshire

Library of Congress Cataloging-in-Publication Data

Business ethics : a European approach / edited by Brian Harvey.
    p. cm.
  Includes bibliographical references and index.
   ISBN 0-13-095696-1
   1. Business ethics—Europe.   I. Harvey, Brian, M. A.
  HF5387.B868 1994
174'.4'094—dc20
                                      94–965
                                        CIP

British Library Cataloguing in Publication Data

A catalogue record for this book is available from
the British Library

ISBN 0-13-095696-1

1 2 3 4 5   98 97 96 95 94

Contents

v

Introduction

A challenging statement was made by a businessman at a recent conference. This is what he said:

> It strikes me that we in America understand little about what business is. Given that business and the free market have become the most dominant social force in this century, and presumably of the one to come, I realize that this is an odd observation. Yet most of us still do not understand how business works. I think our understanding of business — what it does, its effect on society, what makes for healthy commerce — is at about the level that medicine was before Louis Pasteur.

What is it about Paul Hawken's (1992) words that shocks or stimulates?

He is telling us that Americans don't understand what business is about. But isn't America where business as we know it was invented, where most of the economics Nobel Laureates in history have come from, as well as almost all the contemporary business gurus you can think of — Drucker, Peters and Waterman, Michael Porter and Rosabeth Moss-Kanter?

Surely, whether we own them, work in them or buy from them (even in Europe, let alone America), we have a clear idea of what the company or corporation is for — what its role, its responsibilities are. The job of the company is to produce goods and services efficiently and effectively:

- keeping its costs down by not wasting the resources it uses; and
- achieving the sales and revenues needed to reward its shareholders with dividends derived from profits made by responding effectively to demand.

In other words, as Calvin Coolidge said, 'the business of business is business'.

So, our experience and our common sense tell us the same story — surely we understand very well what business is? Why then are we struck by Hawken's statement? Is it the shock of the absurd? Or do we harbour doubts? Is there an insight, an element of truth in what he says? And do his words cause us to focus on the criticisms that are levelled at business? (Every one of us can readily think of recent cases of scandalous fraud or shocking disaster, or the names of long-established

1

pressure groups which keep particular issues permanently in and around the headlines.) Or does what Hawken says excite and inspire us to reflect on the unrealized potential and further evolution of our system of business and society? ('Environmentalists can agitate; governments can regulate; but only industry can innovate,' said the Chairman of Du Pont recently. And Anita Roddick has said that 'Consumers and companies, acting together, can change the world.')

Business and the market

The classical view of the market, as refined in the late nineteenth century, implies a technical role for the business enterprise. It is a 'black box' whose task is to implement decisions on how scarce resources are to be used. Each individual citizen has their own unique set of preferences, their list of wants, and so their own idea on how those limited resources should be used. Through the mechanism of the market, these millions of signals are transmitted and co-ordinated, and are finally converted into action by companies receiving these market signals.

Prices in the marketplace represent both the benefits to consumers of the goods and services they buy, and the necessary compensation to all those in any way involved in the production process. Thus, through the market, including of course the all-important factor of competition, companies are constrained and have a well-defined social purpose. There is no need to ask 'what is the company for?'

But today, we are well aware of the practical possibility of market failure. The market's 'decisions' on what to produce, how and where to produce it and on 'who gets what?', may be considered wrong by some – or even all – of us. This last case is now quite familiar to us in what we might call the 'age of the environment'. For example, rights of property are fundamental to the functioning of the market. Entrepreneurs buy or hire labour, capital, land and materials from their owners. But the air, a river or a stock of fish in the sea has the character of a common-property resource. It will tend to be used as if its use was costless, because that is how it appears to the individual user. It will be *mis*used.

Government intervention, like the proposed carbon tax, is an attempt to overcome market failure by modifying the price signals generated by the market. But the political processes involved in market intervention through taxation, subsidies or regulations are themselves, needless to say, not perfect either – whether within a nation-state, or in the even more complex international arena.

So, the apparently simple scenario painted by neo-classical economics is clearly a misrepresentation of how the world really works. We all know that – yet somehow we are reluctant to accept its implications for our view of the responsibilities of the company – and its managers. The classical model depersonalized company and management – in the iron grip of market forces they had no discretion, no room for manoeuvre. The strong attraction of this model can readily be understood. As a system it has a seductive simplicity, appearing to offer rational solutions to complex social problems by harnessing a presumed basic drive, i.e. self-interest – and all this through an automatically functioning mechanism which acts like a 'hidden hand'.

And for managers themselves, it is arguable that their acceptance of the conventional view of their powerlessness in the face of market and competitive forces is comforting. It may reduce stress, and the need for specifically managerial values and responsibilities.

It is against this background that we feel challenged by Paul Hawken's observation. There have been other times in European history when the managers of society's leading institutions have been reluctant to come to terms with new knowledge and insights into how the world works. Hawken's observations are hardly of Galilean or Copernican proportions, yet they arouse our curiosity, but at the same time we are nervous of where they might lead. Where will it all end? If, as practical managers grappling with the tangible day-to-day realities of competition and the market, we look further into Paul Hawken's speech we might well be nervous. He sums up by saying:

> Business has become, in the last century, the most powerful institution on the planet. The dominant institution in any society needs to take responsibility for the whole. Every decision that is made, every action taken has to be viewed in the light of that kind of responsibility. Business is the only mechanism on the planet today powerful enough to reverse global environmental and social degradation.

But, on the other hand, and to bring us back down to Earth, Paul Hawken's fellow American, Professor Milton Friedman – perhaps the most widely known Nobel Laureate in economics – has said that corporate social responsibility is a 'fundamentally subversive doctrine' in a free society.

Corporate responsibility

The use of the term 'corporate responsibility' to label the debate about the social role of, especially, large business enterprises, originated in the USA. In a democratic society, because of the scale of their impact, private companies came to be regarded as effectively public institutions – but without the same constitutional and democratic checks and balances. We began to read about the threat to corporate legitimacy, and the challenge of constitutionalizing the corporation. An American colleague has suggested that, with roots in the anti-Vietnam war and civil rights protests, the late 1960s saw the beginning of a period of mistrust of large corporations – of direct citizen challenge. Acting initially mainly through the legal channels open to shareholders, corporate activists were successful in politicizing the acts of consumption and investment. Most of us will remember Ralph Nader and Campaign GM on auto-safety.

In effect, another kind of market exists, and probably always has – a market for influence. It is populated today with pressure and interest groups of all sorts, a similar variety of regulatory bodies, and the corporations themselves. This market does not have the attractive simplicity and appeal of the classical market model – but it is real, and cannot be ignored. How should business respond? Given the powerful influence of the dominating market model, the natural response is to 'manage' the external environment of the firm in the interests of current profit performance and long-term survival and profitability. This has become known by the jargon expression 'corporate social responsiveness'. Effectively, it brings changing social demands and expectations into the fold of conventional business management and strategy – they are something else to be managed alongside finance, marketing, production and so on.

So, in our large companies, in corporate affairs or strategic planning departments we often find 'environmental scanning' taking place. A weather eye is kept on changing social and political, as well as technological, trends. Some of these issues will have a direct bearing on the industry concerned. In the case of 'green' issues, for example, knowledge of developing consumer interests and technological possibilities will influence a firm's product development. In this way, through the exercise of sound management as well as a sense of corporate social responsibility, business is part of the 'solution' as well as the 'problem'. In the case of social and political trends, public relations and community involvement programmes may be part of the corporate response – aimed at being acceptable corporate citizens.

Looking now to our own experience in Britain, it is probable that no one today will be taken by surprise by the idea of 'corporate social responsiveness'. Although we accept the market model, it is also now clear to us that the market is set in a particular social and political context – which changes, and for various reasons the well-managed firm must respond – essentially to match the needs and expectations and keep the goodwill of the different groups whose co-operation is needed.

Let us turn now to the concept of corporate responsibility with its wider implications for what business is for. The contemporary idea of corporate responsibility may have come to us a little later than in the States – and an American colleague who enquired into this some years ago offered several possible reasons for that. He mentioned (speaking specifically of Britain, although what he said could be applied more widely in Europe) the presence of a large element of public ownership in Europe; the acceptance and even encouragement by governments of mergers and industrial concentration; the well-established tradition here of government responsibility and intervention in a wide range of social and economic affairs; the historical pre-eminence of non-business elites in society, so that less was expected by way of corporate social leadership; and finally he attributed a role to a management style which he described as typically more informal and intuitive than in the USA.

On this last point, if he is accusing us of amateurism, then I'm sure we would all appeal against that judgement being allowed to stand in the 1980s and 1990s. But, more significantly, the last decade has seen substantial changes in the climate of British business. A period of radical Conservative government began with a strong re-assertion of the constructive social role of free enterprise, emphasizing the possibility of private, free market solutions to an increasing range of what were previously seen as public problems. This confident claim had the effect of increasing the social self-confidence of the business sector. And it has been accompanied by government encouragement for business to become involved in specific areas like education, the inner cities, job creation and the training of the unemployed. We can safely say that for our large firms at least, the concepts of corporate social involvement and investment are now well established.

This process of government leadership and corporate response – and we should add corporate initiative – plus the increased public awareness arising from well-publicized dramatic cases, have all contributed to the raised profile in the public mind of business behaviour and the responsibilities of the corporation – in effect to questions of right and wrong – namely business ethics.

Business ethics

The use of the term 'business ethics' is still not widespread in Britain, certainly not within the business community itself, although this is changing rapidly. But at the most senior levels in business, directors of some major companies have participated with government ministers in setting the tone of a debate about the proper conduct of business. For example, a recent Chancellor of the Exchequer, in a period of our economic history which the Japanese call 'the bubble economy', described a New Britain based on the acceptance of the basic human instinct of self-interest and the economic benefits of the market system, but at the same time he recognized the moral fears which some people may have. His personal belief, however, was that a society based on freedom is inherently stronger and healthier than one based on state coercion, and that self-interest need not lead to selfishness.

At the same time, the Director-General of the Institute of Directors emphasized the crucial moral role which business leaders need to play, not only bearing their responsibilities to stockholders, employees and customers, but also upholding the future of the free-market economy. He said:

> When a business leader brings that free economy into disrepute, he is committing a kind of treason which, in the end, may not only destroy his own reputation but also damage the lives and prospects of millions of other people.

We might react to statements of this sort in several ways. They are somewhat lofty sentiments, although quite appropriate to the positions occupied by their respective authors. In one sense they might have been said at any time, but we can also sense the particular economic circumstances, and political and business headlines of the moment. But although that moment, even so recent as it was, may have passed, business ethics will remain highlighted on our agenda for the foreseeable future. There are several reasons for this – of course ethics in business has always been present in the sense that the theory of the market has itself moral values embedded within it, and similarly so the conduct of everyday business. In Britain we have drawn attention to this moral underpinning by passionately championing the free enterprise system and, although it has become a cliché to say so, the extension of the market and free enterprise into eastern Europe has done so too. Secondly, whatever the fine points of argument about the appropriateness of expecting moral responsibility from the legal entities we call corporations, it is certain that moral responsibility will be ascribed to them by those affected by their operations – and this it seems is a rising tendency in our times. Thirdly, the laws which govern the conduct of business embody moral judgements, and the body of law develops over time – but with inevitable lags – so as responsible professional managers we cannot rely on the market and the law to guide our every step – and neither can those who might be affected by our actions. And even if the law did not take time to catch up with business practice, the legal mechanism itself is not always perfect – and we see today an interest in alternatives to the law. Self-regulation is an example, and is a process where ethics has an important part to play. Finally, in addition to the case where an industry is offered or adopts a self-regulatory alternative to legislation, individual businesses are interested in business ethics as an internal approach to controlling highly decentralized operations in complex, often multi-national environments.

Corporate strategists and planners are interested in the future business environment – the effects of ecological, social and cultural change and the implications for the successful conduct of business, including demands for corporate social responsibility and ethical business. And many others share this interest in the evolving social role of business, and specifically the subject of business ethics; among others these include professional managers, applied philosophers, Christian entre-preneurs, consumers, shareholders, MBA students – and economists. This is the direction from which my own interest in corporate responsibility and business ethics has come, from the 'edges' of the market system where markets and firms fail to perform in textbook fashion. The first focus for this interest was *Environment and Society* (Harvey and Hallett, 1977) which examined the 'everyday political-economic processes which determine the allocation of resources and the environmental problems which are the outcome of such choices'. Then a two-year research project centred on the corporation – the main arena where these socio-economic choices are made as firms interact with evolving social needs and expectations through the market. The fly-leaf of the resulting book gives a pithy account of the issues which concerned me then – the book was called *Managers and Corporate Social Policy: Private solutions to public problems?* (Harvey *et al.*, 1984)

> The central questions this study poses are: does corporate social responsibility exist in actual managerial practice? In addition to the pursuit of commercial goals, are firms involved in providing private solutions to public problems? How do managers perceive the role of their business enterprise in society? Do they feel capable of accepting social responsibilities at all – or some more than others? What is the motivation, both when managers are involved and when they are not? What are the implications of the authors' findings for any future extension of the role of business in the provision of private solutions?

After more than ten years, and in the light of the development of interest in corporate responsibility and business ethics outlined above, that fly-leaf statement seems almost naïve in the directness with which it puts the question 'Does corporate responsibility really exist?' – and today we might also include 'business ethics' in that query. In 1984 the book concluded that:

> The reassertion of the role of *private solutions to public problems* presents an acute dilemma for industrial management. . . . Typically treating the outside (social and political) environment like the weather, managers can feel relieved of some personal moral dilemmas, and espouse the ideology of free enterprise while remaining . . . fundamentally committed to . . . the relatively passive societal role which this implies for the firm. But if the current re-advocacy of *private solutions* is more than rhetorical, then the implicit contradictions in this situation will be highlighted. Without a coherent supporting philosophy, and with little practical guidance or experience, managers would need to become involved in new socially valuable activities. Their personal and political moralities would be tested, the ideological target of State involvement would recede and, in effect, another form of managerial revolution would have to take place.
> (pp. 148–9)

Now, ten years later, is the well-established interest in business ethics a part of such a 'revolution'? The aim of the present book is to offer a European perspective on the subject of business ethics by inviting academic specialists from several European countries to write on the main themes. The first two chapters focus on 'ethical resources' – the fundamental concepts and approaches which can be applied to business ethics; the next three chapters deal with ethical issues arising in the relations between business and three principal 'stakeholders' – employees, share-holders and customers; the following three chapters centre on the ethics of three more abstract, but important relationships – between business and regulation, community and environment; the final chapter reflects on the ethics of our system of markets and business itself – the 'ethics of capitalism'.

Henk van Luijk begins his chapter 'Business ethics: the field and its importance' with several short cases of ethical issues which have arisen in Dutch business – on moral versus contractual obligations; environmental responsibilities; labelling and redundancy policy. He refers to these examples as he defines ethical practice as a conscious appeal to norms and values to which we hold each other obliged as autonomous and entitled members of a 'moral community'. And in the case of *business* ethics this characteristically means weighing the various rights and interests which are at stake in particular circumstances. But how can such decisions be weighed? Professor van Luijk briefly reviews two basic approaches to an ethical dilemma – one appealing to results, benefits or utility, and the other to intrinsically valid principles. Business is about results, but the familiar cost-benefit analysis in business only considers the corporate interest, whereas a utilitarian moral approach includes the rights and interests of others.

Examples of moral reasoning are given in the case of product liability and international business relations. Product liability might be left to contract, but buyers and sellers are often not equals, so perhaps the producer should be reasonably expected to show 'due care' for the interests of the consumer, or even to be held responsible for any, even unforeseen, results of the product's use. That there is no right rule here is illustrated again when Tom Donaldson's 'ethical algorithm' is applied to international business.

Two recent attempts have been made to integrate the moral viewpoint and business practice. The first seeks to list *managerial virtues*, but Professor van Luijk prefers an approach via a *typology of business relations* – self-directed, other-including and other-directed – and he concentrates his discussion on *transactional ethics* because 'the regular exchange transactions and co-operative ventures [of business] require an adherence to the moral principles of equality, honesty and reciprocity'.

So, ethics is a necessary part of business, but Henk van Luijk concludes that more morality is possible in business 'in the sense of a participatory ethics, because social and political developments today open [new] ways to co-operative arrangements for the common good . . . the central question is not *why* be moral in the market, but *how*.'

'How to be ethical: ethics resource management' is the question taken up in Chapter 2 by Professor Jack Mahoney. *Codes of conduct* and the *law* are 'ethical resources', although they do not define what should count as ethical behaviour in business. *Religion* is also an ethical resource, and here principles and rules are defined – but the beliefs from which they are derived may not be shared by everyone. Turning to internal ethical resources, *conscience* and *virtue* are considered, directing our attention 'not just to questions about what is the ethical thing to do, but what it means to be an ethical sort of person'.

In a section he has called 'Thinking matters through' Professor Mahoney outlines and discusses three fundamental ideas in the history of ethics: *utilitarianism*, which looks to the effects of actions, and which 'may appeal particularly to active people, including men and women involved in business'; *duty and obedience to a moral law* 'which any rational person must accept' – what Kant called the Categorical Imperative; and what in the Middle Ages was termed 'natural law', a theory of moral law, based on acting always in accordance with human nature, which has become a powerful modern ethics resource in the form of the appeal to *universal human rights*.

Dr Jef van Gerwen approaches his subject, 'Employers' and employees' rights and duties', from the angle of the employees themselves, 'reflecting a long-standing tradition of European labour movements and legislation. In this respect European business ethics may differ somewhat from its American counterpart [where] . . . business ethics . . . shows a clear management bias when discussing labour issues.' He starts by listing the main rights and duties of employees and employers.

In comparison with the right to a minimum income, the *right to work* 'largely remains confined to the domain of moral principles and ideals', but in European society it is an 'emerging claim which is gaining gradual recognition'. It is a 'meta-right', entitling citizens to require that governments and firms together choose policies which will lead to the highest sustainable level of general employment, and in this form it is included in the Social Charter of the Council of Europe and corresponding national policies.

The chapter concludes by treating the ethics of hiring and firing, and also a range of specific rights of employees such as formal contract, just reward, workplace health and safety, quality of working life, the right to free association and to strike, and employee participation. Dr van Gerwen then illustrates with cases, and considers situations where conflicts arise such as preserving commercial confidentiality, 'whistleblowing', the right to personal privacy, and discrimination at work.

The perspective of Dr Guido Corbetta when dealing with the subject of 'Shareholders' is not the usual one of the responsibilities of managers towards shareholders, but the responsibilities of shareholders themselves. The most important of several reasons given why this has not been common in the past is that the study of business ethics has mainly originated and been developed in the Anglo-American business world, where firms are typically management-controlled. Shareholders here are primarily 'investors', whereas in the case of family businesses – common in Italy and other parts of Europe – the shareholders are also 'governors'. Dr Corbetta discusses the responsibilities of governor-shareholders (including the increasing tendency for large, institutional investors – even in economies dominated by management-controlled corporations – to adopt the role) and in particular the ethical issues which arise when governor-shareholders in the family business, or business empire, put their own interests before those of the company.

Rights of ownership, as in the case of a firm's capital, whose benefits derive from social co-operation, are termed 'conventional rights of ownership' and require the acknowledgement of the rights of other stakeholders.

Professor Kuhlmann begins his treatment of business ethics associated with relations with 'Customers' by highlighting the constitutional 'fiction' of the equilibrium of power in a social market economy and paralleling it with the relationship between buyer and seller. The response to this imbalance has been the development of consumer 'rights', from which can be derived duties of buyers and sellers. The potential for conflict between buyers and sellers is analysed using a 'green' labelling example, and cases are offered to illustrate conflicts in the areas of media advertising, product safety, pricing and terms of contract.

How are these conflicts to be resolved? Self-regulation on the part of the individual firm, and by an industry, are illustrated by the case of the Swiss retail association Migros, and the German Advertising Council. Public strategies of regulation include the growing area of 'soft law', as represented by the UK's Office of Fair Trading, and conventional consumer law. Also, public policy can achieve its intended effect by supporting the active consumer – through education and counselling. Professor Kuhlmann concludes that although conflict is an inherent part of the relationship between suppliers and consumers, shared ethical norms, combined with self-discipline, offer the most efficient way to balance the conflicts of interest, and, to the extent that this ideal is not reached, there must be resort to the less efficient solution represented by law and regulation.

In his chapter, 'Business, law and regulation', Professor Antonio Argandoña begins by justifying the moral duties imposed upon business by the state, and then deals with the ethical problems posed for firms by both business law and regulation:

as they try to . . . observe the law, but also to profit from it, avoid its charges, adapt themselves to the legal and regulatory environment, to change it (if possible), and use it as a shield or as a weapon.

By 'Business and community', Professor Luk Bouckaert means the interaction between business and other elements in the social system – family, education, politics and local culture. Community, state and market are three interpenetrating mechanisms of social co-ordination. So, the application to business of ethics, derived from the moral 'community', should not be seen as coming from 'outside' business; and similarly the firm itself can be seen simultaneously as a creature of the market, but also as the embodiment of a social contract defining the rights and duties of different 'stakeholders', and as a community sharing a common mission and value system. For the firm, this analysis implies a need to accept this 'post-modern' vision of society as a network of flexible and creative structures, to be sensitive to cultural differences, and to institutionalize its moral commitment.

Turning to business and the European Community, Professor Bouckaert argues that Europe is also an integrated market, political structure and cultural space. The rebuilding of Eastern Europe and the challenge of European integration will be the test case of European capability to find a new synthesis of business and community, in which process business itself must play its part in the search for shared transnational values.

Professor Erik Schokkaert and Johan Eyckmans address what they regard as 'the most difficult challenge facing the European business world today' – the 'Environment'. The facts of the state of the European environment, as presented in the EC's 1992 report, are summarized, and the chapter then starts by illustrating with cases the ethical dilemmas which present themselves to business. How, for example, is a pharmaceutical company to balance environmental values and not simply its own profits but also the social costs of higher prices for its product? Other examples include a Belgian case of industrial lead pollution, a Canadian hydro-electric development and the global problem of 'greenhouse' gases. The common thread is that these problems require a choice between different social values: the ethical problem cannot be confined within the four walls of the firm, but must be extended to the market economy itself. The concept of 'external environmental costs', by concentrating on the defects of the price system, 'suggests a concrete way of handling the problem within the structure of the market economy', and the Dutch software company BSO/Origins is given as an illustration of the calculation of external costs. This approach is contrasted with the contribution of environmental philosophies like *eco-centrism* and *sustainability*. Sustainability is judged to be an extremely useful idea which has 'centred the debate on the crucial questions of international and intergenerational justice. But, like many other general concepts, it remains too vague to be of much guidance in concrete situations of ethical dilemma'. Individual firms are thus unable to avoid the need for ethical deliberation and, however difficult, to engage in a process of 'ethical cost-benefit analysis'. Industry-wide initiatives, like the Responsible Care programme of the chemical industry, and business participation in the political debate are also necessary, for example to develop *voluntary covenants*. Inside the firm, environmental management, like Total Quality Management, will need to become an integral part of strategy, with similar requirements for monitoring and reporting.

Schokkaert and Eyckmans remind us of the 'burden of the past' by summarizing disastrous cases like Amoco Cadiz and Seveso, and move on to the international dimensions of finding solutions to environmental problems – burden-sharing between the industrialized and less developed countries; decision-making and co-ordination at the level of the European Community; and the re-integration of the Eastern European economies – in all of which business must play a constructive role. Business is part of the solution as well as the problem. This is illustrated in the concluding section of the chapter which surveys the growth of industries and companies, like the Belgian firm ECOVER, whose products, marketing and labelling are aimed at the growing 'green market'.

In the concluding chapter, Professor Peter Koslowski addresses 'The ethics of capitalism':

> A social philosophy of capitalism must have the same breadth of perspective as [its father] Adam Smith. It must guard against committing the . . . fallacy of believing that an economically efficient system already makes for a good or moral society and that the economy is the whole of society.

By taking goals and preferences as given, the moral problem of the choice of goals is reduced to an economic one, and 'ethics is replaced by economics'. In this, capitalism does not eliminate the problem of value, but puts the burden on the individual, and 'the ability to deceive oneself as to possible relevant aspects of [one's choices] is one of the characteristics of the immoral'.

'There is a certain irrational passion for dispassionate rationality in the economic theory of capitalism which bans any kind of moral motivation or thinking in terms of values,' says Professor Koslowski. Yet it has been shown that trust reduces transaction costs, and that ethics can substitute for direct control in large organizations. 'So, even the mechanistic model of . . . [the] market . . . shows the need for an ethics of capitalism and for evaluating and choosing between goals. It shows the necessity of . . . re-embedding business into ethical and social norms.'

References

Harvey, Brian and John D. Hallett (1977), *Environment and Society: An Introductory Analysis*. London: Macmillan; Cambridge, MA: MIT Press.

Harvey, Brian, Stephen Smith and Barry Wilkinson (1984), *Managers and Corporate Social Policy: Private Solutions to Public Problems*. London: Macmillan.

Hawken, Paul (1992), 'The ecology of commerce', *INC Magazine*, April.

CHAPTER 1

Business ethics: the field and its importance

Henk van Luijk
University of Nijenrode, The Netherlands

1.1   Some real-life cases

● An employee of Corporation X has been the victim of a serious traffic accident. His colleagues subsequently ask the Board of Directors to study the possibility of setting up a collective disability insurance, covering all the employees of the company. Should such a contract not be feasible, then each individual employee could contract his or her personal disability insurance. The Board agrees to find out what the possibilities are. Partly due to reorganization processes in the company, two years go by in which people on the administrative level 'are working on it'. Then one of the initiators of the idea falls seriously ill. As he has been waiting for the Board to come up with information and/or arrangements, he now is uninsured. Does Corporation X have a moral obligation to support the employee in this situation?

● A six-month-old Dutch child suffers from the lethal form of epidermiolysis bullosa, a hereditary skin disease, leading to sticking of fingers and toes, contractions of joints, and obstructions in the bronchial tubes and in the oesophagus – an agony. Children affected by the disease normally die within a few years. There is, as yet, no effective therapy. Sometimes, for a short period, some improvement is achieved by the use of corticosteroids. Up to now, the child in question has stayed most of his short life in hospital. The parents know about the poor prognosis. They then hear about an expert in Spain, a biochemist from Eastern Europe, who runs a clinic for, among others, epidermiolysis patients. They go and see him. The expert treats the child with ointments and a diet. After two weeks, some slight improvements seem noticeable. However, costs are high: $300 a day for a stay in the clinic, $500 a month for the ointments, plus travel expenses to and from Spain. The parents pay the first costs from their savings, but, once back in Holland, they apply to their insurance company. The treatment is not covered by their contract; the expert is, under Dutch law, not authorized to treat patients; and the improvements, while spectacular, are, according to specialists, probably temporary. But the physician looking after the child at home, as well as the association of parents of epidermiolysis

12

patients, are strongly in favour of continuing the treatment. What should the insurance company decide?

● For many years, Albert Heijn, the major Dutch retailer, has been selling potatoes of the variety called 'Bintje', and so have competing supermarkets and special food stores. Bintje is the most popular potato in Holland with, as a consequence, the highest turnover in the potato business. It is also the potato with the highest percentage of profit per hectare, which is why the consumer's price can be kept relatively low. Albert Heijn, a market leader in many respects, is well known as an innovative retailer who tries to play a responsible role in the field of environmental practices, by banning sprays that contain CFCs and packaging made with PVC, for example. Its recently retired third-generation CEO, named again Albert Heijn after his grandfather, in 1992 received an honorary doctorate from Nijenrode University, The Netherlands Business School, in recognition of his distinguished career as a business leader and an innovator in modern retailing. Now the news is spreading that, in growing the Bintje potato, a relatively large amount of pesticides is used that negatively influences the environment and the quality of the ground water. Alternative varieties of potatoes are available. What is Albert Heijn to do?

● Gist-Brocades, one of the major Dutch pharmaceutical companies, has worked for years to develop the enzyme chymosine. By using recombinant DNA technology this enzyme, that traditionally is isolated from the stomach of newborn calves, can now be produced in the laboratory. Chymosine is used in the production process of cheese, to make the milk coagulate. In various countries the product is already for sale. In The Netherlands a registration procedure is still under way. Recently a major consumers association has stipulated that products prepared with the new enzyme should have a label saying something like: 'For this product use is made of a preparation obtained by applying genetic manipulation'. Gist-Brocades does not itself produce the consumer products, it supplies the cheese producers with the chymosine enzyme. Should the corporation comply with the request of the consumers organization?

● In 1988 Fokker Aircraft, as a consequence of a continuing low dollar rate, had to economize in various ways, including reducing the number of employees. The reduction was to be brought about by natural wastage; a stop on recruitment; voluntary early retirement for all employees between 57 and 60 years of age, on equal conditions as those valid for employees over 60; and by forced lay-offs. In total 800 jobs had to disappear, out of which 400 would be forced lay-offs, this on the condition that all employees between 57 and 60 would agree to accept early retirement. Each refusal on their part would cause another forced lay-off of a younger colleague, on top of the 400 already foreseen. In fact, a substantial number of the employees involved refused to co-operate with the proposed arrangement. This raised several questions: Are these employees morally obliged to withdraw voluntarily in order to protect their younger colleagues? Is the company morally entitled to confront their employees with such a dilemma, and to make the number of forced lay-offs dependent on the willingness of elderly people to show solidarity with those threatened by an operation they were not able to influence?[1]

So much seems clear: people in business regularly face dilemmas and tough choices, if not patently of a moral nature, then at least showing some serious moral implications. But what do we mean by *moral* dilemmas and *moral* implications? What do we mean by 'ethics' in the first place?

1.2   Definition of ethics

In common understanding, 'ethics' stands for a *practice* as well as for a *reflection* on that practice. As a practice, ethics can be described as the conscious appeal to norms and values to which, on reasonable grounds, we hold ourselves obliged, as, reciprocally, we hold others obliged to the same norms and values. As a reflection, ethics is the methodical and systematic elaboration of the norms and values we appeal to in our daily activities. Where these activities are organized around business issues, we face ethics in the practical and reflective variety of business ethics.

As a discipline, ethics presents itself as a science of a specific nature, namely as a *normative* science. In a normative science, the emphasis is not primarily on *what is the case*, how a given situation came about and how it can be influenced, but on *what ought to be done or ought not to be done*. The question is not whether the contract between the insurance company and the parents of the child suffering from epidermiolysis bullosa implies the reimbursement of the costs of the special treatment. It does not, as everybody acknowledges. Business ethics asks whether, nevertheless, there are good reasons why, in this specific case, the insurance company should accept some kind of obligation to make the treatment possible, or whether, by assuming such an obligation, we are stretching the realm of moral duties just a bit too far.

Ethics is not the only normative science we are familiar with. Legal, political science and medical experts too come up with normative statements, telling us how to behave and what kind of behaviour to avoid. In so doing, they refer, implicitly or explicitly, to a commonly accepted system of legal standards and principles, to political objectives and ideals shared by at least a fair amount of people, or simply to the basic right of every human being to a reasonable pattern of health-care arrangements. But what exactly are the norms and values ethics is referring to?

The question here is not about the general nature of norms and values, for there is not much discussion on that level. 'Norms', so sociologists teach us, are collective expectations regarding a certain type of behaviour. 'Brush your teeth twice a day' and 'keep your promises' are barely disputed norms. And 'values' are collective representations of what constitutes a good life or a good society. 'Health' is a value, and 'self-respect', and so are 'democracy', 'tolerance' and 'freedom'. The point is, however, that, today, in Western society, norms and values seem to be less stable than they happened to be before. It is a common experience that our era is characterized, even increasingly so, by a pluralism of values and by shifting patterns of norms. The situation should not be exaggerated. Not everything goes, and not all our norms are shifting simultaneously. But people nowadays are accustomed to the fact that, to a certain extent, they have to shape – sometimes even to invent – their norms and values for themselves. Not necessarily *all* by themselves, as isolated individuals – there are groups of significant others to which to apply for moral support. Nor have standards to be constructed from scratch, for, at a basic level, people share moral insights and convictions of a global and yet fairly distinctive nature. Actually, these insights decreasingly stem from religious sources. Few of the elder Fokker employees will feel obliged to a Christian conception of solidarity, telling them to sacrifice their place in the plant on behalf of younger colleagues. The odds are that they feel more prone to stick to the modern humanistic ideal of every man's freedom of choice, refusing, therefore, to be forced to opt for either their job or their self-esteem. And many a person, not only outside but also inside the Albert Heijn retailing organization, will consider the environmental impact of the Bintje potato a point of major concern.

Ethics is about norms and values of a certain seriousness, about standards and ideals, i.e. ones that people cannot easily neglect without harming others, or without being looked at disdainfully by significant others. Ethics is not about brushing your teeth. But it certainly is about keeping your promises, respecting sentient beings, and distributing benefits and burdens in a fair and equitable way. People feel obliged to obey, roughly at least, the rules of morals, partly because they are expected to do so by a forceful moral community, partly because they are entitled to expect others to behave in similar ways, and partly because they acknowledge their status as an autonomous person to imply not only freedom but also responsibility. The *specific content* of moral rules obtaining in a given situation often is a matter of discussion between sensible 'stakeholders'. Quite regularly it is the outcome of a reasonable compromise. In exceptional cases it is a matter of an autonomous decision based on conscience and on one's personal convictions.

Norms and values, reasonableness, moral community, equity and reciprocity, obligation, and responsibility are core concepts in ethical practice as well as in ethical reflection. What does this imply for ethics in *business*?

1.3   Domains of ethics in business

In the production of the enzyme chymosine, Gist-Brocades is operating in perfect accordance with Dutch law and with the specific regulations regarding genetic interventions. Yet, in the public estimation, genetic interventions – let alone 'genetic manipulations' – are easily associated with uneasy feelings of risk and threat. A label on a product, announcing that it has been prepared 'by using genetic manipulation', is the surest way to prevent it from being sold to whomsoever. Therefore, the requirement put forward by the consumers association will have a serious impact on the interests of Gist-Brocades and of the cheese producers using its product. This raises the question to what extent a private organization is entitled to require another private organization to behave according to moral standards the first group considers to be valid, if not generally, then at least under the given circumstances. The consumers association presents itself as the representative of the generalized consumers and as defender of the right to safe products. Is this sufficient to grant the association a moral authority that Gist-Brocades and its clients have to recognize unconditionally, notwithstanding their legitimate economic interests at stake? It seems hardly plausible.

The Board of Directors of Corporation X agreed to study the possibility of setting up a collective disability insurance arrangement, and in so doing accepted a commitment to start research in due course, and to implement the arrangement once its conditions would appear to be suitable. But as long as a collective arrangement has not been brought about, individual employees may be expected not to take unnecessary risks with regard to their health insurances. In the case in question, both parties have been lacking in assiduity. Now that the consequences appear to be far-reaching for the employee, does this imply a moral duty for the company to come to his aid? Or is this a matter of decency more than of moral obligation?

On innumerable occasions, people in business are facing ethical questions in which a balance has to be found between the different and often conflicting rights and interests of the parties involved. One may even say that the weighing of rights and interests, at stake in determinate circumstances, constitutes the common domain of business ethics.

1.4   The common domain of business ethics

Many business practitioners and ethicists alike show a clear competence in handling moral dilemmas. Experience and reflection have taught them how to spot the ethical implications of a given situation, and how to approach them in an orderly way. To track moral elements adequately, one has to take what is called 'the moral point of view'. This means that one tries to determine the specific interests and rights of *all parties involved*. In fact, taking the moral point of view is the first *moral* decision one makes in a process of forming a moral judgement. For how moral one's point of view is depends on how far one is prepared to extend the circle of those individuals and groups that can legitimately claim that their rights and interests too be taken into account. In the case of the child suffering from epidermiolysis bullosa, the parties concerned are not only the child and his parents on the one hand and their insurance company on the other. Involved here are *all* children suffering from the same *or a similar* disease, and involved – albeit in an indirect way – are *all* insurance companies facing lethal illnesses of clients that they, willingly or inadvertently, have excluded from their policies. If equity is a basic moral concept, one cannot accept a moral obligation in one case, and reject it in another that, in all relevant respects, is similar to the first.

It is one thing to determine what the moral core issue is, or what the two or three possible core issues are, in a given situation. Once the core issue has been identified, however, it is another thing to come up with a well-argued position – to give good reasons, that is, for a moral preference in the case. Here the real hard work of ethical analysis takes place, preferably as a joint effort of all those who are in a position to influence the decision, and with the support of some ethical expertise if deemed helpful. It is, however, not easy to predict the outcome of a serious moral discussion. Too much depends on the convincing power of the viewpoints actually brought forward, and on whether the discussants succeed in reaching a consensus or at least a compromise, strong enough to satisfy sufficiently the rights, needs and interests of all parties involved. It is relatively easy, however, to discover a common structure in most moral arguments.

Faced with a moral dilemma, in business relations or elsewhere, people first look for some commonly accepted general principles, fit to be applied in the case under scrutiny, and then try to show that the principles effectively fit the situation – or, more precisely, in what way they do and to what extent. 'One should not attempt to get rid of a responsibility one can reasonably be expected to bear', sounds like a sensible general rule of conduct. So the management of a company should not pass on a lay-off decision to people who are not regularly in a decision-making position. Similarly, the principle of non-discrimination requires equal pay for equal work, so how could one justify a practice in which women are paid less for equal or comparable work? The principle is clear, and so is the action rule proceeding from it. Then let us apply these, as they seem perfectly suited for the case at hand.

The application of the principle or rule to a particular case does not always run smoothly, however. Often there is a gap to bridge, because the general wording of the principle proves not to be adequate to the special conditions of the case. It is a well-respected rule that one should speak the truth to everybody who is entitled to it. But does this imply that, when engaged in a negotiation process, one is not allowed to temporize the transmission of relevant information? When the information one possesses is part of the transaction, the *general* standards about truth-telling may prove to be inadequate.

One way of handling problems occurring in the application of a general principle to a particular situation can be described as *case variance*. To find out if, and if so to what extent, a given principle is applicable in a specific case, one varies slightly the conditions of the case by comparing it to strikingly similar, yet not identical, instances. In so doing one may succeed in determining the margins in between which the rule is valid under the given circumstances. Freedom of religion is a basic human right, included in the Universal Declaration of Human Rights proclaimed by the United Nations in 1948. Consequently, everybody is supposed to stick to the rule, deriving from this special right, that one should not intentionally hurt somebody else's religious feelings. But does this rule imply that it is morally unacceptable to organize a commercial pop-concert in a church building? And does it make a difference if the concert is organized for charity, or if it is going to be a Bach concert on authentic instruments, conducted by Gustav Leonardt, instead of a pop-happening featuring Tina Turner? It is not certain that, varying the case conditions this way, one will arrive at an indisputable conclusion. But at least one stays very close to the specific circumstances. And that is a major preliminary condition for reaching a defensible standpoint.[2]

1.5 Two ways of approaching an ethical dilemma

People in business, once they have acknowledged a certain moral responsibility towards their stakeholders, often succeed in developing a plausible moral stance in a situation of legitimate but conflicting rights and interests. They refer to some well-founded principles, and subsequently apply them, as far as possible, to the given dilemma.

Ethicists here distinguish between *two types of approaches*. The first one is *result-oriented*. It is, in fact, guided by only one principle, known as the principle of *utility or welfare maximization*. It says: 'it is our moral duty to choose *that* alternative action which, in its results, contributes most to the aggregated welfare of all those concerned'. It is also called *the greatest happiness for the greatest number* principle, or the *utilitarian* principle, because it stresses the happiness or utility generated by the chosen action. The utilitarian approach to a moral dilemma has several strong elements. It is democratic, considering equally the interests of all individuals and groups involved. It is practical, by making empirical calculations of the expected effects of an action. It is prospective, comparing possible alternatives and opting for the most effective one. And it has the charm of a single-principle approach. The principle is clear: overall welfare maximization as a moral duty. We only have to implement it under the given circumstances. Here, however, two difficulties arise, one practical and one basic.

The *practical* difficulty is: how to measure happiness and overall welfare? Does the availability of an inexpensive and tasty potato counterbalance the loss in environmental quality caused by the way the potato is grown? Is reluctantly finishing a career at the age of 57 less irksome than being laid off at 37? Is there any common measure enabling us to compare and to decide in cases like this? We often assume there is. Using a cluster of criteria we then accept as morally justified the rule, for example, that, given the scarcity of surgical equipment, the restricted life expectancies and the excessively high costs, mentally retarded people over 55 are put prohibitively low on the waiting list for open heart surgery or intensive care. At the same time we acknowledge that those decisions are not easy to make, partly based as they are on intuition and gut-feelings, and that they are therefore open to criticism and alternative preferences.

There is also a *basic* problem connected with utilitarian approach. One can easily imagine a situation in which it is very profitable for the majority to sacrifice the equal share, the welfare – if not the health and life – of one or a few out of the total population, if their welfare is considered to be of comparatively minor weight. In such a case, the utilitarian approach would tell us to promote the overall welfare by sacrificing somebody's private advantages. And so we accept additional soil pollution for the overwhelming benefit of a cheap potato. Rightly so? It does not really sound convincing. And, above all, we should realize that often more than just potatoes are at stake. There is an old Talmudic saying: 'When the enemy besieges your city, and requires the extradition of one of the citizens whomsoever – otherwise the city will be devastated, all male inhabitants killed and all women and children deported – then nobody may be handed over to the enemy. For it is better that all suffer than that injustice is done to one single person.' The disturbing thing is that the saying continues: 'When, however, the enemy, besieging your city, requires the extradition of a specific person, by name, then the Rabbi has to go to this person, tell him what the rules are, and hand him over to the enemy. For it is better that one dies for the people than that all are given into the hands of the enemy.'

This shows in a precise way the two sides of a moral approach that is *principle-oriented* instead of *result-oriented*. In a principle-oriented approach the basic guideline says: 'it is our moral duty to choose that course of action that is in accordance with an intrinsically valid principle, rule or right, regardless of the consequences'. An intrinsically valid principle indicates an end-state of affairs that is valued for its own sake, be it a fundamental human right, a basic rule of conduct that everybody in our culture, if not every human being, is expected to respect, or some other common standard of decent moral behaviour. The right to live is a fundamental human right; justice done to all people is a basic rule of conduct. Therefore, the life of no single arbitrarily chosen person in the besieged city may be sacrificed on behalf of others, for all can equally claim the fundamental right to live. A principle-oriented moral judgement is based upon the conviction that, in the normal course of events, no consequences are weighty enough to justify the neglect of the principle or rule at stake. In very exceptional circumstances, however, where the price to be paid for sticking to the principle is unreasonably heavy, one may deviate from the principle in view of a higher good. It is an excessively high price to be paid for defending the principle that everybody's life deserves protection if, as a consequence, all are going to die, the person sought by the enemy not excluded.

The appeal to a higher good is, of course, a typically utilitarian approach. Does this mean that, at the end of the day, it is always the result-oriented way of deciding that is decisive? Not necessarily. The two approaches encompass each other. The principle-oriented view enables us to draw clear lines: 'This is what we stand for, here is a limit we do not want to transgress. Sexual harassment is not accepted in this company. You do it, and you're out.' To stand by unambiguous principles can give someone a firm moral hold and yield her a well-deserved respect from others. The principle-oriented view also helps to make clear that, in a utilitarian, result-oriented approach, more things need to be counted and weighed than just costs and benefits. Honour, justice and rights should be allowed to play a major role as well, especially in cases in which specific individuals or vulnerable or unfortunate groups are involved, or where cherished social ideals are at stake that we should not inadvertently put at risk. Conversely, the result-oriented approach can be very effective where the interests and rights of large anonymous groups have to be balanced, or where definite alternatives present themselves. The approach can also serve to prevent principle-oriented decisions from becoming too rigid.

Both methods stem from venerable ethical traditions; both are deeply rooted in Western moral history. They both deserve to get full credit and to be applied simultaneously where possible, cautiously where they threaten to stand in each other's way. Undoubtedly, however, there is, in business practices, a propensity to use the result-oriented type of argument. Several reasons can be given for this seemingly natural preference – none of them totally convincing, however. One reason is the familiarity with cost/benefit analysis in business: isn't that exactly what a moral result-oriented approach is practising also? No, it isn't. For a cost/benefit analysis only takes into account the interests of the analysing party – the entrepreneur, firm, or corporation – whereas a utilitarian approach takes a *moral* point of view, including the rights and interests of *all* parties involved. As a second reason it sometimes is said that, to business ears, the principle-oriented way of arguing sounds a bit too 'principled', too 'moral', too removed from the common business discourse that is about down-to-earth things like market share, continuity and quarterly reports. That is correct – that is exactly how it sounds. That is no reason, however, to restrict the principle-oriented idiom to the President's address on Christmas Eve. Openness to values, rights and principles is a lively expression of the fact that there are more things in heaven and earth than are shown on your spread-sheet.

1.6   The practice of ethical analysis in business

In the next chapter various ethical management resources, including appeals to utility and duty but also to human rights, will be discussed more extensively. Here I indicate how, in practice, the use of fairly general moral principles can clarify specific elements of business behaviour. I give two examples, one related to the field of product liability, the other to business transactions with customers in foreign countries, where the issue may arise whether the saying 'when in Rome do as the Romans do' seems a sound moral action guide. The examples may make clear what are the merits – and the limits – of the classical approach to moral dilemmas in business.

With regard to product quality and moral product liability, three theoretical positions have been developed in recent business ethics writings.[3] The first position is called the *contract theory* of product responsibility. It says, in brief: seller and buyer, or producer and consumer, do have with each other a *contractual relation*, at least implicitly. According to generally accepted norms regarding contracts, the buyer should pay her dues promptly and fully. The seller, for his part, should guarantee the express or implied qualities of the product. He furthermore has a duty to disclose relevant information, a duty not to misrepresent the nature of the commodity or service, and a duty not to coerce his contract partner. These are all requirements to warrant the buyer's free and well-informed choice, which is a necessary condition for a valid contract. Once these conditions are fulfilled, moral obligations of both participants in the contract are considered to be in balance. From then onward, it is up to the buyer to beware.

The contract theory has some difficulties, however. Often the distance between producer and consumer is so vast that one can hardly speak of a *contract* between two parties, not even in a faint, implicit sense. There rather is an asymmetry to be noticed in the relation at stake, leading to a second moral view, called the *due care theory*. Consumers and producers in fact do not meet as equals. The consumer's interests are, in a non-reciprocal way, vulnerable to being harmed by the manufacturer. This entitles her to a *due care* from the side of the producer, over and above the obligation the latter has already accepted on the basis of their assumed contract. The exercise of due care implies that the seller must take adequate steps to prevent whatever injurious effect he can foresee that the use of his product or service may have on the consumer. Implied in this view is a weak version of the dictum 'Let the *seller* beware', based on the vulnerable position of the buyer. The question remains, however, how far due care is supposed to extend itself.

Indefinitely far, says a third theory, called the *social cost theory*. Even after the producer has given all reasonable due care to the design, the production process and the information regarding his product, and after he has taken all possible precautions, he still remains responsible for every damaging effect, be it caused by negligence, stupidity or recklessness. The lady who dries her shampooed poodle in the microwave and after a while finds a very dry but very dead poodle, is entitled to hold the producer of the microwave responsible for her sad experience. The theory is based upon a strict utilitarian argument. If *all* costs connected with the use of the product or service weigh on the producer, forcing him to include these costs in his final price, it soon becomes obvious whether he still wants to produce it and whether the buyer is still inclined to buy. This will lead to a more efficient use of natural resources, which is socially preferable. We face here a strong version of 'Let the seller beware'. The problem here is, of course, that a clear unfairness is part of the arrangement, the seller being saddled with all costs, whatever their origin, and so excluded from a fair market share.

Two remarks need to be made here. First, the principles used in these theories are, indeed, of a fairly general nature. This does not prevent them from being applied in specific circumstances, though. Often, however, the transition from a general principle to a particular decision remains unclarified: sometimes because further clarification is not needed, people feeling perfectly at ease with the unencumbered subsumption of the case under a general rule or standard; sometimes, however, the application is made in an unreflective, intuitive way, as a barely calculated guess. Obviously, such a transition does not strengthen the argument. Second, there is no way to decide, in the abstract, which of the three theories is the more valuable. It all depends on the product, the service, and the relation between seller and buyer. There is no one 'right' theory in these matters.

A second example of how specific issues may be clarified by fairly general moral principles is taken from the realm of international business relations. A recurring problem there is related to the question of to what extent the saying 'When in Rome, do as the Romans do' can be taken to be a solid action guide. Countries differ in the standards they apply with regard to safe labour conditions, wage levels, environmental or pharmaceutical regulations, different positions ascribed to women and to men on the basis of deeply engrained cultural reasons, low-level nepotism, the age at which people – sometimes children – enter the labour market, and 'facilitating payments' offered to officials or customers. Often standards in non-Western countries seem, or really are, lower than we are accustomed to in highly industrialized nations. The question then arises whether, being over there, one is allowed to adhere to the lower local norms, or whether one has to stick to the standards one is bound to in one's home country. In this context, Thomas Donaldson has developed what he calls 'an ethical algorithm', providing us with a yardstick in tricky circumstances.[4]

His proposal runs as follows. First, one has to ask whether the moral reasons underlying the host country's view that a certain practice is permissible, refer to that country's relative level of economic development or, on the contrary, are independent of that level. A Muslim custom prohibiting women to acquire managerial positions in which they would have command over men most probably is not linked to the level of economic development, whereas a low standard regarding air or water pollution in a region on its way to industrialization very often is. Where lower standards are effectively connected to the local level of economic development, then, the algorithm says, the practice – for example of making use of the less demanding environmental regulations – is morally *not* permissible if the members of the home country would *not*, under imaginary home conditions of economic development relevantly similar to those of the host country, regard the practice as permissible. In the case, however, where the lower standards are independent of the level of economic development, two new questions should be raised: first, is it possible to conduct business in the host country while not adhering to the standards that are unacceptable in your home country? And second, does the practice imply a violation of a fundamental human right? If to both questions the answer is negative – it is not possible to conduct business otherwise, and no fundamental human right is involved – then the practice can be considered morally permissible, although the company, while conforming itself to the local standards, keeps a certain obligation to raise its voice in protest. If, however, one of the two questions is answered affirmatively, then the practice must be considered morally impermissible.

Two things deserve special attention with regard to this ethical algorithm. First, it is obvious that a serious attempt is made to do justice to the specific circumstances in which a given moral rule is considered to obtain. The level of economic development and certain deeply rooted cultural rules may not be ultimately decisive from a moral point of view but, nevertheless, deserve to be taken into account thoroughly, whenever we try to form a balanced moral judgement based on sound principles and considered to be appropriate under the circumstances. Second, at the end of the day, it appears that, if in the process of forming a moral judgement anything is decisive, it is the givenness of certain fundamental rights and principles. Where the level of economic development is not at stake, the core question is whether any fundamental rights are violated by adhering to lower local standards. And when, in fact, economic development is an accompanying factor, then the answer whether one should conform oneself to local standards is again linked to basic principles people in the home country feel obliged to uphold. A balance is sought between fundamental moral principles and specific circumstances, but the primary guidelines have to be found on the side of the principles.

We face here a well-known style of ethical thinking. Once the basic principles have been elaborated, one tries to get as close as possible to the particular conditions in order to find out how the principles should be applied under the given circumstances. It is a classical way of approaching moral dilemmas. Ethicists are very fond of this approach, ordinary people are not always, and business people seldom are.

To emphasize the primacy of moral principles gives the impression that other principles of action are all of a secondary nature. Giving primacy to morals risks degrading the legitimacy of motives and intentions which are not commonly qualified as overtly moral but which enjoy a clear acceptability, if not respectability, none the less. Especially in the market the motive of making profit, and the intention to set up, together with others, co-operative ventures for mutual benefit play a central role. If then the impression arises that 'a moral point of view' implies that market transactions are approached from the outside, with a set of prefabricated principles presented as valid under whatever circumstances, business people soon complain that insufficient attention is given to the specificities of their working conditions. Not infrequently the effect is a vague sense of mutual irritation.

Two attempts have been made recently to overcome this uneasy and unpromising relation between business and ethics. One stresses the attitudinal aspects of business behaviour by developing a conception of *'managerial virtues'*, the other elaborates the contours of a *market morality* by distinguishing different action patterns according to the various possible relations between actors, and subsequently connects specific moral principles to the types of action distinguished this way. Both seek to do justice to the moral implications of business as a distinct social practice.

1.7 Managerial virtues

The language of virtues belongs to the classical ethical discourse. One of the great ethical traditions, Aristotelian ethics, is known to be a 'virtue ethics'. Since those early days the concept of virtues was never totally absent from Western ethical thinking, albeit that emphases were distributed differently in different periods. For about two decades, this century's ethics has shown a revival in virtue ethics.[5] In order to fill the gap between concrete practices and general moral principles, ethicists have reintroduced the concept of virtue to describe attitudes that are appropriate whenever moral excellence within a given community is sought. As a matter of fact, virtue, especially in its Aristotelian sense, stands for the qualities of character that make a community member fit to function to an excellent degree within the social fabric. Virtue is as much a communitarian as it is a personal concept. A virtuous person is an excelling community man or woman.

The advantage of the concept of virtue is that morality is conceived as a pattern of attitudes and behaviour expressing the basic commitments of clearly defined groups or communities. A theory of virtues is a theory of distinct and highly respected social practices. The distance often felt between general moral principles and everyday life is overcome as soon as we succeed in elaborating the outlines of the morality that accompanies particular social roles and communities. Just as people find their basic identity by appropriating the mental and emotional capacities their social environment places at their disposal, so do they find their *moral identity* and their own pattern of virtues by adjusting themselves to the moral impulses and expectations their social group or network has to offer them.

It is worth considering whether there is a specific pattern of virtues that characterizes managerial roles and performances. For, once we are able to outline a set of managerial virtues, we will have found a direct access to ethics in business. To behave morally in business will then be equal to acting in accordance with well-defined managerial virtues.

Robert C. Solomon thinks it is possible to elaborate such a cluster of specific business virtues. In a recent study he first of all places himself on plain Aristotelian grounds[6] by stressing the communitarian character of all virtues. He then describes business as a *practice*, in the sense in which MacIntyre uses this term, namely as a social activity based upon a common understanding of goals that deserve to be pursued, and upon a common acceptance of quality standards: 'To say that business is a practice is to say that it is not only a social activity with (at least) several participants but that it has goals and rules and boundaries and a purpose.'[7] Having stated as the basic purpose of business not just 'making a profit' but 'doing well' – fostering welfare, that is, by providing desired services, and, by doing so, making life more enjoyable – he then presents what he considers to be the 'basic business virtues', and he lists them accordingly. The virtues that suit best the proper nature of business transactions and business relations are: honesty, fairness, trust and toughness. To these he adds 'the virtues of the corporate self': friendliness, honour, loyalty and shame. On top of that, in every corporation *caring* constitutes a fundamental attitude, and so does *compassion*. The ultimate virtue of corporate life, however, is *justice*, the fact and perception that all members of the organization and everyone connected with it is 'getting their due'.

There is always a certain amount of arbitrariness involved in the elaboration of such a table of virtues. Plausible as the given list may sound, discussion remains possible about why, for example, toughness is included and no mention is made of *solidarity* with the unfortunate or *stewardship* regarding the environment. On second thoughts, the table looks more or less like the successful American businessman describing his better self. The approach, nevertheless, has a very refreshing touch because it tries to elicit substantial moral insights from a descriptive analysis of real-life business practices. The danger of moral standards coming out of the blue is, to a large extent, avoided. And that is largely new in business ethics.

Two objections can be raised, however, against this attempt to renew the domain of business ethics by reintroducing the concept of business virtues. First, the attempt remains to a very large extent tributary to the Aristotelian version of virtue ethics. Business is conceived as a coherent social practice with well-defined purposes and clear rules. And virtue is seen as the expression and seal of an outstanding community membership. Both conceptions deserve modifications, to say the least. For business activities are moved forward by a host of motives and intentions, not all of them suited to be subsumed under the general purpose of 'doing well' in the sense described above. And businessmen do not conceive themselves first and foremost as members of a community that invokes them to behave according to the standards of excellence valid within this specific community. The texture of business relations is much more open than here suggested.

The second objection points in the same direction. The picture of business virtues is undoubtedly appealing to the already virtuous. The questions remain, however, *how* to join them, and *why* businessmen, under all circumstances, should operate on such a highly virtuous level. If we really want to depict morality as a basic quality of business activities in all their legitimate varieties, our picture must be sensibly more balanced than the one that can be attained by drawing up a relatively short table of business virtues.

1.8   Varieties of business morality

To get hold of the action patterns and their moral qualities that are characteristic of relations in business it may help to sketch the outlines of some basic action types and see how such a typology can clarify the nature and moral content of business activities. I first present three basic action types. Business being essentially a domain in which several people and groups are active at one and the same time, I then ask how, in each of these action patterns, the rights and interests of others are involved. In this way we will discover some basic moral principles inherent in each of the action types. Specifying our findings with regard to business situations, we may be able to acquire a fairly balanced view on varieties of business morality.[8]

Basically, human actions can take three different directions: they can be self-directed, other-including or other-directed. A *self-directed* action is one that intends the actor and the recipient of the benefits of the action to coincide: 'I commit myself to a management course in order to qualify for a future job as manager'. An *other-including* action is one in which the actor intends to share with others the position of being the recipient of the action's benefits. Many business transactions are other-including actions, because both parties are intended to have a deal. An *other-directed* action, finally, is one with which the actor intends results that exclusively benefit one or more other people. Support given to Amnesty International, or allowing a failing employee a second chance is an other-directed action.

This simple model of basic action patterns acquires moral meaning when we take into consideration how the interests and claims of others are involved in each of the different actions.

From a moral point of view, other-directed actions do not require extended comment. We are talking here about actors who, voluntarily, foster the interests of others, whereas the beneficiaries are not entitled to claim, on moral grounds, the performance of the other-directed actions. So we are facing purely altruistic actions, highly respectable and stimulating, but not to be qualified as a moral obligation. Other-directed actions embellish life, people acting in this way can serve as high-standing role models, but moral duties are not at stake.

1.9   Recognitional ethics

To a certain extent the same is true with regard to self-directed actions. As long as the actor is her own beneficiary, and no legitimate claims are raised by others, no specific moral qualifications are due. One may conclude that we face here an ethics of self-development, guided by the principle of fidelity to one's basic self: 'don't spoil the gift of your capacities, become who you are able to be', but for the rest, with this type of actions, we are sailing on a quiet moral sea. Things change, however, and dramatically sometimes, as soon as legitimate rights and interests of others intervene in the pattern of an intendedly self-directed action. For then serious claims are at stake that require recognition on the part of the actor, creating a *moral asymmetry* between the actor and the party affected by the self-directed action. From a moral point of view, where such a situation occurs, the positions of the parties involved can be defined as, respectively, that of a *claimant* on the one side and that of a *duty-bound* actor on the other, the former being morally entitled to the recognition of her claims and interests, the latter being obliged to recognize these claims. In terms of rights the situation can be described as implying one party's moral rights *vis-à-vis* the other party's corresponding moral duty. In terms of interests we face here a situation of conflicting interests and unequal claims, with the tacit supposition that the rights of the party affected have a greater moral weight than the freedom to act of the acting party. I propose to characterize the domain of ethics at stake here as the domain of *recognitional ethics*.

Some basic moral principles characterize the field of recognitional ethics. Basic, of course, is the *principle of recognition* itself – the formal and conscious recognition, that is, that one may get involved in situations of moral asymmetry and then will have to react accordingly. Basic also is what traditionally is called the *principle of beneficence* or the *principle of non-maleficence* – saying that no harm should be done to others, that harm done should be compensated, and that everybody, to a reasonable extent, has the moral duty to avoid harm being done by others.

The domain of recognitional ethics covers a large part of traditional ethical interventions. In the eyes of many, ethics in fact *is* about asymmetrical relations, about the rights or interests of the one generating a duty for another. Practical ethical discussions are, then, about the moral weight of the rights at stake and about the extension of the corresponding duties. Has Albert Heijn the moral duty to refrain from selling Bintje potatoes, given the right of the general public to a safe and sound environment? Are the 57 to 60-year-old employees of Fokker morally obliged to retire on behalf of some younger colleagues who, being in the midst of their careers, can raise a more weighty claim to a job than people approaching retirement anyhow?

Recognitional ethics tries to clarify and support these kinds of discussions, applying the two principles mentioned and other moral convictions that are considered appropriate.

1.10   Transactional ethics

Asymmetrical relations of unequal claims and conflicting interests do not exhaust the arsenal of possible action patterns. I already mentioned the extended field of other-including actions. It is an intricate area that deserves our close attention. In terms of interests one may say that here we face action patterns that obtain among people with common interests and either roughly equal claims or no mutual claims whatsoever.

The concept of common interests needs to be specified because different types of common interests can be distinguished. Interests can be common in the sense of occurring *simultaneously*. Their commonality lies in the fact that they occur at one and the same time and place without, however, being dependent on one another. All parties involved in the action pattern have interests that happen to coincide in time but that do not overtly affect each other. I am pursuing my affairs as you pursue yours. We both are aware of each other's existence, but that is about all the relationship we have – a very thin relationship indeed. There is morality involved in this relation, nevertheless. In order to let each party's transactions run smoothly, all parties have to accept the *principle of equality*, implying that every agent should allow every other the same amount of freedom of action he claims for himself. The moral principle of equality tells us where to refrain from intrusions in the freedom of action of others while following one's own affairs. It is a negative principle, but basic none the less.

Interests can also be common in the stronger sense of being *connected*. Where connected interests are at stake we face the situation that the interests of the one cannot be realized without the interests of the other being satisfied as well. Both parties are needed to arrive at the intended result, namely a co-operative arrangement for mutual benefit, yielding a social surplus that none of the parties on its own is able to produce. As every party is indispensable, every party is equally entitled to an appropriate share in the outcome of the arrangement. Almost all market transactions fall within this category. I need a taxi to catch my train, the taxi-driver needs people like me for a living, so we both are dependent on each other and, as long as we both contribute appropriately, together we generate a surplus that none of us on his own is able to produce. In order to let things run smoothly, here again adherence to two specific moral principles is required: first, to the *principle of honesty*, implying that one should operate in good faith, fairly and equitably, not betraying the confidence received; and second, to the *principle of reciprocity*, saying that one should avoid free-riding on somebody else's efforts.

The domain of ethics covering transactions that are performed on the basis of simultaneous or connected interests and that are governed by the principles of equality, honesty and reciprocity I propose to indicate as the domain of *transactional ethics*.

1.11 Participatory ethics

Within the category of other-including actions guided by common interests we find a third type of actions, specified this time not by simultaneous or connected interests but by *shared interests*. Here parties co-operate in order to produce a more distant common good that has three characteristic features: first, the good can only be realized through the participation of all parties; second, participation cannot be enforced – there is no explicit moral obligation to take part in the project; and third, although participation may be profitable for participating parties as well as for the community at large, none of the parties has to participate in order to survive, every possible participant can abstain without risking a lasting damage for him/herself. We may think here of public/private partnerships of all kinds in view of a local common good, or of covenants between local or national authorities, company branches, single corporations and, maybe, trade unions or public interest groups, shifting alliances to design a common environmental policy, to fight unemployment, or to develop a renovation project for the inner city. The important thing is that parties join the alliance voluntarily, committing themselves to a self-imposed and non-enforceable obligation.

The sphere of non-enforceable obligations entails a specific type of social relations that is guided, once more, by two particular moral principles. The first is the *principle of decency* – a specimen of moral aesthetics, one might say. This principle implies that, where a real opportunity to contribute to the general welfare presents itself and no insurmountable obstacles arise, one should have solid moral reasons *not* to go for it. The second principle at stake is the *principle of emancipation*. This principle states that specific groups deserve the space and means for development that history has unwarrantedly denied them up to now. On the basis of the principle of decency corporations voluntarily contribute to a city development project that aims at an optimal distribution of space devoted to different kinds of housing, to offices, to traffic, cultural and shopping facilities, and to open spaces, preserved for the benefit of all. On the basis of the principle of emancipation special attention is given to the least powerful, in order to defend those who, by themselves, are defenceless.

The domain of ethics covered by co-operative commitments in view of a common good – the domain, that is, of voluntary participations in collective public projects – I propose to indicate as the domain of *participatory ethics*. But haven't we stated before that ethics is not about voluntary actions, actions that are 'beyond the call of duty'? We have indeed. Yet it is misleading to assume that, within the realm of participatory ethics, obligations are strictly non-enforceable. They are *individually* non-enforceable. But that is only part of the story. The evolution of social relations, especially in highly industrialized countries, has also brought with it, together with the increased individuality and autonomy of individuals and corporations, a vastly increased mutual interdependence. That we, as individuals and as corporations, are able to realize our self-determined purposes we owe to a large extent to the institutionalized support of other individuals and instances, the legal system, traffic and telecommunication provisions, and police protection where necessary. Given this lasting public support, this 'gift of society',[9] it is reasonable to assume that those possible participatory arrangements which entail a substantial contribution to the common good rest, as a *collective responsibility*, on *all* participants in public social transactions. Certainly, a collective responsibility is not individually enforceable, a single individual or group cannot be held accountable for every project to which he, she or they could possibly contribute. But an individual, or company, that in no case whatsoever proves to be accessible when invited, is guilty of moral neglect.

Participatory ethics is about the shape of solidarity in an age of individualization. It is the ethics of the *civil society*, recently rediscovered as a solid ground for collective arrangements where both the market and the state fail. By participating, on a regular basis, in common projects on behalf of general welfare, a corporation demonstrates that it takes seriously its corporate citizenship. Participatory ethics is a privileged part of business ethics.

1.12   A balanced approach

Both a theory of business virtues and a taxonomy of action patterns and their moral implications try to produce a moral theory of real-life practices, in our case of business practices. Compared to the virtue-oriented approach the model of action patterns has three advantages.

First, it replaces the short and rather ponderous list of basic moral attitudes by the more flexible and manageable terminology of appropriate moral action guides corresponding to the various types of action in business. Honesty and justice are impressive personal qualities. Every time we see them present in a person we can reasonably predict the general direction that his/her actions will take. If we want to know, however, what justice implies in a setting of connected interests and equal claims, what in the case of conflicting interests and unequal claims, and what in a situation of shared interests and no mutual claims, then more flexible principles are needed.

The second advantage lies in that, in an approach via action types, the field of business need not be conceived as a coherent practice under the sign of commonality, as especially the Aristotelian brand of virtue ethics is inclined to do. Exchange transactions in view of mutual advantage, the recognition of asymmetrical claims between market participants, and the possibility of participatory arrangements, with the accompanying varieties of transactional, recognitional and participatory ethics, are all part of the picture. This way full justice is done to the internal plurality of business activities.

Third, by focusing on the total texture of interests at stake in business relations, ethics can greatly profit from insights generated by related disciplines like economics, politics and social philosophy. For too long business ethics has been confined within its own rather narrow boundaries, set by philosophers as its primary experts. Business ethics, however, is too important an affair to be left to philosophers.

Ethics in business – the practice as well as the theory – faces a basic handicap, namely the distance commonly felt between the business world and ethical discourse. The distance is psychological as well as operational. The psychological distance is related to the difficulty business representatives experience when they see themselves confronted with what they consider to be high-flying and extremely idealistic statements. Admittedly, purely normative principles, especially when elaborated without a firm rooting in daily practice, often have an air of other-worldliness, confirming the noncommittal saying: 'He who preaches the good is always right'. But business ethics as a discipline need not just produce global generalities. In the examples of the product responsibility theories and the ethical algorithm concerning justifiable conduct in host countries, we have seen how moral principles, even of a fairly general nature, are able to direct a moral discussion quite effectively. The theory of business virtues, while still requiring more nuances, is a clear attempt to elicit moral insights from a descriptive analysis of what being in business implies. And the model of action patterns and configurations of interests provides us with a carefully differentiated set of moral principles, suited to be used in the various relational contexts with which people in business are so familiar. Although business ethics as a discipline is a rather recent phenomenon, the progress made already allows us to expect more in the near future. So psychologically the gap between business and ethics does not seem unbridgeable.

The operational distance is more serious. For there the problem is not about understanding but about conduct. It finally comes down to the basic question: 'Why be moral in the market?' People asking this question do not suggest that, in market relations, no moral constraints obtain because 'it's a jungle out there', or because 'in the market, the one and only rule is catch-as-catch-can'. They are willing to admit that, in market operations, in addition to the law, at least the negative moral rule has to be obeyed that is known as the non-maleficence principle, the principle of harm to be avoided. But for the rest, morality seems hardly needed. For with regard to the daily transactions between roughly equal participants, the regulatory discipline of the market itself is largely sufficient. There price mechanisms and the rule of supply and demand teach us how to behave, not morality. And regarding the future shape of society, moral demands are easily stretched too far where business is concerned. For it is the government, and society as a whole, that has to take care of the general welfare, not a single corporation or a single company branch.

Here market morality is unduly restricted to the domain of what we have called recognitional ethics, where we acknowledge that others can have a legitimate claim, overriding our freedom of action, to such an extent that not recognizing this claim would amount to violating the principle of harm to be avoided. But, as we have also seen, there is more morality *needed* in the market than appears to be the case at first sight. And there is more morality *possible* than people sometimes are inclined to notice. There is more morality needed, in the sense of a transactional ethics, because the regular exchange transactions and co-operative ventures require an adherence to the moral principles of equality, honesty and reciprocity. And there is more morality possible, in the sense of a participatory ethics, because social and political developments today open ways to co-operative arrangements for the common good that have long been blocked by the biased structures of our social institutions. So, at the end of the day, and maybe surprisingly, the central question is not *why* be moral in the market, but *how*? By enlarging the domain of market morality, business ethics can greatly contribute to a balanced answer.

Notes

1. The cases have all been provided by participants in a business ethics project that is part of an Executive MBA Programme at Nijenrode University, The Netherlands Business School.
2. F. Neil Brady has described this approach in some detail in his book, *Ethical Managing. Rules and Results* (New York/London: Macmillan, 1990), pp. 115–30. He refers to John Rawls' notion of 'reflective equilibrium' as a balancing of moral intuitions with one's principles for action, and to D. Lyons' 'method of rebuttals' as similar procedures. Recently Theodoor van Willingenburg has devoted a book to this subject: *Inside the Ethical Expert. Problem Solving in Applied Ethics* (Pharos Kampen, 1991).
3. In what follows I succinctly paraphrase Manuel G. Velasquez, *Business Ethics. Concepts and Cases* (Prentice Hall, 1992), 3rd edition, pp. 273–92.
4. See Thomas Donaldson, *The Ethics of International Business* (The Ruffin Series in Business Ethics, Oxford University Press, 1989), pp. 95–108.
5. See Alasdair MacIntyre, *After Virtue. A Study in Moral Theory* (Duckworth, 1981).
6. Robert C. Solomon, *Ethics and Excellence. Cooperation and Integrity in Business* (New York: OUP, 1992, The Ruffin Series in Business Ethics).
7. Solomon, *op. cit.*, p. 119. MacIntyre's definition of 'practice' is sensibly more complicated: 'By a "practice" I am going to mean any coherent and complex form of socially established cooperative human activity through which goods internal to that form of activity are realised in the course of trying to achieve those standards of excellence which are appropriate to, and partially definitive of, that form of activity, with the results that human powers to achieve excellence, and human conceptions of the ends and goods involved, are systematically extended' (*op. cit.*, p. 175). In brief, to be practical in this sense one needs to be virtuous, at least inchoatively.
8. I have elaborated this 'taxonomy of ethical behaviour' in Henk van Luijk' 'Rights and interests in a participatory market society', *Business Ethics Quarterly*, to be published in Vol. 3, 1994.
9. See Alan Wolfe, *Whose Keeper? Social Science and Moral Obligation* (Berkeley/Los Angeles/London: University of California Press, 1989), Ch. 9.

CHAPTER 2

How to be ethical: ethics resource management

Jack Mahoney
London Business School, England

When we come to examine the ethical aspects of business, as of any other area of human behaviour, we do not have to begin with a blank page. We have various ethics resources at our disposal. The purpose of this chapter is to give a new meaning to the term 'ERM' by exploring the challenging field of Ethics Resource Management. It will consider first what external ethics resources are available to people in business; then what internal or personal ethics resources they can draw upon; and finally what contribution may be forthcoming from ordinary reflection about ethics in general and business ethics in particular.

2.1 External ethics resources

2.1.1 Codes of conduct

One attempt to cope with moral issues in business and to secure some agreement in practice is to be found in the increasing number of codes of conduct or of ethical good practice which companies issue for their members. Yet few, if any, of these codes of conduct actually give reasons why people should behave in the various ways they lay down. Of course, operating according to accepted and predictable standards of behaviour is essential to the smooth and efficient running of a business. Acting according to certain principles is increasingly required of business by society, and only by behaving in this way will a business retain a share of the market. Yet none of these is in itself an ethical reason why businesses and the people in them should behave in certain ways and not in others. In other words, the ethical principles on which codes of conduct are based are simply presupposed or taken for granted. As an ethics resource, then, and for the purposes of ethics resource management, a corporate code of conduct can certainly be useful if it enjoins people to behave in ways which are ethical. But it does not provide an answer to the basic ethical question: what is it about various ways of behaving which makes some of them morally right and others morally wrong?

2.1.2   The law and ethics

The law of the land is regarded by many business people as a major ethics resource, so that whatever else acting ethically in business may involve, at least it must include compliance with the law. Some might be inclined to go further, and to maintain that business ethics is no more than a matter of legal compliance – that is, of obeying whatever laws happen to be in force in a country at any given time. Yet laws do not, any more than codes of conduct, offer ethical arguments or justification for what they prohibit or command. In fact, it is widely accepted that it is not the purpose of laws to make people ethical in their behaviour. Their purpose is less ambitious – to compel people to behave or not to behave in certain ways which are designated from time to time either as legally mandatory or as crimes, i.e. as actions which are legally forbidden and punishable.

As a matter of fact, many actions which are judged illegal, or legally wrong, may also be ethically wrong, at least as many people view them, so there can be a certain overlap between legally wrong (or criminal) behaviour and ethically wrong (or immoral) behaviour. Telling lies is not normally considered a crime, although many people, including business people, believe it is unethical. But if it is a lie in court when one has taken an oath to tell the truth, it then becomes the crime of perjury, and will be dealt with accordingly. Similarly, failing to keep a promise is widely disapproved of as immoral behaviour, but it is only when such behaviour takes the form of breaking a contract, or of deliberately disregarding one's statutory (i.e. legal) duties that it becomes liable to criminal proceedings. In other words, some actions which are regarded by many as unethical are also crimes, but this does not apply to all unethical actions.

Moreover, not every crime, or action which is prohibited by a law, is necessarily also an unethical or immoral action. It is not difficult to identify laws around the world today which many would judge to fall far short of ethical standards or principles, whether they do so by excess or by default: by excess, as when South Africa legally compelled people and businesses to practise systematic racial discrimination – so much so that the Sullivan ethical principles for companies having dealings with or in South Africa required people deliberately to break the law of the land; and by default, as when various Third World governments fail to legislate adequate standards of health and safety covering such issues as the dumping of toxic waste, the marketing of dangerous products and the permitting of dangerous or underpaid conditions of work.

Not everything that is legal, then, is necessarily ethical, just as not everything that is unethical is necessarily illegal, or forbidden by some law. In fact, far from laws dictating ethical standards of behaviour, it is increasingly the case that laws themselves are judged by ethical principles and found to be wanting, as the European Court of Human Rights regularly shows. As an ethics resource, then, law may have its uses, but it cannot claim to be an adequate reply to the question of how do we know why some actions should count as ethical behaviour in business and why others should be judged to be unethical business conduct.

2.1.3   Religion as an ethics resource

Many business people belonging to one or the other of the great world religions, including Judaism, Christianity and Islam, believe that their religion provides them with ethical principles and standards which can be applied in business. The outstanding example of such religious ethical teaching is what both the Jewish tradition and the Christian tradition refer to as the Ten Commandments, which are believed to have been divinely revealed as the will of God.

Apart from those Commandments which govern religious behaviour, the ethical commands which the Jewish and the Christian religions accept as the will of God are: 'you shall not kill; you shall not commit adultery; you shall not steal; you shall not bear false witness against your neighbour; you shall not covet your neighbour's house'. On the whole, tradition in both cases – and reinforced for Christians by the teaching of Jesus – has come to view these Commandments from God as ethical principles which forbid doing anything to destroy or harm another person's life or marriage or reputation or property.

Religion can also for many people include beliefs about God's other actions which have ethical implications. In the Judaeo-Christian tradition, God is regarded as the supreme being who created the universe and continues to keep it in existence. It follows ethically that humans should respect the physical and natural world as God's property, and should act as stewards responsible to God for the ways in which they use his world. Again, the belief that human beings are each, in the words of the Hebrew Bible, especially made 'in the image of God' leads to the ethical conclusion that every human individual without exception has an innate and inalienable dignity which ought to be respected. And the belief that all human beings are God's creatures with a shared destiny results in the ethical conclusions that this basic human kinship be recognized by all political forms of human society, as well as by all economic systems, so that the resources of God's earth are developed for the common benefit of the whole human family.

One obvious difficulty about the ethics resource which is available from religion is what ethical rules and principles derived from religious beliefs have to say to people who do not share those beliefs. For if some ways of behaving are to be considered right or wrong just because a god has decided so at some time in human history, then such teaching appears either acceptable only on faith or else debatable or even arbitrary. On the other hand, if the god in question proclaims that various ways of behaving are right or wrong because they actually are the right and wrong ways for human beings to treat each other, then perhaps it ought to be possible for human beings to work that out for themselves, without the need of a divine revelation.

Christians are themselves divided over how accessible the content of their ethical teaching is to those who are not Christians, largely depending on what emphasis they place on the Christian belief in human sinfulness and frailty. One influential current of Western Christian thought, which can be mainly identified with sixteenth-century and later strict Protestant Christianity, holds the view that the only way in which sinful human beings can be confident of knowing moral truth is by accepting the law of God, especially in the teaching and the example of Jesus, and by regarding any other claims to achieve or provide ethical knowledge as to be treated with reserve and suspicion. Some adherents of this pessimistic account of human nature regard society and various secular activities, including engaging in business, as in need of regular 'prophetic' denunciation for being fertile ground for greed, self-delusion and exploitation, which can be avoided only with difficulty and only through strict 'evangelical' adherence to the teaching of God as revealed in the Bible, and often as understood in a literal – even fundamentalist – fashion.

The other major current of Christian thought on these matters, found at its strongest in various expressions of Catholic Christianity, takes a less extreme view of human moral disability arising from and leading to sin. As a result it is more optimistic, at least in theory, about the ability of all human beings to draw on their god-given resources of mind and will to discover moral truth even apart from a special revelation, and to put it into effect in their lives – including their business lives – with at least some measure of success.

Other differences are to be found among Christians in the ways in which they understand their tradition and its ethical content or implications affecting business. It took official Christianity centuries to come to ethical terms with the whole idea of charging for credit. Some Christians today are profoundly opposed to capitalism and the market, while others are stout, or qualified, defenders of both; some find competition and the profit motive morally objectionable, yet others accept it either willingly or realistically; some find the whole business of making money distasteful and morally dangerous, and others see it as creative and desirable.

Despite these various difficulties involved even for its adherents in regarding religion as an ethics resource, however, it is possible to draw some more optimistic conclusions. For one thing, the Judaeo-Christian tradition is at one in subscribing to certain basic moral insights and values, such as the inalienable dignity of every human being without exception, and the importance of human relationships for the well-being and flourishing both of individuals and of the human family as a whole. Where honest moral disagreement occurs today among Christians it tends to be not so much over the importance in general of such ethical values and principles as, at least in many cases, over how they can best be given practical expression in day-to-day decisions, especially when there appears to be a conflict of those values or principles which are held in common.

In this respect, then, ethics resource management which includes religion as a possible resource can provide scope among its adherents for agreement on the importance of certain basic values at what might be termed the level of strategic ethical awareness, while still leaving considerable room for differences or for manoeuvre on the tactical judgements and decisions which have to be made about how those basic ethical values ought to be realized in actual situations. Nor is this considered by many an in-house activity or a debate confined to believers. Their concern for those values and for applying them in business, as in all other public activities, also leads them to explore whether such ethical values can be agreed upon with others in society as common ground on which to base the conduct of business, even if those values may be held by others for reasons which are not – or not entirely – based upon religious beliefs.

2.2   Internal ethics resources

It is a commonplace of business to prefer self-regulation to any other form of control over one's behaviour; and this prompts the question whether in the field of ethics also, as applied in business, this might be an important or even preferred aspect of ethics resource management.

2.2.1   *Ethical self-regulation: recourse to conscience*

For many people the simplest and often spontaneous answer to the question of how do we know what is the right thing to do in any given situation, is to consult or to follow one's conscience. Yet on reflection the appeal to one's conscience is not quite so simple. To begin with, conscience appears to mean quite different things to different people. Some describe it as a 'feeling' about what is right and wrong; others call it a 'sense' of right and wrong; while yet others refer to it as 'something inside us' which enables us to 'judge' whether a particular action is, or was, right or wrong. Conscience is also commonly referred to as a 'guide', a 'law' or a 'voice' within us, something we should 'consult' or 'follow' or 'obey'. One thing which various descriptions of conscience have in common is to indicate that our conscience has a certain, quite unique ethical claim upon us to which we as individuals feel obliged to pay heed. Yet why should conscience claim such authority?

Religion has a ready answer when it describes conscience as 'the voice of God' or when, less metaphorically, it explains conscience as the interpreter of divine moral laws and commands. For those, however, who do not look to religion to explain the phenomenon of conscience, and even for many who do, its actual authority and binding force appear ultimately to derive from the fact that it is *my* conscience or, more precisely, what *I* judge I ought to do or ought not to do. In other words, the basic authority of the individual's conscience appears to derive from the importance and dignity of the human individual as she or he comes to a fully personal decision in conscience about how they should behave. This means there is certainly room in our understanding of conscience for feelings about various sorts of actions, or for a sense of right and wrong about different types of behaviours, or for a general awareness of some things as being right and others as being wrong. Yet, central to the experience of conscience appears to be the idea of making a judgement about certain ways of behaving in general, or a judgement about a particular action which is being considered.

If it is a judgement about morality it will probably have the same characteristics which we can identify in all human judgements. Few important human judgements or decisions, or at least few which are considered praiseworthy, are snap decisions taken out of the blue. They are the culmination of a process. They come after the problem or the decision to be taken has been clearly identified and analysed, after all the relevant facts have been obtained, after due consideration has been given to the resources and the various alternatives available, after consulting others and seeking advice where necessary, and after weighing all the evidence. Until all that has been done, in the popular phrase, 'the jury is still out'.

In traditional ethical language this process of coming carefully to a moral judgement is referred to as 'educating' or 'forming' our conscience – taking all the steps identified above so that as we eventually decide what action we should take we do so with as informed a conscience as possible. Part of the input at this stage of building up to an ethical decision will come from the various ethics resources which we have already considered, which are fed into our moral information-gathering and sifting, and become the subject of our consideration and deliberation. Other resources which we shall be considering later include the various theories of ethics which have been applied and argued about in some form or other for centuries.

Two immediate conclusions follow from recognizing the importance of this conscience-forming process. One is that our conscience, our capacity to make moral judgements, is not just a given which we possess from birth. It can grow or develop, given favourable conditions and suitably nourished; or it can be neglected and be abused, and even atrophy. Perhaps the old computer maxim, GIGO – garbage in, garbage out – can also apply to our sense of moral deliberation and judgement. If it is consistently given a diet of junk, it will produce junk.

The other conclusion which follows from this realization that conscience works as a normal decision-making process which includes many variables is that, as with any other human decision, we can get it wrong. Just because people feel something intensely or strongly doesn't mean they are correct, and no matter how convinced they are, this does not prove that their conviction is infallible and cannot possibly be mistaken. The interesting thing is that, according to much traditional ethical thought, even if my conscience is mistaken I am bound to follow it and others are bound to respect it. For this makes a lot of sense if conscience is recognized to be, as suggested above, the human person coming to a moral judgement. If this is what he or she after due consideration genuinely judges to be what they ought to do or ought not to do, then personal consistency and moral responsibility require that they act accordingly. Moreover, their dignity as a human person requires that they should be respected by others in so doing, even if others consider them mistaken, and even if they actually are – as a matter of cold fact – mistaken.

Finally, if conscience is the human person in his or her moral mode of decision, then one essential component remains to be considered in order to reach an adequate understanding of what conscience is. For human beings are not just moral calculating machines. The fact that some people view conscience as a matter of moral feelings can alert us to the fact that as in all decision-making, so also in ethical decisions, emotions, feelings and other influences can come into play and need to be taken into account. Sometimes it is a fellow-feeling or an emotion of sympathy or of moral outrage which can alert people to the need for decision and action; sometimes it is a feeling of contentment or peace which can encourage one to take certain decisions for action or approve them in others. Feelings and emotions, then, are important in matters of ethics if we are to do justice to the idea that conscience is the whole human person stimulated to come to a moral conclusion. For if conscience is the human person in his or her mode of moral deliberation, then much will depend on the sort of human person each one is, not just with regard to their emotions and feelings, but also more broadly with regard to their whole individual personal make-up and history. Our consideration of conscience as an inner ethics resource cannot, then, be complete until we explore the role which our character plays in the whole process of approaching and reaching a moral decision.

2.2.2   Self-regulation: moral skills

Since the eighteenth century and what we call the Age of Reason and the Enlightenment, most attention in ethical reflection has been devoted to exploring what human reasoning and the human mind can provide by way of analysing and resolving ethical challenges without the need for religion or any other outside resource. This approach to ethics as an 'autonomous' discipline and the product of human reasoning long antedates the Age of Reason, of course, and forms a long and honourable tradition in the history of ethics, as well as being the presupposition behind the development of the major ethical theories of utilitarianism, duty ethics, natural law and human rights ethics which we shall shortly be considering.

In the history of Western ethics, however, there has also been another tradition which has been lost to view since about the time of the Enlightenment and which is in process of being recovered today by philosophers and theologians. It is the tradition which directs our attention not to what is the moral action which is called for in certain typical situations, but to the moral agent, or the person who is faced with moral choices. If the previous type of ethical thinking is known today as 'quandary' ethics or, less pessimistically, 'issue' ethics, then increasing attention is now being given again to the ethical thinking and reflection which goes by the name of 'virtue' ethics, or 'character' ethics. It directs our attention not just to questions about what is the ethical thing to do, but what it means to be an ethical sort of person. It recognizes that to be honest, loyal, sympathetic and fair as a person is an important inner resource for discovering what is the honest, loyal, sympathetic and fair thing to do and for actually doing it. It recognizes that we must follow our conscience on the occasions when it tells us what to do and what not to do, and that one who habitually does this is rightly described as actually being 'conscientious'. It acknowledges the importance of asking the question, what should I do, but it seeks a deeper level of the moral human being and his or her inner resources in asking the question, what sort of person should I be, or should I be aiming to become?

The traditional approach to such 'virtue' ethics looks on a virtue as a permanent tendency which a person may possess to react in a particular way when faced with various situations, almost, in a significant phrase, as if it were 'second nature'. This is why some writers refer to virtues as habits, such as the habit – or the almost instinctive reaction – of telling the truth when asked a question, or a feeling of resistance or reluctance when tempted to betray a confidence or a colleague. A virtue can also be seen as a sort of moral skill, an ability to deal with various situations with a certain measure of facility, or at least without a great deal of difficulty.

This way of talking of virtues as moral habits and skills also brings out the fact that a virtue is not just a matter of knowledge. I may well know how to make an omelette, or drive a car, because I have read an article or a book on the subject. But that doesn't necessarily mean that I actually can make an omelette or drive a car. Actually to be able to do it requires not just know-how, but also familiarity and practice in acquiring the ability to do it. Finally, such moral tendencies or skills are also seen not just as personal ethics resources which enable us to act or behave readily in certain ways. They are in fact personal qualities, aspects of the individual who can not only act justly or generously when the situation requires it, but who actually *is* just or generous. For many people the possession or the pursuit of virtues as personal qualities sums up what it means to lead a good life, or actually to be a morally good person, which they would view as the ultimate in human flourishing and indeed what constitutes genuinely human fulfilment.

The whole approach to ethical behaviour in terms of personal qualities and dispositions which equip one to bring about appropriate ethical states of affairs goes back to Plato, and to his famous quartet of what came to be called the 'cardinal' human moral qualities on which all the rest hinge: the four basic virtues of wisdom, justice, temperance and fortitude, which were later taken up by the Judaeo-Christian Book of Wisdom and thus acquired immense religious as well as philosophical authority in the history of Western ethical thought.

The idea, then, of internal dispositions within us to do the right thing in various situations has a long history and can be considered an important ethics resource, particularly as a means of ethical self-regulation, in business as in all other walks of life. Yet it raises two basic questions which need to be considered. One is: are we born with these desirable dispositions of character, or can such skills and predispositions be acquired? And the other is: does being virtuous, fair, honest, loyal and so on, actually tell us what is the fair, honest or loyal thing to do in various situations?

The fact that virtues can be regarded as moral skills implies that they can be acquired through practice and can become, as was said above, not a natural trait but 'second nature' and a matter of almost instinctive reaction, like driving a car out of a busy car park. In fact, the whole point of moral education of young people can best be viewed as much more than moral instruction, or than just teaching them to do what they are told, where the only inner dispositions which are cultivated may be those of obedience and conformity. The point of moral education is to help young people become inner-directed and self-regulating by acquiring and consolidating basic social habits of being thoughtful for other people, of respecting their interests and wishes, their property, privacy, reputation and so forth. Again, of course, such moral education is not simply a matter of knowledge, or knowing what is the right thing to do. It is a mixture of familiarity through practice, of reflection and discussion, of following the example of others whom one admires and of forming certain ideals or goals in life.

Do such internal dispositions to do what is right, loyal, honest and fair actually tell us in various circumstances what is the right or loyal or honest or fair course of behaviour which we should follow? Does habitually being honest help me to know whether to tell the truth when there might be something to be said on moral grounds for telling a lie, for instance to someone who is dying? Does the ingrained habit of acting loyally help me to know what to do when I have conflicting loyalties, one to a friend or a colleague and another to an employer?

Aristotle, who was the first philosopher to develop in detail the idea of virtues as internal ethics resources, made two points which can be helpful here. The first was his argument that a virtue occupies the middle ground between two extremes. He made much, for instance, of the virtue of moral courage, or of coping with one's fears when faced with a difficult moral decision; and few people would argue with his observation that courage is what helps us overcome cowardice or timidity, when we can be overwhelmed by fears of the consequences for us or for others of acting ethically. On the other hand, we do not call a person courageous when they take stupid risks; we call them reckless drivers, or we condemn people as rash in other fields of behaviour if they do not stop to think, or do not give enough forethought to the possible risks of their actions. Strange as it may sound, then, courage lies midway between timidity and impulsiveness; it consists in working out the balance, or the golden mean, between paying too much attention to our fears and ignoring them altogether. It seems, then, that actually possessing the virtue can help us be alert to extremes and to find, as well as follow, the middle path between them.

The other point which Aristotle made about moral virtues which may throw light on whether they can provide us with moral knowledge is to be found in his statement that if we want to know what is the just thing to do in certain circumstances, we will get our answer from observing a just person. One thing which this brings out is the importance of role models in acquiring our own personal ethics resources. But, as many people have pointed out, Aristotle's argument appears to be a circular one, because we would not call anyone just in the first place unless we already knew that what they were doing was just.

Perhaps one answer to this objection is that we do not need the example of just people to instruct us in cases where it seems obvious and widely accepted that a certain course of behaviour is the just thing to do. When the situation is more complicated, however, as when the rights or the stakes of various parties appear to be in conflict and compete for our moral attention, then the person whom we have come to respect and trust as one who regularly acts justly in the more obvious cases may be the person from whom to take a lead in the more complex cases. He or she may be said to have a well-developed sense of justice, or a 'feel' or an 'eye' for the right course of action which enables them to recognize it where others might not, just as the skilled or trained draughtsperson, manager or financier can have an acquired capital of experience and practice on which to draw to solve particular tricky problems in their field of expertise as these crop up outside the routine course of events. A person able to draw on such experience and inner ethical resources can justifiably claim a certain measure of moral confidence, and even possess moral authority, in the face of new ethical challenges which may arise from changing circumstances. He or she will also be capable of moral inventiveness and imagination, as well as moral courage, in exploring such challenges in ways which may not be open to others whose major ethics resources come from outside in the shape of codes of practice, laws and religious rules of behaviour.

Accumulating ethical capital through regular investment in acting virtuously can, then, provide one with a capacity for moral insight into various ethical issues as they arise in the course of life, including business, and for identifying the just, honest or loyal course of action in such situations. It does not, however, automatically follow that one will always be correct. Abraham Lincoln spoke about acting 'with firmness in the right, as God gives us to see the right'. And it is a matter of history and experience that even virtuous people can get things wrong, either because they share the ethical limitations of a particular culture, or because of their own history and upbringing and the ingrained ways of thinking and behaving which they have acquired in the process. To the question of ethics resources, then – how do we know what is the ethical course of action, and how can we be sure of it – the moral virtue and ethical character approach appears to have an important contribution to make which has been ignored for too long, but it does not appear completely adequate as an answer. At the very least it still appears, as do the approaches by way of codes, laws, religion and conscience which we have considered, to require as a backstop the additional and indispensable resource of human thinking and reasoning about what is ethical, and why in the various situations and circumstances of life some actions are the right ones to perform while others are to be avoided as morally wrong.

2.3   Thinking matters through

Why is it wrong to tell lies, to injure other people, to break one's promises? Why should we go out of our way to help other people? A major part of the history of ethics has consisted in various attempts to provide satisfactory – and intellectually satisfying – answers to such questions. The most popular attempt at an answer as to what makes various actions ethically right or wrong, and one which may appeal particularly to active people, including men and women involved in business, is one which is result-oriented, looking to the effects of one's actions on other people. It is a remark commonly heard that such-and-such a way of behaving is not wrong because no one is hurt by it, ranging from homosexual activity between consenting adults in private to 'white lies' to various other 'victimless' actions, which is how some business people would describe insider trading. By contrast, in this line of argument, what makes such actions as fraudulent accounting, misleading advertisements, poor-quality or dangerous products, unfair employment and promotion practices and late payment of suppliers all ethically wrong is that they will result in harm to various people. From these considerations the general principle can be formulated that ethically wrong behaviour is *harmful* behaviour: anything which causes deliberate harm to someone is for that reason unethical, and the more harm it causes, the more unethical it becomes.

Such considerations about not causing harm can be generalized in what has been called the *principle of non-maleficence* governing all human behaviour which wishes to be considered ethically sensitive. Its best-known practical expression is to be found in the injunction addressed to the medical profession: *primum non nocere* – the first thing is not to cause harm to the patient. However, doctors are expected to do more for their patients than not to kill them or not to make their condition worse. More positively, they are expected also to do everything they can to cure their patients, or at least to improve their state of health. Similarly, in the whole field of ethical behaviour this is found expressed in the more constructive *principle of beneficence*, and the view that ethics consists in actually doing good to others as a matter of principle. Thus, anything which helps others is for that reason ethical, and the right thing to do.

To avoid harming people and on the contrary to do good to them, then, appears to sum up what many people mean by acting ethically. As such it is expressed at a fairly high level of abstraction. Yet from it we can develop more specific conclusions, by identifying various possible actions towards others as either harmful or helpful, and on that basis concluding that such actions are ethically right or wrong.

Part of the function of moral philosophy is to probe the various general ethical theories which have been or are proposed, in order to assess their strengths, but also to consider what weaknesses they may possess in terms of being unreasonable or inconsistent or 'counter-intuitive', i.e. at variance with popular unreflective judgements of what counts as ethically right or wrong behaviour. Thus, attractive as a basic ethical theory of avoiding harm and of doing good to others appears, it has also been judged to suffer from certain weaknesses – or at least certain imprecisions – which can be summed up in two questions: how do we identify what actually is harmful or helpful to other people at any given time, and how do we choose between people when we cannot do good to all of them or when we cannot avoid harming some of them?

2.3.1   Promoting human well-being

One highly influential attempt to answer both these questions was popularized and systematically developed by the English constitutional lawyer and social reformer Jeremy Bentham, who claimed that the guiding legal and ethical principle in society should be always to seek 'the greatest happiness of the greatest number'. For him ethics was a simple practical matter of identifying and calculating the advantages and disadvantages which would be produced by a law or an action and concluding that the best law or the right thing to do would be that which resulted in the greatest net utility for as many people as possible. Equally famous in this early form of utilitarianism were Bentham's definition of utility as happiness, which he maintained consisted in pleasure and the absence of pain, and his contention that all pleasurable experiences are quantifiable, and all individuals are to be counted as of strictly equal importance. Thus, in his view morality is no more and no less than a matter of cost-benefit analysis in terms of human happiness and unhappiness.

Not everyone, however, agreed at the time, or would agree today, that all human happiness can be levelled out to enjoyable states of mind which are all strictly comparable. Far less can agreement be found for the underlying argument that everyone invariably pursues their own happiness as the basis of all their actions, and therefore everyone is morally obliged to make others happy, and that this is what ethics is all about. Yet if human happiness is more than enjoyable states of mind, how is one to identify what makes people happy? In various attempts to answer this question – which is obviously crucial to the theory of utilitarianism being of any practical use as an ethics resource – the idea of utility can be expanded to include other states of affairs which are regarded as worth pursuing, not because they are pleasurable (for they may not always be), but because they are valuable or admirable in their own right, including social harmony and order, friendship, knowledge, the arts, equality, freedom and even self-sacrifice. No doubt the pursuit and the realizing of such values can produce a sense of satisfaction or of mental well-being, at least at times, but most people would seem to agree that gratification is not always without exception the reason – or the main reason – why one pursues such worthwhile aims.

It might be possible, then, to broaden one's understanding of happiness to include a great variety of values of which pleasure may be only one, and to speak more in terms of bringing about the optimum and the maximum of general human welfare or flourishing as the single principle which provides a foundation for all ethical decisions. However, such a more reasonable approach only introduces a further complication. If we are to aim to produce the optimum of general human flourishing for as many people as possible, we are in danger of being paternalistic in claiming to be able to decide what will be best for other people. People have differing clusters of values and personal priorities which will make it immensely more complicated than crude utilitarianism realizes to maximize the general happiness, as that term is now understood here. Moreover, it has become increasingly recognized in the modern world that people's freedom to decide for themselves must figure prominently as an important value in any picture of true human flourishing. Perhaps, then, the most appropriate form of utilitarianism for the modern world is to view ethics as basically doing literally everything with the aim of maximizing human freedom of choice. Rather than work for what we in our wisdom think will be the best outcome for others, we should give ethical pride of place to the greatest possible promotion of people's *own* preferences, by providing conditions for them to decide for themselves and pursue what will give them satisfaction and what they – and not others – consider will make them fulfilled and happy.

This ethical equivalent of maximizing consumer choice may well appeal to the business mentality which is familiar with the aim of respecting the sovereignty of the consumer. In addition, it appears to have the merit of recovering the simplicity, and therefore the empirical usefulness, of early utilitarianism by seeing the foundation of ethics not in terms of producing pleasurable states of mind, which we have seen to be unsatisfactory, nor in aiming as an alternative to maximize a bewildering variety of human and social desirable situations, but simply in regarding as the only moral absolute the goal of increasing the scope and the extent of human freedom and choices. Anything which on balance favours this is *ipso facto* ethically the right thing to do, and any actions which bring about a net diminishing of the satisfying of human preferences are by that very fact ethically wrong.

Yet, attractively liberal and democratic as such a simple and empirically verifiable foundation for ethics sounds, it could very well lead to certain conclusions which a great many people would find morally unpalatable and counter-intuitive. If all or most of the members of a particular society place great store on the value of human sacrifice, utilitarianism would now claim that it is ethically incumbent on everyone to maximize the opportunities for those people choosing to engage in such behaviour. More realistically today, if a given society prefers on the whole that the moral tenets of a particular religion or branch of religion, whether Jewish or Christian or Muslim, should be strictly observed by all who live and work in that society, even for a time, then utilitarianism as now understood obliges everyone to abide by that preference and that strict ethical code, and to do so on ethical and not just on legally enforceable grounds. Giving the customer what he wants may not be such good ethics after all, especially if he has a preference for child abuse or marketing hard drugs or practising racial or sexual discrimination.

It seems, then, that the ethical absolute of maximizing and facilitating human freedom of choice needs to be subject to certain qualifications. If that is so, then it is no longer an absolute, nor is it the single foundation for all actions which are to qualify as ethically right or wrong. This apparent need for some other principle to control the maximizing of preferences, if this is to be considered an ethical goal, brings us to the other major question to which utilitarianism in any form has great difficulty in replying: the whole issue of how to distribute happiness or human flourishing in order to meet the principle of the greatest happiness of the greatest number of individuals.

2.3.2   Who profits?

It is a commonplace to realize that in our various actions we cannot satisfy everyone. A company faced with a financial crisis is involved in a series of decisions which have to be selective in deciding who is to be satisfied in these new circumstances – the owner or shareholders, the workforce, the banks and other creditors, and so on. In fact, if it is a strength of modern stakeholder theory that it recognizes the ethical claims of the various constituencies whose interests are at stake when company decisions are being made and executed, one of the weaknesses of the theory is that it gives no indication as to how priorities should be identified among the various stakeholders.

In the same way, it may be said, the basic principle of utilitarianism – or aiming in all our behaviour to bring about the greatest good (however that is understood) for the greatest number of people – has the merit of stressing that ethics is deeply concerned with how our actions may affect other people, and with expanding our horizons of interest beyond ourselves and our own immediate circle of friends, colleagues or cronies to include the greatest possible number of beneficiaries. It also involves the real possibility that the greatest number I am bound to benefit in any given case may not include me personally, or those close to me. Utilitarianism thus contains at least the possibility of requiring people to be altruistic and even of requiring the sacrifice of my personal interests in order to secure those of as many people as possible.

But it does carry a genuine problem of distribution and how to decide who shall benefit, and how much, and who shall not. One rather theoretical, but none the less real, expression of this weakness is that the total amount of satisfaction aimed at contains two interconnected variables: it cannot tell us whether we should aim to satisfy a small group of people to an intense degree or a larger group of people to a moderate extent, if either course would produce an equal total of satisfaction. It is a moot point for utilitarianism whether record profits ought to go entirely in lucrative dividends to delighted shareholders, or whether profits should be shared out or spread around in the form of increased salaries or wages or reduced prices or capital investment for the future.

The main distributional weakness of any form of utilitarianism, however, is its win/lose aspect. If the basic ethical principle of bringing about the greatest happiness of the relative majority of people can be achieved only at the expense of those who are by comparison in a minority, then the ethical thing to do is to disregard the interests of that minority. Such principled behaviour would thus ethically justify safeguarding the survival of a company which is in legal or public difficulties by creating a scapegoat who will get the company out of its mess, or, if the difficulty is financial, by squeezing a small supplier into ruin by not meeting its bills. It would also justify a large conglomerate in using any means at its disposal, including bribery and espionage, to take over a smaller company and strip it of its assets as a prelude to closing it down.

One reaction to such logical conclusions is to regard them as counter-intuitive, as morally repugnant, and to conclude in turn that if that is what utilitarianism can lead to, then so much the worse for utilitarianism as a claim to be an ethics resource in business or in any other field of human activity. Another reaction, however, would be to counter that utilitarianism as properly understood need not lead to such conclusions. The 'greatest number' of possible beneficiaries in each of the above situations applies only within a group which is somewhat arbitrarily identified as those people whose interests are immediately and directly involved. However, if we widen the constituency to include the possible knock-on consequences of scapegoating, bribery or asset-stripping within a greater number of people or within a whole society, we may well come to quite different ethical conclusions as to what will bring about the greatest happiness of the greatest number *as now identified*, compared with the amount of harm, dissatisfaction or restricted freedom which also results. And if such practices become regular business procedure in society then the resulting consequences will be universally destructive.

One consequence of this widening of the circle of people affected by one's actions is to shift the focus of utilitarianism from concentrating on what particular actions will maximize utility for the majority to advocating and accepting those general practices which society has found from experience do optimize and maximize human well-being. However, this shift from act-utilitarianism to rule-utilitarianism – accepting as practical ethical yardsticks such tested social practices as telling the truth, keeping promises, respecting property and so on – runs into difficulties when particular situations arise in which, according to the strict utilitarian principle, one actually *should* tell a lie or break a promise. Moreover, expanding the moral community in order to gain a wider perspective and a longer view of what does, or will, maximize human well-being for the most people, and must therefore be absolutely accepted as an ethical rule, logically entails taking into account the interests of future generations as well as those alive at present.

In itself concern for future generations is an important factor to be built into ethical reflection, as we have become increasingly aware in relation to the earth's limited supply of natural resources and to the environmental and ecological legacy which future generations will inherit from us. Yet, introducing our descendants as a factor in order to work out what ethical rules should be accepted by the whole of present society and should be rigorously applied by individuals in their every business action, has taken us a long way from the attractively simple principle from which we started, that ethics is a matter of avoiding causing harm to others and of doing good to them. Moreover, widening the circle of those whose well-being ought to be considered raises considerable difficulties about where the cut-off point should lie. It also only serves to accentuate the basic distributional difficulty of utilitarianism in all its forms, and to confirm that as a morality aimed at satisfying the majority it has a logical built-in capacity, as we have seen, to disadvantage or even to victimize minorities and individuals in ways which many find ethically offensive.

2.3.3   The call of duty

Not everyone sees ethics as a matter of making people happy. Some see it much more in terms of doing one's duty or of respecting absolute moral principles or obeying moral laws, however disadvantageous that may be for oneself or for others. The basic danger which such people see in using the happiness or welfare or preferences of others as a yardstick to decide what is the ethical thing to do is that it focuses attention completely on the consequences of what we do and gives no thought to the deeds we actually perform as a means to bringing about those desired consequences. In other words, in this view the approach to ethics by way of 'consequentialism', of which utilitarianism is the most obvious example, is simply an elaborate way of arguing that 'the end justifies the means'. It maintains that situations can arise when we are morally obliged, not just permitted, to harm innocent people, to tell untruths, to break promises, to take or destroy what belongs to others or to do anything else, provided it will produce a good net result.

The important question which such people raise is: why should all the emphasis in ethics be put on the results of our actions, on what we aim to bring about, and no importance whatever be given to what we in fact do, the actual *content* of our actions? For are there not some types of actions which can never be justified and which it is ethically wrong to perform because they are intrinsically wrong, however beneficial their results might be?

A difficulty which has to be faced by people who hold that there are such ethical absolutes is that most of our day-to-day actions and decisions can have unfortunate results for someone or other and will often involve people being harmed, or misled, or disappointed or deprived. Instances in business can range from being absent from a meeting to not honouring a deadline, to beating a competitor for a contract to cutting back on staff or closing down a local branch, to filing for bankruptcy – all apparently examples of infringing what we identified earlier as the principle of non-maleficence, or avoiding inflicting harm on other people. In more extreme ethical dilemmas waging a defensive war will inevitably result in innocent civilians being killed and their property being destroyed, choosing some patients for scarce medical treatment will result in others dying, building a new factory in one region may result in increased unemployment in another. It seems as if holding absolutely to the principle of never harming other people is a recipe for paralysis and is totally unrealistic.

To meet such difficulties those who maintain that one may never inflict harm on others point out that the unfortunate results of some or many of our actions are actually side-effects rather than deliberately desired. We do not miss a meeting in order deliberately to disappoint others: we do it to go to a funeral. We do not lay staff off in order to impoverish them: we do it in order to cut costs. We do not choose some patients for kidney transplants so that the others will die: we aim to make the best use of scarce resources. Life is full of such difficult choices. In fact, often the difficulty and the moral reluctance involved in such choices arise precisely from the fact that in addition to the good results which they are aimed at bringing about, they will also produce regrettable side-effects – results which we would rather not bring about, yet which seem inevitably the price to be paid for the good effects we really want to achieve.

The important point in this line of argument, which is traditionally known as the *principle of double effect*, is that it respects the view that certain harmful actions cannot be performed deliberately, since they are inherently unethical, but that it also allows for harmful 'collateral' consequences to follow from an ethical action which is performed for its good consequences, so long as those harmful consequences are unavoidable side-effects and so long as they do not outweigh the beneficial good results. It could be argued that this is simply a matter of cost-benefit analysis of all the consequences, both good and bad, of a possible action, such as we have already examined, in order to decide whether the action should be performed or not. That, however, would be to blunt the point of the analysis. If the net consequences will be harmful, that is too high a price to pay for the action, even if it is not wrong in itself. But if the net consequences will be beneficial that would still not justify doing something which in itself is considered unethical, irrespective of its possible consequences.

Various reasons are proposed for considering some types of behaviour as absolutely wrong and never justifiable, whatever good consequences they might bring about. For instance, recourse to the religious ethics resource of the Bible which is accepted by Jews and Christians, as we have seen, can lead one to conclude that God has utterly forbidden ways of behaving towards other people which endanger their lives, damage or take their property or destroy their reputation. And for many people the belief that God has delivered such absolute prohibitions and wishes them to be obeyed is sufficient justification for accepting them and trying to act by them. It is also possible on religious and biblical grounds, as we have also seen, to argue from the inherent dignity of all human beings as created 'in the image of God' that any way of treating a fellow human being which is offensive to his or her inalienable dignity is also offensive to their creator and therefore absolutely wrong.

Again, however, as we have noted, such divine absolute prohibitions will carry no weight as such with people who do not accept the religious beliefs on which they are based. Consequently they will be disinclined to accept the idea of moral absolutes in general, or that certain types of behaviour are absolutely wrong, unless this can be established by human reasoning without recourse to religion. One famous and influential attempt to do this was undertaken in the name of reason by the German Enlightenment philosopher, Immanuel Kant, who was convinced that ethics has nothing to do with consequences or human well-being, but comes purely from a sense of duty and of obedience to a moral law which any rational person must accept. What Kant called the Categorical, or Absolute, Imperative of morality is expressed in various ways, of which for him the most important was that any type of action we are thinking of performing will be morally wrong unless we would wish to make it a law that everyone behave in that way. Thus, when we tell a lie, we do not want everyone to tell lies; when we steal, we would not wish to make it a law that no one should respect another's belongings; when we break a promise, we still want everyone else to keep their promises. Unless our action can be 'universalized', it will be wrong.

The objection could be raised against Kant at this stage that his theory based on everyone telling lies, or stealing or breaking their promises, is the popular one of 'what would happen if everyone did that?' in terms of the social chaos which would result. And that would be an argument from consequences, which for Kant have nothing to do with ethics. As he understands the argument, however, it seems to be based more on the thought that it is pointless to make promises unless people have grounds for believing them, that it is irrational for people in general to propose something *as* the truth unless it actually *is* the truth. And above all, it is unreasonable and self-contradictory for anyone to hold that others ought to keep their promises and ought to make only truthful statements, while wanting an exception to be made in his or her particular case. Whatever else one might think about this particular reasoned defence of moral absolutes, it does have the merit of emphasizing that ethics should be impartial and based on universal considerations, i.e. on arguments which would apply to everyone in similar situations, and that one would need to have very good grounds – and grounds which can be rationally justified at that – to claim that such universal considerations do not apply in one's own particular case.

It was in the second formulation of his Categorical Imperative, however, that Kant coined what has become his most famous maxim and one which has had considerable influence on many people who would not otherwise accept, or even be aware of, his ethical theory: act in such a way that you treat human beings never just as a means but always also as ends. It is important to notice, of course, that Kant does not say we should never treat each other as a means to particular ends. We do it all the time, when we employ people to perform certain tasks, ranging from chairing meetings to posting letters. Kant's point is that our treatment of people in this way should never be merely as means, for this would dehumanize them, and there is something about human beings which requires that they should never be degraded or manipulated or disregarded for what they are. The point is a familiar one in enlightened human resource management, even if the impersonal phrase is in danger of offending against it, and it is reinforced by Kant's third formulation of the Categorical Imperative, that we ought always to act as if all human beings together constitute a 'kingdom of ends' and treat each other as such.

Kant's maxims concerning the need for ethical considerations to be universal and impartial and above all affirming the dignity of individuals have stood the test of time and criticism rather better than his arguments that it is always wrong to tell lies, or to commit suicide or neglect one's talents or refrain from helping others in need. For one thing – and this is a problem for anyone who maintains that there are absolute moral prohibitions – his theory is unable to solve the dilemma which occurs when two such absolutes come into conflict, such as the duty to help an innocent person in need when this requires telling a lie to protect them. No doubt there are ways of justifying a lie in such a situation, but Kantian theory does not allow for them.

2.3.4   Respecting the human

Kant attempted to establish moral absolutes, without regard to consequences, by an exercise of what he called the 'practical reason'. Others who are equally opposed to deriving ethics purely from the results of our actions attempt various ways of doing the same by considering not just our reason but human nature as a whole, and exploring whether it has any ethical implications which we ought to respect.

Some early Greek philosophers concluded from observation that there is an order and harmony in nature, and that the moral life for individuals is to 'act in accordance with nature' and not against it, in ways which have interestingly come back into fashion in some environmentalist and New Age thinking today. Christian thinking in the Middle Ages and later built on the idea of human nature to develop the so-called 'natural law'. According to this ethical theory the fundamental human drives in individuals, such as to survive, to procreate and to pursue truth in common with others, give rise to corresponding ethical obligations enjoining the care of life, appropriate sexual conduct, respect for truth and the promotion of human society.

This theory of a moral law based on acting always in accordance with the fundamental orientations of human nature has been subject to various criticisms. It has been accused of having a static and unhistorical view of human nature and of tending to confuse nature with a particular culture, and it has difficulty in establishing its basic premise that simply because human beings have certain fundamental drives there is an ethical obligation to respect and protect those drives. Nevertheless, the attempts of a natural law theory to base ethics on a recognition of what it is to be human, and to link ethics with human development and flourishing, found a certain continuity and much more acceptance in the theory of natural rights and human rights which has developed since the sixteenth century through the ages of English, American and European political and social revolution to its popularity and powerful appeal today in the aftermath of the Second World War.

Not that the recognition, protection and promotion of human rights meets with universal acceptance as an ethical theory in the modern world. Jeremy Bentham thought natural rights the height of nonsense. Some complain that the human rights theory is used to make unreal and even comparatively trivial ethical claims on others. Others point to the confusing and differing ways in which rights are understood. Some consider that the rhetoric of rights actually says no more than the less inflammatory language of justice. But perhaps the major problem involved in the theory of human rights is how one can prove that they actually exist; that is, that all human beings without exception, simply by virtue of being human, have valid grounds for making certain claims on how they ought to be treated.

The appeal to universal human rights has become a powerful modern resource for many Christians in their insistence on justice for the poor and powerless wherever they suffer throughout the world; and their religious tradition enables them to claim that this situation is not as God intended or intends his human creatures to be treated. Made in the divine image, all men and women have thus been endowed with an inalienable value and dignity simply as his creatures; and furthermore they have been given a destiny and a task which entitle them to claim of other humans the freedom and the other resources required for each of them to find her or his personal fulfilment in pursuing that calling. It is interesting to note that John Locke's pioneering justification of the Glorious Revolution in England, the American Declaration of Independence and the French Declaration of the Rights of Man, each in turn appealed to a religious belief in the creation of human beings by God to justify their claims for God-given natural, or human, rights which must take precedence over any humanly offensive laws and claims of kings and governments.

Apart from such a religious foundation, the major line of purely rational argument to establish the existence of human rights lies in the appeal to a sort of social contract, or a conventional agreement that such rights should be recognized as an essential condition of general social harmony. What this utilitarian type of argument does not take into account, apart from its rather nebulous character, is that one of the most powerful functions of appeals to human rights is to stand up on behalf of individuals or minority groups of human beings against the bland discrimination of utilitarian considerations in general, and the tyranny of majorities in particular.

More often than not, the claim to certain human rights is a move against the tide, a protest or a safeguard on behalf of the weak against a long-standing or entrenched misuse of political, social or economic power.

Perhaps, in default of any convincing rational argument to justify the existence of human rights, the most one might claim is that they are simply self-evident and require no proof of existence. Human beings just have an intrinsic and unique dignity, and this simply entitles them to be treated in certain ways and not in others. Appeals to intuition, i.e. to a direct awareness of a state of affairs or to an immediate perception of the truth of a statement, tend to be suspect in philosophy. For one thing, they cannot be argued about, or explained in terms of something else, or debated, and therefore it is difficult to see how they can be corrected or qualified. For they are not necessarily correct. People can claim contradictory intuitions: one 'just knows' one thing and another 'just knows' the opposite, to their mutual bafflement and irritation that the other can be so blind to the obvious truth.

Nevertheless, for all the rational dissatisfaction expressed about the elusive nature of moral intuitions, it seems difficult to avoid the conclusion that at least on occasion a person or a group of people can have a moral awareness of something which is not, or not yet, capable of being explained in reasoned terms, but which may be none the less true for all that. The dawning realization of the rights of black human beings, of female human beings, and of various minority groups of human beings in society, may be cases in point. And certainly there seems an impressive moral authority about the steady and growing persuasion of so many people and groups in the modern world, even if it cannot be 'proved', that human beings ought to be treated, and ought to treat each other, only in ways which will respect their inherent value and dignity.

What forms such respect might or should take, and what human rights can be claimed on the basis of human dignity, are open to debate, of course. The right to life and the right to live according as one chooses are as basic as one can get. Yet it is important to realize that all human beings without exception possess such rights to life and freedom, and that therefore no one can exercise them ethically in ways which will infringe the equivalent rights of others. Again, the question is hotly debated, and underlies fundamental differences of political opinion, whether the claims which such rights entitle one to make are limited to creating corresponding obligations in others not to interfere with the individual's life and freedom and not to prevent them from having equal access to the means necessary to live in a way worthy of human beings; or whether more positively such basic rights entitle one to require that others actively provide the facilities and resources for an appropriately human standard of living.

Finally, the exploring of ethical behaviour in terms of the human rights possessed by all individuals to be treated in ways consonant with their dignity and to lead lives which are humanly satisfying has the merit of clearly identifying at least some of the basic features of what counts as human 'happiness' and well-being – an idea, or a moral aim, which otherwise remains tantalizing and vague, as we have seen. It provides strong counter-evidence to the contention that human cultures around the globe are so different in their standards and ways of acting that it is impossible to find some ethical common ground on which they might all agree. And it counters the argument that it would be ethical imperialism for one culture or country or business corporation to impose its standards and ways of behaving elsewhere. The point of the ethical theory of basic human rights and the contention that they apply equally to all men, women and children wherever they live, as the Universal and other Declarations of Human Rights make clear, is not that one culture is necessarily superior to others, but that all human cultures alike are subject to their constant scrutiny, evaluation and correction. The Latin poet, Terence, put the point more succinctly when he wrote, 'I am a human being; and I count nothing human as alien to me' (*Heauton Timorumenos*, I.1.25).

2.4   Ethics resource management

This survey of the ethics resources available to business people who want, or feel obliged, to bring ethical considerations to bear on the conduct of business by individuals or by corporations as a whole does not claim to be exhaustive. Its more modest purpose has been to identify and explore some of the major and relevant ways in which what can be called ethics resource management in business can be undertaken. Those who are experts in the field of ethics, and further reading, discussion and deliberation on the part of those who are not, will certainly bring out other approaches or refinements which can be considered in pursuing the human ethical enterprise. Yet perhaps sufficient has been identified and discussed here to illustrate the considerable ethics resources which are available to help people in business decide for themselves how to behave ethically, whether those resources are to be found in the public domain of codes, laws and religious beliefs, or whether they lie in the more intimate reaches of the human conscience and personal moral skills, or whether, finally, such resources lie in ordinary sustained thinking about what counts as ethical behaviour and why.

2.4.1   *Putting it all together*

Subsequent chapters of this book are designed to explore in detail the ethical aspects of various typical or significant business situations which may give cause for ethical interest or concern. In the light of the variety of approaches illustrated and discussed in this chapter, it should not surprise the reader to find considerable differences and even differing conclusions in such exercises of applied ethics. Nevertheless, from the various approaches to ethics resource management which we have considered it might be possible and useful to conclude by highlighting some of the more salient and even agreed features which our study has identified.

The external ethics resources of corporate codes of practice and laws governing behaviour show on the whole a certain unanimity in the approval or disapproval which they accord to certain ways of behaving, whether these are encountered in the day-to-day conduct of business or whether they are such gross or widespread forms of socially harmful behaviour, in business or elsewhere, as to be declared crimes. To that extent they can be considered as providing a useful, if limited, check-list against which to measure business practices or conduct. The same can be said of the external ethics resource of religion, at least for those who are of that religion. However, in the case of codes and laws, and also in the way some people understand the ethical teaching of their religion, no explicit justification other than that of authority is offered for why certain ways of behaving are required and others prohibited.

Among the internal ethics resources which are also accessible to help evaluate the ethical quality of various ways of behaving, pride of place is traditionally given, as we have seen, to the individual's conscience. Yet here too it is possible to stop short at the authoritative judgement of one's conscience, without reflecting on the decision-forming process which precedes it and on the qualities and moral skills of the individual human person which together form the grounds for the authority popularly ascribed to conscience and for the actual decisions of conscience.

What all these considerations appear to indicate is that if the pursuit of ethics is a typically human activity, it cannot dispense with human reflection and debate, and ultimately it will not be satisfied with anything short of enquiry into the basic intrinsic reason or reasons why some types of human behaviour should be considered morally right and others morally wrong. Only by such reasoned reflection, it appears, can human beings fully understand ethics and intelligently address new ethical opportunities and challenges which arise in changing social, cultural and techno-logical situations.

Most ethical theories are concerned with how our behaviour affects other people. It is true that Kant looks more for internal rational consistency, but most commentators on his theory find it strangely empty of content and remote from reality. Yet strikingly it is Kant who insists, in a way which many think rings true, that we must be impartial in our ethical decisions and never seek to make private rules to our own advantage. And it is he who famously bequeathed to all who are more explicitly concerned for the well-being of others the maxim that no one may ever be dehumanized or treated as less than a person in the interests of others.

For many people this is exactly the qualification which is required to make utilitarianism or any other form of consequentialism more ethically acceptable. It was probably the strength of Bentham's theory that he linked ethical behaviour so closely to the effects of our actions on others, whether for good or ill, and that he saw a profound ethical value in minimizing pain and suffering (including the sufferings of animals) and in seeking to expand the sum of human welfare. When the colours on his ethical palette were increased to include more than pleasurable experiences and to offer a range of other values such as truth, gratitude, friendship, equality and freedom, then his picture of what makes for human happiness, and human ethical behaviour, became a richer and, for many people, a more truly human one to inspire ethical imagination and to motivate ethical behaviour.

Yet the very broadness of the consequentialist ethical perspective carries with it, for many people, dangers of being too sweeping. It has little room in the overall composition for individuals or groups whose interests are overshadowed for the more striking effect. And it ignores the individual brush strokes, the many individual actions which together create and build up the scene of human well-being.

More prosaically, it has been observed that as a programme of ethics utilitarianism and consequentialism are nearly right. Yet in that 'nearly' they may go tragically wrong. The necessary corrective and control, it seems, can best be found in the idea of human rights, with a religious basis in the Judaeo-Christian belief in the dignity of all human creatures, a philosophical basis in the Kantian maxim of treating every member of humanity as an end, and with impressive support from the repeated affirmations in many quarters today that every single human being, simply by virtue of being human, has a value and a dignity which call for recognition, protection and promotion, perhaps increasingly in the conditions of modern society and of modern business.

2.4.2   Adding ethical value

In the light of these considerations it may be possible to suggest, finally, that ethics is ultimately about moral values, the sheer worth of human beings as such, as well as of their fulfilment in a variety of activities as individuals and in concert. From this point of view ethics is not primarily about laws, whether divine or human, or about codes of conduct. A law or a clause in a code of behaviour is nothing other than a single-value pressure group, aimed at impressing upon all concerned the importance of one particular human and moral value, whether it be human life, honesty, property, loyalty or the like, and the need to bear it in mind in all our decisions and actions. When ethical dilemmas occur, as they frequently do, whether in dramatic or more mundane ways, it is ethically superficial to view this as a matter of deciding whether to observe or infringe a code or to break a law, even a divine law. Dilemmas are more profoundly and more maturely a challenge of which values to opt for in a forced choice while attempting to accord as much recognition as possible to others.

Various attempts have been made in the history of ethics to make such value choices easier by identifying a hierarchy of moral values, such as considering those people nearest us in terms of kinship as having a prior claim on our ethical attention; or judging that values of the human spirit are superior and therefore preferable to those to do with physical existence, which in turn are to be preferred to property values. All such attempts are basically unrealistic in any but the most abstract sense. Yet they do raise the question of whether, not necessarily in general but in particular situations, it is possible to consider some moral values as carrying more weight than others. It is perhaps here particularly that the importance of the ethical theory of human rights becomes most apparent. While there may very well be room and scope for manoeuvre and debate where other moral values are concerned, it is in fact the purpose – and may be the major ethical attraction – of human rights to give particular prominence and overwhelming weight to the basic characteristics of human living as particular and precise ethical values which should never be permitted to be eclipsed by any other considerations.

Further reading

The literature dealing with ethics is immense. The following general studies are particularly recommended: Bernard Williams, *Morality. An Introduction to Ethics* (London: Penguin, 1973); D. D. Raphel, *Moral Philosophy* (Oxford University Press, 1981); and William Lillie, *An Introduction to Ethics* (London: Methuen, 1971). Several excellent articles are to be found on religious (and philosophical) topics in James F. Childress and John Macquarrie (eds.), *A New Dictionary of Christian Ethics* (London: SCM Press, 1986). On ethics and legal compliance, see David Lyons, *Ethics and the Rule of Law* (Cambridge University Press, 1984).

CHAPTER 3

Employers' and employees' rights and duties[1]

Jef van Gerwen
UFSIA, Belgium

Any type of relationship within the firm calls for specific ethical qualities and responsibilities of the agents; such is the case for producer/customer relationships, for relations with trade partners and competitors and, of course, also for employer/ employee relationships, which we will be discussing here. We will look at this subject in the first place from the angle of the employees, reflecting a long-standing tradition of European labour movements and legislation. In this respect European business ethics may differ somewhat from its American counterpart, if not in theory, at least in practice. Whereas American business ethics on average shows a clear management bias when discussing labour issues, European ethicists tend to refuse to define labour relations too exclusively from the employers' viewpoint, stressing instead the workers' role as fully entitled participants in the decision-making process of the firm.[2] A preferential focus on the workers' position does not imply, however, that our view will be biased in the opposite direction. It should be clear from the start that both employers and employees do have reciprocal rights and duties.

Because we are treating a vast subject-matter, it may be useful to start with a schematic outline of the major rights and duties (see Table 3.1). From this overview we may draw the following conclusions:

1.   The rights and duties of employers and employees are complementary: a right of one party implies the imposition of a duty to the other one, and vice versa. This seems logical: a right will always remain a void and purely theoretical concept, unless one also defines the agent who will be held responsible for carrying out the matching duties.

2.   The symmetry between both parties' rights and duties is incomplete. Some rights at one side, such as the right to work, are not matched by a proportional obligation on the other side. This lack of symmetry indicates, first of all, that a supplementary effort of society as a whole may be required in order to fully guarantee certain rights. Secondly, it illustrates that a number of rights and duties are still evolving within history. Economic ethics cannot be conceived as a once-and-for-all finished product. New economic rights and duties are likely to emerge in the future.

Table 3.1 Employees' and employers' rights and duties

Employees' rights and duties	Employers' rights and duties
● Right to work	● No-discrimination rules for recruitment; conditions for firing
● Right to just remuneration	● Duty to fair compensation
● Right to free association and to strike	● Respect for union presence and activities
● Right to privacy and to normal family life	● Work-oriented code of conduct
● Freedom of conscience, and freedom of of speech	● Acceptance of criticism from workers, without repression
● Right to due process	● Acceptance of labour court jurisprudence in conflicts
● Right to participation	● Duty to inform and to consult workers
● Right to healthy and safe working conditions	● Duty to guarantee same
● Right to work quality (job satisfaction)	● Duty to improve quality of work
● Duty to comply with labour contract	● Demand of minimal productivity of employees
● Loyalty to the firm	● Right to loyal co-operation
● Respect for current legal and moral norms	● Requirement of correct behaviour at the workplace

3. The rights and duties of employers and employees may also conflict with one another. The right to privacy of an employee, for example, may collide with the right of the employer to control the quality of the employee's performance; or the loyalty of employees towards their firm may not coincide with their duty to serve the general interest or with the promotion of their own private interests.

Without offering an exhaustive treatment of all these issues, we will systematically deal with the main subjects of labour ethics. First of all, we will discuss the meaning of the right to work; then we will describe some specific rights and duties that can be deduced from this basic right. Finally, we will look at some typical conflicts of rights occurring between employers and employees.

3.1   The right to work

A full analysis of the right to work belongs to the field of fundamental social ethics, rather than that of business ethics. However, since a correct understanding of the specific rights and duties of employees and employers presupposes an adequate interpretation of this fundamental ethical standard, we will start by briefly defining the significance of the right to work. For a more detailed study we refer to the appropriate literature on the subject.[3]

3.1.1 The meaning of the concept

Both components of the expression of 'a right to work' can be used with different meanings.

The right to 'work'
The term 'work' may refer to any kind of purposive and creative activity by which people meet their needs (labour in a broad sense), as well as to the more restricted field of institutionalized activities, which are socially and economically valued as 'employment' (labour in a restricted sense). In our context we use 'work' in the latter sense of the term, so we are referring to 'a right to employment', indicating a guaranteed access to a job which is being performed to earn an income. A person can be self-employed, earning income out of the surplus value of the goods or services produced and sold by his/her own initiative, or s/he can enter into a wage-labour contract, being employed by someone else.

The above distinction will help us to clarify some important conflicts of interpretation of the right to work. In the context of the free market economy it will not be readily accepted that every active member of the population who presents him/herself at the labour market should have an equal and actual chance to be employed, so that no single person would remain unemployed against his/her own will. On the contrary, adepts of the free market will tend to interpret the right to work in our first sense of the term, as a right to active participation in social life, without implying a right to employment. Moreover, when they do talk about the right to employment, adherents of the free market philosophy will tend to interpret it as a negative right: namely, the right of those who have a job and are willing to work not to be hindered by others to execute it (because of strikes, picketing, lock-outs, or prohibitive legislation).

In planned economies and in countries with a strong socialist tradition, on the other hand, the right to work will be understood as a positive right to employment, i.e. as a guaranteed access for all those who are ready and qualified to be employed through private or public initiatives. Within the context of industrial society, the right to participation in social life remains an illusory aim for the majority of people, unless it concretely includes a guaranteed access to employment. This is the case because labour, in its institutionalized form of employment, has become for most citizens the primary factor of active membership in society, of economic power and social status, rather than the ownership of capital or land, or the possession of valuable information.

The 'right' to work
The expression of a 'right' is ambiguous as well. First of all, we should distinguish between a juridical and a moral right. A basic right may already be morally valid within a certain society without being fully codified within the body of law. Only after moving through the full legislative process will a moral principle also be sanctioned as a positive law, and present a full right in the juridical sense. To take an

example in the field of social rights, the right to a guaranteed minimum income has only recently entered into European legislations. Four of the twelve European Community member states have not passed such a law yet; but as a moral principle the same right has been accepted in Europe for a long time: local public authorities have enacted its concrete application before national or international provisions came into effect.

When compared with the right to minimum income, the right to employment is still evolving at an earlier stage and it largely remains confined to the domain of moral principles and ideals. An unemployed person who has proved that s/he is willing and able to perform a job cannot file a claim before a court, demanding that some party in the private or public sector provide an adequate job offer for them. As long as this opportunity is excluded, the right to employment will not become a full juridical right.

It does not follow, however, that it is devoid of all moral and political meaning. On the contrary, the right to employment in our society is an emerging claim which is gaining gradual recognition. In this respect, the economist and moral philosopher Amartya Sen introduced the useful distinction between a right and a 'meta-right'. A right implies access to the good itself, whereas a meta-right offers a guarantee to implement policies that will promote the gradual realization of the good, within the limits of what is politically and economically possible.[4] The right to employment as a meta-right, therefore, means that citizens have a right to require responsible organizations (in the first place the government, and in the second place private employers) to choose those policies that will lead to the highest maintainable level of general employment. In this sense the right to employment has already been defined in an operational way, e.g. in the Social Charter of the Council of Europe, and in the corresponding national employment policies, which are defined and executed in close consultation and co-ordination with employers' organizations and trade unions (the so-called 'social dialogue' or 'consultation economy').[5]

The European Social Charter

It was signed by member states of the Council of Europe at Turin, Italy, on 18 October 1961, and came into effect on 26 February 1965. On the general right to work, it includes the following provisions:

The Contracting Parties accept as the aim of their policy, to be pursued by all appropriate means, both national and international in character, the attainment of conditions in which the following rights and principles may be effectively realized:

Part I

1. Everyone shall have the opportunity to earn his living in an occupation freely entered upon. (. . .)

Part II

Article 1

The right to work. With a view to ensuring the effective exercise of the right to work, the Contracting Parties undertake:

1. To accept as one of their primary aims and responsibilities the achievement and maintenance of as high and stable a level of employment as possible, with a view to the attainment of full employment;
2. To protect effectively the right of the worker to earn his living in an occupation freely entered upon;
3. To establish or maintain free employment services for all workers;
4. To provide or promote appropriate vocational guidance, training and rehabilitation. (. . .)

3.1.2   *The right to work within a business context*

What are the concrete consequences of the right to work at the level of corporations? Three general indications will be given, followed by some particular rules regarding hiring and firing, as well as by a more detailed discussion of specific labour rights (section 3.2).

1. The responsibility for realizing the right to work does not exclusively belong to the employers. A continuous co-operative effort is required, involving all economic agents of society. In order to guarantee the implementation of a policy of maximal employment, a sustained effort of dialogue and of co-ordination between the social partners (representatives of employers, trade unions and the government) is a first requirement. Accepting a definite active role for the public authority as a subsidiary provider of employment (so-called 'mixed economy' model) is a second one.

2. Under the present economic conditions one cannot – nor should one – press any particular employer to create more jobs, or to keep employees at work at a loss. One can only encourage the creation of extra jobs, or the maintenance of the existing level of employment, offering social and financial incentives to those who do so. A similar restraint can be formulated regarding the orientation of prospective employees: they should never be forced to accept a job which they refuse, or which lies far outside the scope of their qualifications. One is allowed, however, to stimulate workers to get retrained for qualifications which are more in demand.

3. Employees are not a mere commodity; they are human beings with inalienable rights and dignity. Consequently, one cannot engage or fire employees at will. Apart from profit considerations, a number of moral requirements have to be met.

Any employee deserves basic respect as a fellow human being. This implies, first of all, that those recruiting personnel use impartial criteria to evaluate the candidates with regard to their ability to perform the job; and, secondly, that the employer recognizes its specific moral obligations to those employees who have been working in the firm for a considerable period of time. Indeed, specific moral obligations of the employer become apparent both at the start and at the end of a labour contract.

Hiring

Though it would seem obvious to many, one cannot hold without further qualification the principle that the employer should always recruit the most qualified candidate for a job. The employer, indeed, does have a right to include other motives in the decision to enlist a candidate, such as kinship (e.g. in family firms) or the family background of the candidate. An employer may prefer to offer a job to a breadwinner, who has to support their family, rather than to a single person. The inclusion of other criteria than job qualification, therefore, does not necessarily prejudice the employee. Nevertheless, when practising partial or arbitrary judgement in recruitment, employers should be aware that they infringe upon the moral right of the applicants to equal and fair treatment. This is the case, e.g., when employers exclude candidates only on the basis of gender, or accept candidates lacking the necessary qualifications for a particular job when qualified applicants are available.[6]

Firing

The longer an employee has been working, the lower will their average chances be to find a new job after dismissal. Consequently, the employer has a moral duty to try (within the limits of what is economically possible) to keep its long-term employees in the firm up to retirement. This is a matter of basic social security for the employee, who most often has to rely on the stability of their job in order to meet social obligations and to succeed as a person. Moreover, one has to consider that the same employee has also invested a great deal of their life and energy in the firm, contributing to its results.

Loyalty to one's employees implies that one should never dismiss employees without a valid reason. Moreover, when terminating a contract, the relevant terms of notice should be respected. And finally, when economic conditions make it imperative to close a plant, or to reduce the number of employees, the employer should offer the maximum guarantees of social security, including possibilities of transfer to a new position, or of retraining. The latter moral requirement is gradually being translated in juridical terms in the European directives on information and consultation of workers in situations of collective redundancy, of restructuration of the firm (including closure or sale), or of important technological innovations.[7]

An ethical way of dismissal?

The French ethicist Michel Falise coined the concept of the 'ethics of dismissal' ('une éthique dans le licenciement').[8] He illustrates the issue with the following case: a textile mill, which is producing for the domestic market as well as for export, offered work to about 950 persons in the early 1980s. Because the demand for textile products remained constant during those years, whereas imports from foreign competitors were increasing, the entire national textile sector was facing hard times. Its sale figures decreased by 20 per cent. Moreover, the French economy as a whole was in a period of recession. In those circumstances the employer had to face some harsh choices: should they dismiss a number of workers in due time, in order to retain a sufficient degree of productivity with a reduced workforce producing for a smaller market segment? Or should they continue with the present workforce, with the possible prospect of having to close down completely?

At this point, some extra ethical clarification is required: moral conduct and ethical responsibility presuppose a situation of free choice: making an ethical decision implies that we choose appropriately between those alternatives that are available to us as conscious and free agents. We cannot be held responsible for those events which lie beyond our scope of power or consciousness. When applying this insight to the case of the textile mill employers, we may presuppose that it is not within their power to avoid the consequences of the general recession, nor to change the structural decline in the textile sector in the short term. Consequently, we cannot demand that they should act as if they could do so, e.g. by asking them to keep producing with the same capacity, or to enlist more new employees.

The degree of free choice which is available to the members of the firm (employer, employees, shareholders, etc.) and which defines the limit of their moral responsibility, is determined by the prevailing macro-economic circumstances. So, the employers are only responsible for the way in which they choose between the alternatives which remain open to them: either restructuring the firm (including job cuts) or imminent closure.

However, the same members enjoy some real freedom to act within those confined limits, and have thus a real responsibility in deciding on a number of questions:

- Will they discuss the policy alternatives in due time in the assembly of shareholders, agreeing on some planning of necessary changes, instead of allowing the situation to deteriorate until the firm is definitely lost?
- Will they inform and consult all the concerned parties, and explicitly the workers, discussing all available alternatives?
- Who will be made redundant, and according to which criteria?
- Do they respect due times of advance notice for redundancies?
- Do they use all available possibilities to relocate workers in other plants, or to retrain them, helping them to enter into new jobs?

In Falise's example, the partners come to the tentative conclusion that a reduction of 10 per cent of the workforce is needed in order to grant the mill a real chance to stay in business. In order to reach this objective, the following measures are accepted:

1. Employees who are ready for retirement will not be replaced.

2. Employees older than 55 have to accept early retirement, which is accompanied by the usual social benefits.
3. Employees older than 50 are not forced to quit their jobs, but may also apply for early retirement.
4. If the total number of employees under categories 1, 2 and 3 does not add up to 10 per cent, an additional number of employees younger than 50 will be discharged. In doing so, the employer will take into account their social situation (family background, age, seniority) and their merits (service record).

After a consultation period of about six months, the final restructuring of the workforce in the textile mill looked as follows: 50 employees accepted early retirement, 21 were dismissed, and 150 were retrained to take up new jobs within the firm.

The importance of an 'ethics of firing' becomes evident when one compares the above example with the many occurrences of immediate dismissal of employees without advance notice. For example, according to Belgian law, an employee may be dismissed without respecting the usual terms of notice only when s/he has shown serious shortcomings precluding further professional co-operation immediately and definitively. Those who are fired in this way are also excluded from receiving unemployment benefits or assistance of public employment services. The employee has the right to contest the charges before the labour court, in which case the employer has to deliver proof that the dismissal was indeed well founded on a serious shortcoming of the employee.

Clearly, one is justified in immediately dismissing any employee who has knowingly and willingly shown serious shortcomings in the execution of his/her contract, especially to avoid further damage to the production process, to other workers or to the public interest. But on several occasions, employers have been inclined to give too broad an interpretation to the term 'serious neglect', so that employees have been dismissed for minor infringements of the work code, such as stealing a discarded specimen out of the production chain (a damaged bag of chips, some sandwiches), for disobedience in matters not directly related to the quality of work (a typist who preferred to work in a room with an open window, against the will of her/his boss), or for withholding information at the moment of application (militants of a leftist organization not mentioning their academic degrees when applying for a job as a semi- or unskilled worker).

Employees may also abuse the same procedure in order to obtain an immediate dismissal from their job. This may happen when they intend to take up another job elsewhere: by provoking immediate dismissal, they could count on receiving compensation for the termination of their contract, which they would certainly not receive if they themselves took the initiative to resign.

We may conclude that the procedure of immediate dismissal for serious shortcomings should always remain an exceptional practice, which can only be invoked in order to remove immediately those employees who by their very conduct pose a serious threat to the adequate functioning of the firm. A 'serious shortcoming', thus, should include some form of neglect or misconduct which is directly related to the work process (and not only to the private life of the employee) and which would have an enduring negative effect on the adequate functioning of the production process.

3.2   Specific rights of employees

3.2.1   The right to receive a written contract

As soon as a person has accepted a job offer, he or she becomes the carrier of a number of specific rights and obligations. Several of those rights and duties should be formulated explicitly in due juridical form in a labour contract.[9] The drafting of a labour contract is in itself an act with moral relevance: it grants legal security to the parties involved and, insofar as it presents a complete, explicit and concrete definition of the terms of the contract, it will provide a basis of mutual confidence for the subsequent period of co-operation between employer and employee.

Because the drafting of a contract is a moral good in itself, one should accept as a general principle that all sorts of labour, also on an interim or part-time basis, should be subject to a written contract in due form. This is especially required in the context of small firms and family firms. There it may occur that members of the family, friends or acquaintances, are employed based on informal agreements. Often the lack of formal labour contracts is justified by referring to moral values: between friends and kin members one should be able to rely on mutual trust and voluntary commitment as a sufficient basis for working relations. This, however, is a clear example of bad judgement. In the professional sphere one should rather avoid relying too extensively on moral attitudes that belong to the private sphere of family and friendship relations (gifts, voluntary work, etc.). Respect for impartial, universally applicable criteria, acceptance of objective and business-like arrangements, which are contractually defined and are therefore juridically enforceable: those are moral attitudes that are most fitting to the sphere of professional life.

Having affirmed the moral qualities of labour contracts, we will now look at the specific ethical norms that play a major role in orienting labour relations. We will consecutively discuss the rights to just remuneration, to safe working conditions, to work quality, to free association, to participation, and to due process (section 3.3).

3.2.2   The right to a just remuneration

The right to a just remuneration, and more specifically the right to a just wage, has been a primary aim of the labour movement since its very start. The wage, indeed, is in the first place an expression of the exchange value which every employee receives in exchange for his performance, but it is also the main source of income and basic security for most workers, and most often the result of a co-operative and collective effort. As soon as more than one criterion is invoked to define wages (performance, needs, distributive justice) conflicts of weighing different criteria will occur. Thus, adepts of the liberal and social democratic schools have always differed on the ways to define just wages. According to the latter, a wage is fair and sufficient only if it grants to every employee his proportional part of the realized surplus value of the firm. A wage should present a share in the profits which the workers have helped to realize. Moreover, a just wage should not only be proportionate to performance, but also satisfy the basic needs of the employee and his/her family (those who depend on the wage-earner for income). Because the wage is often the only source of income for the employee and his/her family, it should be sufficiently high and stable to guarantee a decent standard of living.

According to the liberal tradition, however, a wage should only provide compensation for a given job performance, the price of which is determined by the interplay of supply and demand on the labour markets. The price of labour is in principle unrelated to the profit realized by a company, or to the needs of the employee. Within the liberal vision, indeed, profits rightly belong to the owners of the firm, i.e. to those who have accepted the risk to invest capital in the firm. Social needs, such as income security, should be met through the initiatives of civil society and the government. Social security transfers should not be connected to the wage mechanism, because they tend to make wages too rigid and labour costs too high.

Obviously, the definition of a 'just wage' is a complex issue. It involves detailed analysis and policy choices concerning the relationship between capital and labour, between labour and income, and between the use of need and merit criteria for determining income.[10] Without further elaborating these fundamental issues, we adopt the following tentative list of pragmatic criteria for evaluating the fairness of wages:

1. The legally guaranteed minimum income.
2. The difficulty of the job
3. The principle of equal treatment
4. The average wage in a given sector
5. The capacity of the firm
6. The acceptance of collective wage agreements.

Other, more circumstantial, criteria could be added:

7. The average cost of living in the region
8. Tenure, or guaranteed job stability
9. Seniority.[11]

The guaranteed minimum wage

A legal minimum wage, which is defined by law in most European countries (except the United Kingdom), provides a first indication of a just remuneration. Wages falling below the legal minimum are judged to be unfair, not necessarily because they would not offer a correct expression of the market value of the job, but because they do not allow fully employed people who lack additional resources to live with minimal dignity. Thus, the legal minimum wage sets a socio-ethical limit to the free interplay of market forces, and rightly so.

We should add here that, following standard practice in most European countries, wages are supplemented by substantial social security benefits (child allowances, health insurance, unemployment benefits, retirement pensions, insurance in case of labour accidents or occupational diseases) paid by common funds to which employers and employees are obliged to contribute. These social security benefits provide an essential correction to the primary wage, so that the final, secondary wages (after social security transfers) offer a more correct reflection of payment according to the needs of employees and their families, and not only according to performance. Since these benefits form an integral part of the guaranteed minimum wage, nobody should be allowed to dodge the regular payment of social security contributions.

The difficulty of the job
To the degree that the execution of a job requires a higher standard of technical skills or knowledge, that it involves a higher risk for the employee, or a greater amount of responsibility for other people's safety or property, it should be better remunerated.

The principle of equal pay
This, of course, is directly related to the previous criterion. Employees having to perform identical jobs, or jobs with a similar degree of difficulty, should receive equal treatment, including equal pay. Gender discrimination, ethnic discrimination, or any other form of unequal remuneration of employees which cannot be justified by manifest differences of work performance, are unacceptable.

The average wage in the sector
One of the unavoidable consequences of market economics is the unequal payment for comparable levels of performance due to sector differences in average added value: e.g., average wages in the textile sector will be much lower than in chemistry. Even though the actual labour markets often do not offer an adequate indication of what would be the true average wage in a situation of perfect competition, they may provide a rough estimate of a fair wage in a given sector.

The profit realized by the firm
Although a sufficient part of the wage should be fixed, guaranteeing a stable income to the employees, it is becoming more and more acceptable that a substantial part of wages should be proportionate to profit, both because workers have contributed to its realization, and because a good result for the firm should be reflected in wages, as an incentive for future performance. Profit-sharing among all employees of the same plant or firm seems preferable to compensation according to individual performances, especially in those circumstances where higher performance is the net result of co-operation rather than of individual efforts.

The result of collective agreements

Precisely because markets in general, and labour markets in particular, do not by themselves lead to fair wage levels, the results of labour negotiations between union and employer representatives will often grant a useful secondary indication of a just wage in the sector. Wages which are the outcome of balanced negotiations between opposite interest groups tend to offer a more nuanced estimate of due remuneration than wages which have been determined unilaterally by one party.

Apart from the above (more or less) universally accepted criteria, we may add a few others, whose validity is more contested, but which still play a considerable role in the European context.

The average cost of living

Until the recent past it was generally accepted that wages could differ substantially not only between different sectors, but also between regions. Employees living in areas with a lower standard of living (rural areas, Third World countries) could rightly be paid lower wages than their colleagues living in more expensive conditions. The rationale behind this was not only market-oriented (the labour cost being higher in the wealthier areas) but also of a social nature: wages should reflect the purchasing power of employees as consumers in a given area. By paying different wages, one was offering them roughly equal purchasing power. Nevertheless, under the influence of European unification and of free circulation of workers, the validity of this criterion will probably diminish. Moreover, remaining differences in remuneration, e.g. between German and Portuguese workers in a comparable job, will be based on different levels of average productivity, rather than on differences in the standard of living.

Tenure, and guaranteed job stability

In many countries, it is a commonly accepted practice to pay an employee less in the public sector than in the private sector for similar work, e.g. as an engineer, a physician or a lawyer. In order to justify this policy, it is argued that the public administration serves other ends than the mere maximization of utility (profit) and, consequently, that public servants are remunerated according to a competitive labour model. Moreover, the employee in public service will be compensated by means of secondary wage benefits for the comparable disadvantages of their primary wage: in comparison with colleagues in the private sector, s/he will enjoy greater stability in the job (fixed tenure, no unemployment risks) and higher social security benefits (higher pension). These arguments offer a partial justification of the prevalent policy. Indeed, there may be specific deontological reasons (the ethical code of public service, impartiality requirements, etc.) for providing a professional statute different from the private sector, including wage guarantees. Yet it seems to be in the interest of both the private and the public sectors to keep the differences in remuneration between both as limited as possible. Indeed, too rigid a system of tenure will inevitably lead to inertia and discouragement among civil servants lacking a sufficient amount of competitive impulses. On the other hand, a lower level of social security benefits within the private sector can hardly be praised as a great moral achievement, either.

Seniority

In many countries wage levels will increase in proportion to the number of years the employee has been in service; this seniority qualification may even be carried from one job contract into another when the employee changes firms. This difference in pay for the same job is justified as a reward for loyalty to the firm, and as a recompense for the higher level of job experience of senior employees. One could question, however, if these justifications apply equally in all circumstances, and if seniority should be accepted as a generally valid criterion for determining the fairness of wages. Counter-arguments could be put forward: younger employees could demonstrate other qualities to a higher degree than their more senior colleagues, such as having gone through professional training at a more recent date, being more dynamic and introducing new insights and suggestions onto the shop floor. These qualities could equally justify pay differentials. Moreover, seniority has a negative secondary effect for older employees applying for new jobs, or attempting to hold on to their existing job in times of decreasing labour demand. Because the labour cost of senior employees is relatively higher for the same job, employers may be tempted to prefer younger candidates. Of course, as we have mentioned above, an employer also has a moral duty to offer job security and maximum stability of employment, especially to those employees who have served the company for a long time. But the fulfilment of this obligation should not be thwarted further by adding to the general cost of employment an extra cost for senior employees.

3.2.3   The right to safe and healthy working conditions

It seems evident that all workers have the fundamental right to execute their job contract in safe and healthy conditions. Many international directives and regulations are enforced to implement this aim; most important of these is the set of binding health and safety provisions that has been put forward by the European Commission for all Member States.[12] Nevertheless, in practice, infractions do still occur. In Belgium, for example, 175 lethal accidents have been registered at the workplace during a one-year period, and 153,000 employees have been injured (1986 figures, collected on an overall population of 2,225,000 employees). Moreover, in the same year, 2,497 new cases of victims of occupational disease were counted, bringing the accumulated amount from 1963 to 1986 to 83,558.[13] The highest proportion of accidents and occupational diseases is to be found in mining industries, whose overall numbers of employment are declining steeply for the moment. But apart from the 'mining factor', a significant percentage of accidents and diseases is due to structural deficiencies in production processes or in the organization of the workplace (for which employers are responsible) and, secondly, to neglectful behaviour by a number of employees. This observation is confirmed by the fact that a growing proportion of accidents is being registered in small firms, where the implementation of safety measures seems harder to reinforce than in larger ones.

Health and safety infractions cover a very complex area of conduct. Employees are not only running 'obvious' risks such as cutting or crushing injuries, electrocution, burns or fractures. They are also exposed to extreme heat or cold, excessive noise levels, dust, chemical agents, metal poisoning, or radiation; or they may be pushed to a work rhythm causing nerve damage. The existing regulations, the labour-related medical services, and the so-called 'Committees for Safety, Health and Improvement of the Work Place' (obligatory in each firm employing more than 49 people) do not automatically provide a sufficient guarantee. The crucial 'missing link' is often to be found in a deficient corporate culture, in which a general attitude of negligence is allowed to flourish until severe accidents have occurred.

In March 1989 the Penal Court of Antwerp (Chamber 25bis) was treating the case of unsafe working conditions in a benzene plant of the AMOCOFINA corporation. The plant had been closed in 1985; however, in 1980 a first case of cancer had been found among the workers. One year later, another plant worker died of leukaemia; soon afterwards, significant deviances in blood patterns were observed also among employees working in the administrative office of the plant. Even though the physician who was responsible for regular health checks of the workers had contacted the safety manager and the director of the plant as early as 1978 in order to demand extra protective measures, these executives had failed to take initiative. On the contrary, the director had urged the physician not to spread the news to the outside world, even not to inform the official Fund for occupational diseases (as he should have done). In the meantime, benzene concentrations of 420 ppm could be measured on the work floor of the plant, whereas the legal norm allowed for a maximum of only 25 ppm.[14]

Of course, one has to keep in mind that safety risks can never be excluded completely in the production process. If employers and employees were forbidden to run any risk, many essential products and services could no longer be provided to the larger community. So, in many cases, some prudential judgement will be required, balancing the real need of the community to obtain some product and the gravity of risks for those providing it. In all circumstances the following conditions should be met:

1. Employees should be informed from the start about the health and safety risks they are exposed to when accepting a certain job.
2. They should accept to take the risk freely, without any coercion.
3. They should be compensated sufficiently for the risk they are asked to take, both through direct wage increases and through appropriate insurance and social security provisions.
4. A health and safety risk should not be accepted recklessly, but only to produce a good with a clear public utility.
5. Both employer and employee should apply the best available knowledge and technology in order to reduce the present risk.

3.2.4   The right to work quality

The object of labour ethics is not confined to matters of just remuneration after the job has been completed, or to protect the health of the worker during execution. It is also a matter of moral concern that the time spent at work should be intrinsically rewarding, so that the employees are not forced to experience their job as a senseless activity, and as a form of alienation which they only accept to endure because of the related income. They should be able to be satisfied with the result of their work. Partly, the realization of this aim will depend on macro-economic variables which remain beyond the control of individual firms and employers. Many sorts of stress and alienation are indeed produced as side-effects of macro-economic processes of automation, power concentration, bureaucracy and the introduction of economies of scale.

However, the average employer may enjoy a sufficient degree of freedom within the existing economic limits to increase the quality of work of the employees within the firm. A key role in increasing job satisfaction will be played by taking counter-measures to repetitive work at the assembly line or in bureaucratic settings. Indeed, job quality strategies often show a clear anti-Tayloristic bent. (Taylorism: a management philosophy stressing the productivity-enhancing effects of mechanized production processes including assembly-line work, division of complex tasks in minuscule, repetitive performances delivered at high speed.) However, the aim of increasing job quality stretches beyond the issue of defining alternatives to conveyor-belt production processes.

Increasing autonomy on the job

Most employment follows a rationale of 'heteronomy', which means that employees are essentially told by hierarchical superiors what to do, and when and how to do it. This hierarchical structure of command may be an unavoidable characteristic of the complex division of labour and of information control within firms. However, if it is not balanced by giving maximal opportunities to the employees for exercising their free judgement on the job, excessive heteronomy will not only hurt ethically but also economically. Autonomy implies that employers are able to delegate maximum responsibility to their employees, making positive use of the personal experience of employees on the job. Initiatives and corrections by employees are encouraged and are included in the decision-making process. Employees are regularly briefed and consulted about possible innovations.

Further strategies

The basic requirement of maximizing autonomy may be further implemented through strategies of *feedback*, *task significance* and *task identity* clarification, and of *flexibility on the job*.[15] The first two strategies are intended to increase the amount of critical information employees receive about their production tasks: by adapting their product to criticisms or suggestions coming from consumers or co-workers (feedback), and by receiving some prior explanation on the significance of their tasks within the larger framework of the firm's production aims and processes (task significance). The latter two strategies are meant to increase identification with the final product, allowing any particular employee to follow the production process over a larger segment, or to shift functions along the production line. Flexibility, however, can become a mixed blessing for employees, as it may be used not only to add variety to the job (shifting working hours, changing tasks) but also to increase overall productivity, thereby putting extra pressure on all employees and imposing shifting working conditions on those who may not want them.

3.2.5   The right to free association and to strike

The right to free association, i.e. to legitimately organize trade union activities within the firm, and the right to strike are two closely related employee rights. Employers enjoy corresponding rights to free professional association and to lock out workers.

The right of employees to organize in trade unions in order to defend their professional interests proceeds from the basic right of free association. As such it is explicitly mentioned in the Universal Declaration of Human Rights (1948), in the Social Charter of the Council of Europe (1961) and in the European Community Charter of Fundamental Social Rights of Workers (1989). This recognition is a relatively novel phenomenon. During the nineteenth century trade unions were considered illegitimate in most countries, because they were supposed to undermine the freedom of enterprise and the freedom of contracting (free, uncontrolled individual labour contracts). In practice, this interpretation led to inhuman living and working conditions, prohibiting the weaker parties on the free market from defending their interests collectively. The mass of unskilled workers hardly possessed any bargaining power for negotiating fair labour contracts, whereas industrial employers could recruit at will out of the abundant supply of cheap labour emigrating from overpopulated agrarian areas to the new industrial centres. Only after a prolonged social struggle, reaching far into this century, did workers receive the right to organize in independent unions in order to correct the power balance in industrial labour relations. The same principles of free association were later expanded to include employees of other economic sectors, and employees of smaller firms (which often maintain a typical non-union climate).

A trade union serves a moral purpose, namely to promote the interests of the employees working within a certain economic sector, region or firm. This promotion of a group interest is a legitimate moral end; it should also take into account, however, the following ethical orientations:

1.   Trade unions are representatives, not of the general interest, but of an important particular interest. Consequently, they should not act or impose themselves in the place of the government, which is the primary agent acting to promote the general interest of all citizens. It seems appropriate, rather, that some form of institutionalized bargaining be organized between representatives of the government, the unions and

employers' organizations, in order to co-ordinate the respective initiatives and policies. Any functional or administrative mixture or confusion between trade union and governmental activities should be avoided.

2.   Trade unions have to defend the interests of all concerned workers within a given firm or sector, and not only those of their members. Although it may seem obvious that unions offer preferential treatment to those who in fact support them, and though one has to criticize morally those employees who like to profit from union action without actively contributing to its organization, it should be kept in mind that unions are morally required to defend all workers' interests within a given context. Closed-shop practices (whereby employers are pressured by a union to recruit only among union members) are morally unacceptable. Also, it is most important that unions do not only defend those in jobs, but also include the unemployed of the same sector.

3.   Trade unions should respect the freedom of choice and expression of non-union workers. This includes the freedom to keep working under conditions other than those proposed by the union, to organize in other associations or interest groups, or to refrain from enlisting in the union. Unions cannot claim a monopolistic position in representing the employees of a given firm or sector. They can only strive to increase their membership without using coercion in order to become as representative as possible for a given population of employees. Employees, on the other hand, have a moral obligation to act in solidarity with their colleagues. Even if they cannot be forced to join any particular union, non-members should ask themselves whether, by their very conduct, they do not damage the legitimate cause of their fellow workers.

The right to strike has always been considered an ultimate consequence of the right to free professional organization, and of the related right to collective bargaining. A strike, indeed, is conceived as a legitimate means of last resort in the context of a conflict-regulation process. As such, it has been explicitly mentioned in the United Nations' International Convention on Economic, Social and Cultural Rights (1966, art. 8), and in the European Charters of the Council of Europe (1961, art. 6) and of the European Community (1989, art. 13).

European Social Charter

Article 6: The right to bargain collectively

With a view to ensuring the effective exercise of the right to bargain collectively, the Contracting Parties undertake:

1.   to promote joint consultation between workers and employers;
2.   to promote, where necessary and appropriate, machinery for voluntary negotiations between employers or employers' organizations and workers' organizations, with a view to the regulation of terms and conditions of employment by means of collective agreements;

3. to promote the establishment and use of appropriate machinery for conciliation and voluntary arbitration for the settlement of labour disputes; and to recognize:
4. the right of workers and employers to collective action in cases of conflicts of interest, including the right to strike, subject to obligations that might arise out of collective agreements previously entered into.

Contrary to popular opinion, the right to strike does not properly belong to trade unions, but rather to the employees as a whole. A strike, indeed, is a collective, democratically decided refusal of the workers to execute their job as defined in their labour contracts, in order to defend their collective professional interests.

This implies that the employees have a moral right to suspend the execution of their work unilaterally (not identical to breaking their contracts!) for an indefinite period of time, once the following conditions have been met:

1. There exists a reasonable chance that some legitimate professional demands of the employees will be met by this means.

2. Other, less radical means of negotiation, arbitration and reconciliation have been exhausted. A strike is only justifiable as a means of last resort.

3. The importance of the common cause or demand should be proportional to the use of a strike, which implies that the aim of the strikers should be to obtain some objective of participative or distributive justice, which can justify the hardships and damages which the parties concerned will probably suffer as a consequence of the strike.

4. The strikers have taken all necessary precautions in order to avoid irreparable damage to third parties (consumers, the larger public, the environment) and to the means of production of the firm (maintenance of capital goods, machines).

The last criterion implies that some professional groups may be forbidden to enter into a general strike, because any unlimited suspension of their work would inevitably cause extreme damage to the general interest. This is the case, e.g., for physicians, police agents, soldiers, whose rights may be legitimately limited at this particular point. Members of such occupations can use alternative means of pressure which come close to the model of a regular strike, without having the same negative effects for the public – such as work-to-rule, or limited strike actions with reduced personnel on active duty, or reduced working time.

The risk of irreparable damage done to the firm may offer a legitimate incentive to employers to lock out employees, and to recruit other candidates instead. There is no agreement within the juridical and ethical literature on the use of lock-outs. For some authors, the right to lock out is a logical correlate of the right to strike: employers are free to use it as an ultimate means of pressure in labour conflicts, under conditions similar to those when workers may enter a strike. According to others, however, any ethical judgement should take into account the structurally weaker position of workers with regard to property rights and control over the means of production; consequently, the right to lock out should not receive equal standing with the right to strike. Rather, an unwarranted lock-out could provide a legitimate ground for workers to occupy the firm. The different stances on this issue are related to the different interpretations that are given to the participation rights of employees.

3.2.6   The right to participation

Employee rights of information and consultation, co-ownership, co-operative management, co-decision-making, structural participation, profit-sharing, financial participation in the capital of the firm, etc. – these are all different elements relating to the same fundamental question: to which degree, and by what means, do employees have a right to take part in the general control of the firm? 'Control' may imply two distinct capacities: participation in the decision-making process (structural partici-pation), or co-ownership of the means of production (financial participation). In the final analysis, both aspects will be related, of course, since participation on one level without taking part on the other would not be very effective. Yet it may seem useful to distinguish both aspects, if only because national schemes of participation tend to accentuate one or the other dimension, since an overall European model is still lacking.[16]

Within our present Western economic system, there is fundamental disagreement on the concrete content of workers' participation rights. The basic unresolved issue which lies at the root of this problem has to do with property rights, more precisely with the just ascription of property rights of the firm and its products to the different co-operating parties. Who should exercise ultimate control over the firm? The shareholders, who provide the capital? The directors and the management, who invest their expertise? All the employees, who invest a large part of their lives and energy in the same firm? Or government representatives, defending the general interest? Should any of these parties claim a predominant role, or should they exercise control in a combined, co-operative manner? The answers to these questions can be classified into two opposing categories, as follows:

1.   Adherents of liberal and capitalist currents of thought will give priority to the principle of private property, including the private ownership of capital and of capital goods such as firms. They see the firm in the first place as a commodity, which should be sold and purchased freely on the market. The right to dispose of such commodity should be held undividedly by the one party who owns the capital (this one party may be a physical person, a group, or a legal fiction).

In this perspective labour appears equally as a commodity and, moreover, as a hired factor, not as a component equal to capital within the structure of the firm. The owner of the company hires workers for a limited purpose and time, offering in exchange a limited compensation and nothing else. Therefore, employees have no right to claim any part in the ownership or the decision-making process of the firm, just as the employer has no right to claim any control over the private affairs of his employees. When applied to the extreme, the capitalist approach leads to a complete exclusion of the social economics which are implied within the functioning of the firm, and it is incompatible with any job security.

The only meaning which workers' participation may still receive within this school of thought is that of a right to receive correct information about the firm. Employees have a right to be well informed about any facts relating to their working conditions (productivity goals, wages, safety, product quality, expected results and developments of the firm). One should not hide any information from them which might affect their interests as a person. But as a matter of principle they need not be given a consultative or determining voice in company policy. In the liberal vision, exceptions to this rule can only be justified by utilitarian motives – because some employees could become more productive or more highly motivated by participative strategies. Thus, worker consultation and participation may become acceptable almost as 'a lesser evil' in this perspective, but certainly not as a general rule, as a 'basic right'.

2. According to the advocates of a socially corrected market economy (a line of thought which is shared by social democrats, Christian democrats, and expressed within the social teaching of the churches, as well as socialist traditions), the principle of private property of capital should not be completely rejected, but corrected by complementary regulation, so that the firm is being managed taking into account the interests of all parties concerned, including employees. Two sorts of arguments are put forward in order to defend this position.

(a) Firms are in essence social goods, not merely private commodities. Firms are being conceived, formed and reformed with the overall purpose to produce goods and services for society. Although it may be most efficient (in order to stimulate creative initiatives, and to maximize profit in a competitive setting) that firms are privately owned, this line of argument does not provide the entire truth about the status of the firm. Once established through the initiative of one private party, a firm ceases to be a mere instrument in the hands of some individual(s), becoming an institution, i.e. the net result of co-operation of many parties and interests, and a socially valued reality by itself.[17] This social character of the firm implies that it can no longer be controlled unilaterally by one party, since all the parties who are related to the continuous functioning of the firm should have their say in its management and ownership. They obtain this right to participate insofar as they contribute to the success of the firm, and as they depend on the firm for satisfying some essential needs, such as security of existence, income, health and self-development.

(b) Every person is entitled to own the fruits of his or her labour. The accumulated surplus value which is created in a firm is the net result of the co-operative effort of all parties involved. Consequently, profits are not adequately distributed if all property rights, including a claim to the residual income, belong to the capital owners, whereas the workers can only claim a fixed compensation. Employees should be regarded as full partners, rather than as hired labour. Their voice should be taken into account, directly or indirectly, through employee representatives on the board of directors, when deciding on company policy. Evidently, such participation in the decision-making process should be accompanied by participation in the ownership of the firm (by means of share ownership, co-operative ownership, employee investment funds, rather than through simple forms of bonus payment and profit-sharing).

The socio-economic approach to participation was institutionalized mostly on the European continent, especially after the Second World War. The clearest example is provided by the German system of 'Mitbestimmung', but also French, Dutch, and Belgian economic law contain some specific models. The process of arriving at a consistent and uniform transnational model of participation has been hampered, however, not only by ideological opposition, but also by legal difficulties.[18] In many legal traditions, especially those influenced by the Napoleonic Code, a clear conceptual separation is maintained between the firm as an economic entity on the one hand, and the company (i.e. the firm as an object of property) on the other. As long as this legal 'cleavage' is maintained, participation of employees is likely to remain an exceptional practice, and limited to exceptional policy decisions (such as firm closures, restructuration or bankruptcy).

3.3   Arbitrating between conflicting rights

Any time when different rights are being invoked in a particular case, conflicts of rights are likely to occur. The question will inevitably arise, then, as to which right should receive priority. Should one prefer higher wages or better health conditions at the workplace, if one cannot improve both at the same time? Discord can equally appear when one needs to define the party which will be held responsible for guaranteeing a right: is it the employer, or the social partners, or the government? And, last but not least, a series of conflicts between the rights of employers and the opposite rights of employees needs arbitration. The overall question here will be: to which degree does a right of one party put a limit on the right of the other one? Where do we draw the line between conflicting interests for the good of all? We will discuss some exemplary cases of this latter type of conflict in this section.

3.3.1   Speaking out or keeping silent?

Firms can only function well if certain costly and crucial types of information remain well protected within their confines. The deserved return on research and development investment would be lost if research results or production techniques that have been gradually acquired within the firm are being revealed to outsiders and communicated to possible competitors. Legally speaking, such information is most often protected by patents and charters; it should be clear, however, that such regulations are based on a moral principle: employees are required to respect trade secrets as part of their obligation of loyalty to the firm, because this valuable information truly belongs to the firm. A requirement of confidentiality may or may not be explicitly formulated within the deontological code of the employee's profession (e.g. accountants or lawyers). It can equally be justified on utilitarian grounds to apply to all who work within the firm: the employer and the fellow workers should have the moral certainty that no member of the firm will steal any information which truly belongs to their common enterprise, and, in doing so, withhold any rewards to which they are entitled. This obligation of loyalty may come into conflict, however, (a) with the general interest of the public, and (b) with the personal interest of the employee.

We will subsequently consider both possibilities.

Informing the public

First, we will consider the case in which loyalty to the firm comes into conflict with the general interest.

Leaking information on leaking barrels

A chemical plant produces a considerable amount of unrecyclable waste. The company which owns the plant has a contract for waste disposal with a local public authority, which provides for the waste to be buried under certain environmental safety conditions. The waste is crated in the appropriate barrels at the plant before it is transported to the waste disposal site. Two engineers are responsible for supervising this process, and checking the quality of the barrels before transport. When arriving at the site, incoming barrels may be counterchecked by public administration officials, but this is often done in a routine fashion only.

At a particular moment the engineers come to the conclusion that a new chemical by-product cannot be disposed of in the kind of barrels they customarily use, because laboratory analysis has confirmed a small but significant probability that the product will gradually seep through the container and spread into the soil. After some time, this could cause severe damage to the drinking-water supply of the region. They inform the chief executive officer of the plant about their observations, and propose to reload the content of the unsafe barrels into a new type of container, which still has to be made or bought by the firm.

The chief executive officer of the plant, however, refuses to go along with the engineers' proposal. He prefers to deliver the usual load of barrels to the waste disposal site at the customary time; any change would imply extra costs and could cause suspicion among the public officials, who could be inclined to impose extra control procedures or conditions on all the waste being delivered. Moreover, the CEO estimates that the safety risk, though statistically significant, is too small to urge a fundamental change of policy. He assures the engineers that he will accept accountability for this decision if it should be put into question at a later date. Finally, he asks them to consider the issue as closed.

The two engineers do not accept this outcome. They send a written report to the board of directors of the company, asking them to reconsider the CEO's decision. They argue it is in the company's as well as in the public interest to strictly abide with safety regulations as they have been written into the contract with the public authority. At the board's meeting, however, the CEO is able to convince the majority of the board to endorse his line of policy.

At that point, after hearing of the board's decision, both engineers have divergent opinions on the next step to take. Engineer A is convinced he has done his duty; he does not favour informing the wider public on the matter, because he fears he will lose his job as a consequence. He decides to keep silent.

Engineer B, on the contrary, estimates that the gravity of the matter does not allow her to stop at this point. She decides to send a copy of her report to the municipal official who is responsible for public health in the area. Once the information is presented to public officials, however, it is also leaked to the local press and to environmental action groups. As a consequence, the municipal officials enter a lawsuit against the chemical company; engineer B is fired for breaking confidentiality. She equally sues her employer, asking for compensation. But even if the court decides in her favour, it may take years before she receives reparation; in the meantime, she has a hard time finding a new employer because of her reputation as a whistleblower.[19]

Situations like the one above are most usually indicated in the literature with the whistleblowing metaphor. They are all characterized by a conflict between two norms: loyalty to the firm on the one hand, and the duty to avoid harm to the public interest, on the other hand. How does one balance obedience to both norms, once they enter into conflict? How can one arbitrate in such cases? Concretely, in the above case, was engineer A right to keep silent, once he had informed his superiors, and had seemingly been discharged of his responsibility for the further risks? Or was it engineer B who took the best possible line of action?

Under the circumstances described in the above case, the latter alternative seems to be preferred. Engineer B has acted rightly. But in order to justify her action, a number of conditions have to be met:

1. *Ultimate resort.* All chances of correcting the defective policy via internal critique and decision-making procedures within the firm have been used. The employee has tried in vain to convince his/her superiors or colleagues to correct the faulty policy,

or s/he has a serious reason to suppose that the critique will only be met by reprisals from their side.

2. *Systematic or permanent damage.* The damage being done is not incidental; it is a structural failure, which is inherent to the product or the production process.

3. *Harming a third party.* The party which is likely to suffer damage is not informed about the risk or consenting to it. Specifically, it is the public interest of consumers and of the wider community or the environment which will be harmed in the first place.

4. *Factual certainty.* The employee refers to specific and reliable data to prove his/her allegations.

Only if all these conditions have been met, may the employee legitimately 'blow the whistle', revealing confidential information regarding the firm to outsiders. The employee should also be prudent in the choice of recipient for the information, directing it in the first place to those officials who bear some public responsibility for the matter in hand. Nevertheless, the employee should not be held accountable for subsequent leaks of information to the press or the wider public that may occur as a secondary consequence of his/her initiative.

Under the above conditions an employee is allowed to break the rule of confidentiality; but is s/he also morally obliged to do so? As we have seen in the above case, engineer B had to endure some serious hardships as a consequence of her conduct. Should one require all employees to accept those disadvantages when finding themselves in similar circumstances? Or can one also follow engineer A's line of conduct as a morally acceptable practice?

Indeed, mitigating circumstances should be taken into account in the process of decision-making. If they are serious enough, they may justify the decision of an employee *not* to blow the whistle, even when all the above-mentioned criteria have been met. This could be the case, e.g., if the chance to avoid further damage to the public by speaking out is particularly small, or if the employee has sufficient reason to suspect that she or her family may suffer serious personal damage as a consequence, such as dismissal, difficulties in finding a new job, intimidation of family members, physical violence, or ostracism. In such circumstances an employee may opt for material co-operation, rather than for speaking out.

Material and formal co-operation

The distinction between material and formal co-operation is well known in ethics. Formal co-operation is offered by those persons who commit an evil knowingly and willingly; therefore they are the ones who bear full responsibility for this act and its consequences. But those who are not completely free to refuse co-operation, or who lack complete insight in the quality of the evil act to which they contribute, are co-operating materially. Morally speaking, one can only be held accountable insofar as one is acting voluntarily and consciously.

This consideration of mitigating circumstances neither refutes nor contradicts the earlier argument on the justification of whistleblowing. It rather indicates that the fulfilment of some moral obligations in society may call for heroism and a readiness to bear sacrifices which we cannot impose as a general rule on all citizens. When a person is asked to accept serious personal risks in order to serve her community, one can only encourage and praise her for freely choosing to do so. One cannot enforce such supererogatory type of conduct as a norm.

The latter consideration leads us also to a final conclusion at the level of corporate ethics. Precisely because individual employees tend to be overcharged in such a conflict of loyalties, it should be a priority for corporate managers to introduce preventive measures in the decision-making process of the firm, in order to avoid the critical situation of one single employee having to decide in private to break confidentiality. If employees receive various possibilities to express criticism and to suggest corrections within their firm as a normal part of the operating procedures, without having to fear any reprisal or sanctions as long as their intention is clearly to defend the public interest, they will no longer have to resort to the ultimate means of whistleblowing. Each firm should include within its standard decision-making processes some forms of regular consultation of employees, and some reporting on the safety and quality of the production process, so that conflicts can be dealt with collectively.

Conflicts of interest between the firm and its employees

Confidentiality can, of course, also be broken to serve the private interest of the employee, to make some personal profit, to take revenge, or to give a favourable treatment to friends or family members. These practices are referred to with the term 'conflict of interest'. Conflicts of interest emerge when an employee (also a director, or an executive officer) is making a transaction in the name of the firm, while also having some distinct private interest in a particular outcome of the same transaction. In those situations where the private interest of the employee conflicts with the best outcome for the firm, the conditions for a loyal and impartial execution of the labour contract may be threatened.

Conflicts of interest can be of a financial as well as a relational nature: an employee can have mixed interests because he or she possesses a considerable amount of shares in a competing company, or because he or she has the occasion to conclude a contract with some acquaintances in the name of the company.

The employers have a right to defend themselves against these occurrences. To this end they can ask their employees to disclose the relevant private information in order to be informed of potential conflicts of interest: e.g., employees can be asked to disclose the content of their share portfolio. The employer can formulate a number of conditions with regard to the ownership of shares by its employees, stating that certain categories of employee should own no shares from a competitor, or only a limited amount. Likewise, it can be accepted as standard practice that no employee should conclude a company contract with friends or family members (regarding sales, recruitment, etc.). At the least, the conclusion of these contracts should be supervised by a third party, guaranteeing due respect for the interests of the firm.

. Employees, on the other hand, are obliged to inform their employers in advance about potential conflicts of interest, and to avoid the occurrence of actual ones.

Insider trading, or the use of insider information, represents a special case within this category: it involves the use of confidential information about the firm's future performances by the employee on the financial market, in order to realize a speculative gain for himself or for some third party. Such practices are to be condemned for two reasons:

1. The employer is in fact robbing his or her own firm, since she could only receive the crucial information as a member of it. Moreover, he or she only received this information under the condition that s/he would use it to serve the corporate interest.

2. Third parties have also been damaged: those agents who were deprived of the information while dealing on the same financial markets or contracting with the same firm will unjustly suffer losses as a consequence of the practice.

The regulation of conflicts of interest cannot be limited, however, to the control of employees and to preventive measures against abuses from their side. Employees are also entitled to claim due respect for their interests within a co-operative setting. This is the case, for example, in disputes on the so-called 'intellectual property rights'. If the firm has acquired some valuable information, such as research results, or a new production procedure, as a result of the creative contribution of some employee, then the latter has a right to just remuneration, or to some share in the profit which will be realized as a result of his or her contribution. Any explicit regulation with regard to this sharing of benefits should preferably be fixed beforehand, and mentioned in the labour contract.

On the other hand, when certain types of employees, such as researchers, managers, qualified programmers, leave the firm in order to engage in a new labour contract with a competitor, a particular problem arises. How will one distinguish between the sort of information the employee is allowed to claim as his or her own (and to use freely in her or his next job) and that which properly belongs to the firm s/he leaves (and which should not be disclosed to the next employer)? In general, such conflicts can be solved at the best by contractually defining a fixed term during which the firm holds an exclusive right to the use of particular information (analogical to patents). Afterwards, the employee is free to use the sensitive data in another context. It is in the interest of both parties, and also a matter of equity, that the above-mentioned term is limited to that period of time in which one may reasonably expect the firm to earn back the costs of the research or the production effort related to the acquisition of the valuable information.[20]

3.3.2   *Privacy and the control of workers' performance*

Employees are bound by their labour contracts to reach a certain level of performance on the job. They should co-operate loyally in order to achieve the goals which are formally agreed upon. This commitment offers the basis for a complementary right of the employer: he or she is free to recruit those employees whom s/he expects most likely to perform well, and s/he has a subsequent right to control the workers' performances, in order to ascertain that the original goals are met.

The implementation of these employers' rights, however, can lead to a new series of conflicts, either at the moment of recruitment or during later quality controls:

1.   Employers may wish to increase productivity to such a degree that they put excessive demands on their employees; or they may want to control the workers' conduct in such a way that they infringe upon the employees' right to privacy.

2.   The employees, from their side, have other obligations to fulfil besides their occupational duties: as citizens, or family members, or simply as autonomous individuals with a fundamental right to freedom. Each employee has the right to demand the necessary time, privacy and freedom of action in order to meet his or her moral obligations outside the job context. Employees cannot be morally required to put their entire lives at the service of work and productivity. Consequently, the employees can rightly ask to balance the claims of the production process with those that arise from the fulfilment of other role obligations. But they can also be tempted, of course, to invoke these role conflicts incorrectly, using working time or company facilities to promote their personal interests.

Two cases of privacy conflicts

Marc is working as a clerk at a chemical plant. At a certain moment he is called by the office manager. The manager asks if Marc is in regular contact with a local group of ecological activists. Is he an active member of the group? Does he share their convictions? Did he ever leak inside information about the functioning of the plant to them? Marc retorts that the manager does not have the right to question the political or social commitments of employees outside the factory. To which the manager replies that the local ecology group is connected to a network of organizations, including Greenpeace, which are publicly campaigning against the chemical corporation which employs Marc, so that he will be considered an untrustworthy and disloyal employee if he continues to participate in the activities of the ecologists. Maybe he has already been playing a role as an informer for them? Marc denies the last point. The manager, however, does not accept this denial as sufficient evidence of loyalty, and demands that Marc abandon any commitment to or membership of the group. Marc refuses to do so. He is convinced that his ecological activities are a private matter. The manager disagrees; he threatens to dismiss Marc at the first occasion, if necessary by invoking another formal reason as an excuse.

Ann is employed as a secretary in an import-export firm. She has been trained to work at the computer, using a wide variety of software programs. Ann's employer has recently discovered that she keeps working on her own account after the normal working hours. He also noticed that Ann has copied some computer programs of the firm in order to do secretarial work at home for other parties. He has asked Ann to cease these activities. Ann recognizes she is using some copies of the firm's computer programs at home. But she assumes that she does not hurt the firm's interests in doing so, since these activities happen during her free time. She also points out that she is not the only employee to take home some instruments of the firm for personal use. She suggests this kind of 'borrowing' by employees is a normal type of conduct, and regrets she has been selected out of the crowd to become subject to this particular criticism.

The above cases lead to some concrete questions regarding the type of conduct an employer is allowed to demand from employees. Generally speaking, one can accept as a guiding principle that an employer only has a right to demand a particular type of conduct when it is directly related to the desired job performance of the employee.

Moreover, an employer should not collect information on the employee without the latter's knowledge and consent.[21]

Some recurrent points of conflict can be mentioned explicitly here; they are the following:

The appearance of the employee

In a number of occupations it is important that employees present themselves in an agreeable way, that they are well dressed, or that they are able to express themselves correctly and politely (e.g. in a sales department). As soon as there exists a direct link between such aesthetic qualities and good job performance, employer demands are permitted in this respect. Aesthetic requirements should be balanced, however, by taking into account the other relevant rights and values which may receive priority attention. It should not be accepted, for instance, that air hostesses, or public relations personnel, be dismissed at a certain age, merely because the employer systematically prefers to recruit younger and more attractive personnel for public relations purposes. Apart from anti-discrimination regulations, there is an inherent duty to remain loyal to the senior employee, who will certainly not have lost all his or her previous qualities by a certain age.[22]

Adherence to a religious or political conviction

This qualification can only be invoked as a condition of employment in institutions which explicitly are intended to deliver a product or a service with a particular ideological quality. This is the case, for example, in a Christian school, a socialist adult education programme, or a liberal trade union. Corporations which do not offer goods or services with a particular religious or political quality should respect the freedom of conviction of their employees, and employ them regardless of their ideological differences.

Sexual orientation
There exists no valid a priori reason for refusing to recruit persons on account of their sexual orientation (e.g. homosexuals, transsexuals). However, all employees are rightly requested to abstain from sexual contacts and courting at the workplace. Sexual harassment is evidently forbidden.

Discrimination against women in employment
Some employers justify discriminatory treatment of women during the selection or promotion of employees on grounds of the likelihood that female employees will be more likely to apply for leave of absence for family reasons (pregnancy, care for children). This is not a legitimate reason for discriminating against female candidates, however. Moreover, employers can never make an employment offer conditional upon the commitment of the employee not to become pregnant during the period of the labour contract.

Affirmative action policies, on the other hand, which are meant to correct previous discrimination against female employees by giving preferential treatment to present candidates until equal representation is reached at all levels, seems equally a morally questionable line of conduct. This is the case, first, because better-qualified male candidates may be put aside as a consequence and, secondly, because it does not serve the just cause of emancipation to appoint less-qualified candidates simply on the basis of gender. One should rather stick to the principle that job selection and quality control should be based on the professional qualities of the candidate only, regardless of external characteristics such as gender. Discriminatory practices against women should be corrected by the introduction of anti-discriminatory regulation, rather than by affirmative action.

Racial or ethnic discrimination
As a consequence of the above, these practices are also morally unacceptable. The same considerations regarding affirmative action policies or anti-discriminatory regulation also apply to this point.

Residence requirements
The employer is only allowed to require that employees live near the workplace, or that they can be reached at odd hours to be called to the workplace, when it can be proven that these requirements are inherently related to the good performance of a particular job.

Employees' activities outside normal working time
Apart from overtime work, for which there exist specific regulations, employers

cannot ask supplementary commitments of their employees besides the loyal execution of the labour contract. They should not demand, for example, that employees buy products of the firm for private use, or make publicity for the firm among relatives, or offer part of their free time for voluntary services related to the firm.

On the other hand, an employer does have a right to forbid full-time employees from accepting additional jobs outside their normal working time. Such an exclusivity condition, which will often be mentioned explicitly in the labour contract, is directed specifically against employees who would continue to work for another employer during their 'free time'.

Health requirements

The employer has a right to demand that the employee be subject to the necessary medical checks to prove his or her physical and mental fitness for the job. However, rather than personally collecting the necessary medical data, the employer should leave this task to the accredited physicians and medical services. Confidentiality of personal medical data should be respected by all parties. Having been informed of the physical requirements for a particular job and after due examination of the employee, the physician will report to the employer his or her evaluation of the fitness of the employee without disclosing the details of the medical dossier. The employee has a right to refuse medical tests or disclosure of information on his or her health, when no clear proof has been given of a link between the demanded information and good performance of the job. In case of doubt the advice of the physician should be heard and respected.

A last remark: in fighting discrimination, one should distinguish between those forms of discrimination which are morally unacceptable, and those which are part of the selection process in a competitive environment. One can hardly object to the fact, for instance, that an employer prefers to promote those employees who have accepted overtime work, or who have excelled in their past state of service. This distinction is not a theoretical one; it is influenced by concrete and changing socio-historical circumstances. There exists a strong long-term tendency in modern Western society to limit further the range of acceptable forms of discrimination on the job. Discrimination on grounds of gender, race or nationality is no longer acceptable, although it has been current practice up to the recent past; discriminatory treatment based on outward appearance or social status is also more and more illegitimate, whereas selection based on experience, knowledge and assertiveness of the candidates seems to receive greater acceptance. In this respect one can observe the paradoxical use of age as a discriminatory factor in the selection process: the ideal employee often should not be too old (preferably between 25 and 35), but he or she should nevertheless demonstrate a wide range of experience on the job! The 'youth factor' may become a new dominant type of discrimination in future labour relations.

Notes

1. This chapter is a revised translation of chapter 5 of a Dutch business ethics manual: Verstraeten, Johan & Van Gerwen, Jef, *Business en ethiek. Spelre-gels voor het ethisch ondernemen* (Tielt: Lannoo, 1990), pp. 123–65.

2. This judgement should be interpreted as reflecting the different history of labour relations in Europe and the United States, rather than as a critique of the work of American ethicists.

3. See Tanghe, Fernand, *Le droit au travail entre histoire et utopie* (Brussels: Publications FUSL, 1989); Moltmann, Juergen (ed.), *Recht auf Arbeit, Sinn der Arbeit* (Munich, 1979); Mieth, Dietmar & Pohier, Jacques (eds.), 'Unemployment and the right to work', *Concilium*, vol. 18, 10, Dec. 1982.

4. Sen, Amartya, 'The right not to be hungry', in G. Floistad (ed.), *Contemporary Philosophy* (The Hague: M. Nijhoff, 1982), vol. 2, pp. 343–60.

5. One may compare here the full texts of the European Social Charter of the Council of Europe at Strasburg (1961) with the United Nations' International Convention on Economic, Social and Cultural Rights (16 December 1966; see also article 23 of the Universal Declaration of Human Rights, 1948) and with the European Community Charter of Fundamental Social Rights of Workers (9 December 1989).

6. These principles have been implemented in European Community regulations regarding equal treatment for women and men, and regarding free circulation of workers: cf. *First Report on the Application of the Community Charter of the Fundamental Social Rights of Workers*, Commission of the European Communities, COM(91) 511, Brussels, 5 December 1991.

7. The terms of this regulation are spelt out in Articles 17–18 of the EC Community Charter, and in the proposal for a *Directive on the Establishment of a European Works Council in Community-scale Undertakings*, COM(90) 581, Brussels, 25 January 1991.

8. Falise, Michel, *Une pratique chrétienne de l'économie* (Paris: Centurion, 1985), pp. 104–20.

9. See, e.g., 'The E.C. Council Directive on the Introduction of a Form to Serve as Proof of an Employment Contract or Relationship, 14 October 1991', *Official Journal of the European Communities*, L 288, pp. 32–5.

10. See, e.g., the work of André Gorz, *Métamorphoses du travail. Quête du sens. Critique de la raison économique* (Paris: Galilée, 1988).

11. A comparable list of criteria is provided by Manuel Velasquez, *Business Ethics. Concepts and cases* (Prentice Hall, 1982), p. 310, referring to earlier works of Wirtenberger, Garrett and Barry (p. 310, footnote 14).

12. Cf. the so-called framework *Directive on Health and Safety Protection for Workers*, 89/391/CEE, which has been followed by a number of specific safety regulations for different industries.

13. Figures quoted from ir. H. de Lange, *Statistics of Labor Accidents and Occupational Diseases* (NVVA, 1989), Dossier D 24. The statistical figures probably underestimate the real amount of accidents by about 50% (both because of incomplete coverage of all labour sectors and because of unreported accidents).

14 Data reported by the Flemish daily *Het Volk*, 22 March 1989, p. 3.

15. M. Velasquez, *op. cit.*, p. 315, referring to R. Hackman, G. Oldham, R. Jansen and K. Purdy, 'A new strategy for job enrichment', *California Management Review*, vol. 17, 4, 1975, pp. 58–9.

16. See, e.g., F. Van den Bulcke, *Beloon inzet met kapitaal. L'actionnariat du personnel*

(Antwerp: Tijd NV, 1989); Oswald von Nell-Breuning, 'Robinson und Freitag – Möglichkeiten und grenzen wirtschaftlicher Mittbestimmung', in I. Brusis and M. Groenefeld (eds.), *Unbequeme Grenzbeziehung. Streitschriften von Oswald von Nell-Breuning* (Cologne: Bund Verlag, 1990), pp. 66–79.

17. I have also encountered this line of argument in Philip Selznick, *Leadership in Administration* (Harper and Row, 1957). See also 'property rights analysis', e.g. Yoram Barzel, *Economic Analysis of Property Rights* (Cambridge University Press, 1989), and Louis Putterman, 'The firm as association versus the firm as commodity. Efficiency, rights and ownership', in *Economics and Philosophy*, 4, 1988, pp. 243–66.

18. Proposals for a European Directive on workers' participation have been circulating through the EC administration for more than two decades without ever being adopted by the Council of Ministers. Among the most recent proposals are a *Directive on the European Works Council* (document COM(91) 581 of the EC Commission) and a *Recommendation on Equity Sharing and Financial Participation by Workers* (document COM(91) 259).

19. This is a fictive story, based, however, on concrete events. For an analogous case, see Norman Bowie, *Business Ethics* (Prentice Hall, 1982), pp. 140–9 (BART case).

20. Velasquez, *op. cit.*, pp. 306–9; Richard de George, *Business Ethics* (New York: Macmillan, 1990), 2nd edition, pp. 291–301.

21. Savatier, Jean, 'La protection de la vie privée des salariés', *Droit Social*, 4, April 1992, pp. 329–36.

22. A famous case in this respect was presented before the Court of the European Community at Luxemburg in 1971, in the so-called Arrest Defrenne (25 May 1971; later arrests in 1976 and 1978). Mrs Defrenne was employed as an air hostess by the Belgian airline company SABENA, and routinely sent into retirement at the age of 40; similar measures were not foreseen for male air stewards. The practice has been abandoned in the aviation sector since the court decision. See, e.g., Gérard Lyon-Caen and Antoine Lyon-Caen, *Droit social international et européen* (Paris: Dalloz, 1991), 7th edition, p. 360.

CHAPTER 4

Shareholders

Guido Corbetta
Bocconi University, Italy

The ethical questions raised by the relationship between shareholders and the firm have not been widely considered in studies on business ethics.[1] Some publications dealing with this area do not even have a chapter on the subject: in M. G. Velasquez' book there are chapters on types of market, relations between companies and environment, companies and consumers and companies and workers, as well as on employees' rights and duties, but there is nothing at all about shareholders.[2] Other publications deal with the question of shareholders' responsibility, but only in terms of the moral implications of investment decisions.[3]

There are several reasons why this aspect of the question has been passed over. In the first place, business ethics is a relatively new focus of study, and has yet to be fully developed. Secondly, priority has so far been placed on the moral legitimacy of the various social and market systems (macro level) and on the behaviour patterns of individuals (micro level); less attention has been paid to the moral assessment of forms of enterprise and intermediate organizations (meso level). Thirdly – and this is perhaps the most important reason – business ethics came into being and continues to develop mainly in the Anglo-American business world where a great proportion of enterprises are management-controlled firms in which shareholders have always had a less important role.

This chapter sets out to consider shareholders' rights and duties. After making the necessary distinctions between the different types of capitalism and between governor-shareholders and investor-shareholders, the chapter goes on to single out the issues involved in cases of family businesses, a form of capitalism that is common in Italy and other parts of Europe; lastly, an insight is offered into the contribution made by business ethics to the specific question of the behaviour of shareholders who put their own interests before those of the company.

4.1 Types of capitalism

The well-known theory formulated in the early part of this century which envisaged a gradual separation of ownership and management[4] concluded that a company's success or failure was in the hands of its professional managers, and that ownership of companies would be shared among thousands of investors who, through the capital markets, would finance only those firms which demonstrated superior management skills and profits.

Although this theory of the separation of ownership and control contained some elements of truth, on a practical plane it was not universally applicable in countries where different forms of corporate ownership had taken root. Each of these forms originated in different cultural, religious, political and economic backgrounds. Each, in its turn, has important consequences for the structure and evolution of national industrial systems, international competitiveness, the distribution of incomes, the degree of openness or inward-lookingness of the economic system and – of course – for the organization of companies.

Among the most common forms of ownership of medium-sized and large companies are the following main types:

1.   *Family-based capitalism*: ownership is concentrated in the hands of one or a few families which are frequently related to one another. Sometimes one or more members of the family is directly involved in running the company; in other cases non-family senior managers are appointed to top management posts and the owning family merely participates in board of directors' meetings. This form of ownership is particularly common in Italy, but there are large family businesses practically everywhere.

2.   *Financial capitalism*:[5] ownership is concentrated in the hands of one or just a few private and public financial institutions which, through a system of cross-holdings, control companies and intervene in their management. In these cases the role of owner is not limited to the financing of firms: ownership also implies powers to appoint management and steer corporate strategy and the right of veto when management decisions are opposed. This form of ownership (with some slight differences) prevails in Germany, Japan and some other countries like Holland and Switzerland; it is rapidly becoming more common in France too.

3.   *Managerial capitalism*: ownership is shared among numerous stockholders, none of whom exercises any significant control over the activity of the managers who run the companies. The management of these companies therefore becomes a kind of self-regenerating structure. This form of capitalism is clearly the sort envisaged by the theory of the separation of ownership and control and it is particularly important in the Anglo-American business world, though with some important ongoing changes which we shall examine later.

4.   *State capitalism*: through central and peripheral agencies or corporations set up *ad hoc* (as in the case of, for instance, IRI and ENI[6] in Italy), the state has direct control over companies. The existence of this form of capitalism clearly stems from

a certain view of state intervention in the economy. In Italy, France and Spain there are major groups belonging to this category.

Data relating to the number of companies with stock exchange listing and the ratio between average capitalization of the listed companies and Gross Domestic Product (Table 4.1) highlight the big gap between capital markets in the USA and UK and those in the other main countries of Europe. These figures confirm the preponderance in the USA and UK of the 'public company' model typical of managerial capitalism; in these countries companies make extensive use of their stock exchange listing to obtain the financial means needed for development; in other countries types of capitalism have come to the fore that make only limited use of the financial sources available on the capital market.

Going on to consider the way in which companies are organized, it is evident that appointment criteria, composition, powers and mode of functioning of companies' boards of directors vary considerably according to the type of capitalism.

In cases of family-based capitalism and financial capitalism, for example, boards of directors are appointed by the majority shareholder or by a coalition of shareholders who are often themselves members of the boards, which appear to be the real organs of corporate governance.

In cases of managerial capitalism, board members are instead 'co-opted' by the management itself. Save a few noteworthy exceptions, the choice falls on people whose most important characteristic appears to be their willingness to endorse without question whatever proposals the top managers who are also board members may submit. The board of directors thus eventually loses its role as collective organ of corporate governance and often becomes a false front used to give greater authority to decisions made by others.[7]

Table 4.1   Figures relating to several bourses (1990)

	New York	London	Germany	Paris	Milan
No. of national companies listed	1,678	2,006	413	443	220
Average capitalization of national companies listed/GDP (%)*	45.5	74.9	17.4	19.8	10.2

Source: 'Il Sole-24 Ore', figures and estimates based on Irs/OECD data
*Estimates for 1991

4.2   Governor-shareholders and investor-shareholders

Anyone who has a shareholding in a company can be called an owner of the capital of that company. The rights and duties connected with the role of ownership can be summed up as follows:

- defining the company's mission;
- deciding the objectives of its operations;
- personally running the company or appointing and appraising its management;
- providing the company with the financial resources necessary for the pursuit of its objectives;
- obtaining a return on one's investment that is in line with the risk incurred;
- transferring ownership of the company's capital.

A company's shareholders do not always exercise all these rights/duties. It is evident even from a preliminary analysis of the various forms of ownership considered that we can identify different shareholder roles and responsibilities. For example, the distinction between governors and investors can serve to classify the behaviour of the different shareholders within a particular type of firm – be it family-based, management-controlled or any other – but it is clear that, whatever the corporate model, one particular type of shareholder prevails.

In family businesses, a few people each own a significant portion of the total capital – possibly inherited from the previous generation – and are often involved in the day-to-day running of the firm. The decisions of a single shareholder can have an important influence on the development of the company. At the same time, changing economic and competitive conditions can have far-reaching effects on the lives of the firm's owner-families. Mobility of stock is limited by sentimental ties, by rules established within the ownership 'fraternity' and by the fact that a family shareholder has little to gain by selling minority holdings to shareholders outside the family without the consent of the other partners. The bond that exists between shareholder and firm is therefore a close and long-lasting one.

The situation is totally different for a shareholder who has a small (percentage) share in a listed company. In this case the person invests just a part of his or her savings in a company's stock in the expectation of a fair dividend or a rise in stock value. In general there is no possibility that decisions taken by this shareholder will influence the running of the company. Disinvestment is easy and depends solely on assessments of economic advantage. The bond between shareholder and firm is therefore loose and transitory.

Financial capitalism represents yet another case. Here the shareholder is a financial institution which holds a significant share of a company's capital stock. These shareholders are involved in the running of the company, or at least in its supervisory bodies, and their decisions can lead to major changes in corporate strategy. Any variation in the economic and competitive conditions of the company can cause significant variations in the value of the investment. The mobility of the shareholding is limited and is tied to restructuring operations which may even involve some of the foremost financial and industrial organizations in a country. The bond forged between company and shareholder is therefore very similar to that existing in cases of family-based capitalism although obviously, in this case, the person in the financial institution who is responsible for taking decisions is a manager who personally has no major shareholding.

We can now summarize the distinguishing characteristics of the different types of shareholders and differentiate between the 'governor' and the 'investor' (Table 4.2).

We define the shareholder as a 'governor' when:

- the (percentage) share of capital stock owned is high;
- development of the firm is substantially dependent on the economic resources made available by the shareholder and, likewise, the economic fortunes of the shareholder depend significantly on the firm's profitability;
- the shareholder exercises his or her power to intervene in decision-making processes by appointing the firm's management, steering corporate strategy and monitoring and appraising the management's performance;
- any decision to sell the shareholding is limited by sentimental reasons, in the case of family businesses, or by complex strategic assessments which may occasionally even have implications for national equilibrium (as was recently the case with operations conducted in Germany and France).

We define the shareholder as an 'investor' when:

- the (percentage) share of capital stock owned is small, often a fraction of a percentage point;
- the link between the development and profitability of the firm and the fortunes of the shareholder is not very close: the company gathers its resources from a very large number of shareholders, each of whom makes only a limited contribution to the firm's needs; likewise, the income of each individual shareholder does not come from the dividends distributed by one firm;
- there is little likelihood that shareholders' opinions about management appointments and corporate strategy will influence decisions. On a practical level a 'shareholders' democracy' – i.e. effective control over management by numerous small shareholders - is not feasible;[8]
- the decision to sell the shareholding is taken only on the basis of assessments of returns. 'Abandoning' is often preferable to 'expressing dissent' and, even more so, to 'remaining bound.[9]

Table 4.2   Distinguishing characteristics of governors and investors

	Governors	Investors
Size of shareholding	Large	Small
Respective economic importance	High	Limited
Intervention in decision-making	Frequent	Rare
Mobility of stock owned	Limited by sentimental motivations and strategic assessments	High and motivated solely by appraisal of the profitability of the investment

Within each of the two classes – governor-shareholders and investor-shareholders – it is possible to differentiate cases in which the shareholder is a physical person (directly or through a company which has the holding in question as its main activity) from cases in which the shareholder is an institution such as a bank or pension fund.

Cases of family-based capitalism and financial capitalism can therefore be classified within the governor-shareholder category whereas cases of managerial capitalism are to be found within the investor-shareholder category, both when the shares are owned by institutions and when they are owned by individuals.

On a practical level the way in which governor-shareholders and investor-shareholders perform their ownership role varies. Table 4.3 shows that, while governor-shareholders exercise all the rights/duties of ownership, investor-shareholders exercise only some of them. Thus different ethical issues are raised by the behaviour of the two types of shareholders.

Table 4.3   Rights and duties exercised by the different types of shareholders.

	Ownership rights and duties exercised by:	
	Governor-shareholders	Investor-shareholders
Defining the company's mission	YES	NO
Deciding the objectives of its operations	YES	NO
Personally running the company or appointing and appraising its management	YES	NO
Providing the company with the necessary financial resources	YES	YES
Obtaining a commensurate return	YES	YES
Transferring the shareholding owned	YES	YES

4.3   The evolution of managerial capitalism

Major changes are currently taking place in managerial capitalism. Poor economic and competitive results in the 1970s and 1980s have led to takeovers and leveraged buyouts in which controlling stakes in the capital of large companies are acquired. In the case of takeovers, the acquiring shareholders take on the job of rapidly reorganizing the company's activities (sometimes selling off parts of the company in the process); in the case of leveraged buyouts, they take over the medium/long-term running of the company.

These ownership restructuring operations – which are not always favourably commented upon – have been stimulated by several factors.[10] One is the change that occurred during the preceding decades in the shareholder structure of corporations. From the 1950s onwards in many companies small shareholders were replaced in part by a limited number of large, institutional shareholders like pension and mutual funds; using the savings of thousands of small investors, these organizations succeeded in acquiring huge (percentage) shares of the capital stock of important management-controlled companies.

The arrival of these big investors contributed to changing a fundamental element in the working of the classic managerial capitalism model: for institutional investors the option of 'expressing dissent' sometimes implied greater advantage than 'abandoning'. In other words, it was no longer easy for investors to make changes to their securities portfolio, since the value of the shares they owned was very high and selling some of them might cause a substantial reduction in the overall value of the remaining holding. Institutional investors were therefore obliged – often unwillingly – to examine the possibility of behaving like governor-shareholders.

This meant that managerial capitalism was already getting closer to financial capitalism. But institutional investors still maintained a largely 'non-interventionist' approach to the operations of firms, leaving managers in charge of running the business and merely keeping a fairly distant watch on things. So the transition from investors to governors is slow, since fund managers have to acquire the attitudes and business skills needed to operate as governor-shareholders. The skills can be acquired by putting together a team of people to assess companies' development plans. But developing a governor attitude depends mainly on the willingness to assume responsibility for intervening in corporate governance processes. This stage can be reached only by abandoning the typical attitude of the investor-shareholder, disinterested in the company's affairs, and establishing a relationship with management that is geared to confrontation and may even lead to the management's dismissal should it prove incapable of doing its job.[11]

There is every evidence, moreover, that the managements of management-controlled companies are reluctant to hand over any of their autonomy to the shareholders. According to the findings of a recent survey[12] based on a sample of over 200 finance managers of British companies, the managers interviewed endorsed the need for change in relations between institutional investors and management. However, when asked what changes they considered appropriate, the great majority of respondents merely spoke of the need for a better information flow from management to investors, while they emphasized the dangers implicit in investors' intervention in the definition of corporate strategies and in board of directors' 'compensation committees'.

Yet, where shareholders fail to exercise control over management, this increases the possibility of anti-company behaviour on the part of the managers, who are concerned only with getting the maximum personal gain even when this puts the very survival of the company in jeopardy.

The case of Allegheny Ludlum Industries[13] – a Pittsburgh-based manufacturer of special steels with a 1982 turnover of $2.6 billion – presents an all-too-vivid picture of the greed of a senior management team. As well as generous salaries, the senior managers of ALI allowed themselves the following 'fringe benefits':

- an elegant Tudor-style mansion in Pittsburgh, worth $450,000, and furnishings worth several hundred thousand dollars more;
- a fleet of five planes, very frequently used by the senior managers' families;
- over $30 million in personal loans obtained from the firm at an interest rate of 2 per cent;
- the appointment of the son of the chief executive officer as manager of the Dover Hotel in central Manhattan, bought by ALI for $5.7 million;
- the purchase for $500,000 of a resort condominium often used by the company's senior managers as a holiday home;
- an ALI investment in a badly executed building development in Florida, in which the senior managers owned property.

The CEO of ALI got his just deserts and was sacked but he was nevertheless granted a golden handshake of about $107,000 and receives a monthly pension of $12,900. ALI was declared bankrupt in 1988 and the value of its shares dropped by 75 per cent.

4.4   Governor-shareholders

In management-controlled firms where the capital stock is owned by hundreds or thousands of small shareholders, the investor-shareholders have no possibility of intervening in corporate governance processes: it is the firm's management that performs the key role of reconciling the interests of the various stakeholders and it alone takes responsibility for the long-term development of the firm. Because the senior management team has the power to determine corporate policies, it becomes the key decision-making party. As such it is the behaviour of management which needs to be investigated to assess whether it complies with the following specific economic and ethical criteria:

- What is the legitimate framework of managerial power?
- What are the ends of managerial activity and how can they be justified?
- On the basis of what principles does management take its decisions and deal out advantages and disadvantages to the various stakeholders?

Governor-shareholders, however, are obliged to think deeply about the responsibilities they acquire as owners of significant shares of companies' capital stock. A number of issues emerge that specifically regard this type of shareholder:

- What are the responsibilities that stem from ownership of significant shares of a company's capital stock?
- What are the limits of ownership rights?
- How can the interests of a company's owners and those of its other stakeholders be reconciled?
- How must relations between shareholders and managers be conceived and organized?

These issues clearly come into play in the cases of family-based and financial capitalism. In these models there is a strong bond between company and shareholders. On the basis of their holding in the capital stock, shareholders have the power to influence the operations of the company, and they put this power into practice. They therefore perform a completely different role to the other stakeholders – and also to the managers of management-controlled firms. This is because governor-shareholders derive their power directly from their right of ownership and not from a position to which they are appointed.

From this point on we shall focus our attention on the behaviour of governor-shareholders, who loom large in non-Anglo-American economic systems and who are now – as we have seen – gaining importance in the USA and UK as well.

Before considering relations between governor-shareholders and companies from a general standpoint, it is worth examining a number of moral issues that can emerge in cases of family-based capitalism. The issues involved here differ from those related to managerial capitalism and thus give a clearer appreciation of the distinctions previously introduced between the different models of capitalism, as well as between governor- and investor-shareholders.

In Italy all the leading private groups are controlled by families which pass ownership of the business down from one generation to the next (the Agnellis and Ferruzzis, for example) or which are still in the hands of their founder (Berlusconi and De Benedetti). Members of the family control the shareholders' meetings, they are members of the boards of directors and they are sometimes personally in charge of running the companies. Management plays an important but clearly subordinate role.

If these families have succeeded in hanging on to control of the capital of the companies throughout their developing years, it is thanks in part to special conditions that have made things easier for them. In the first place, the legislative system has enabled them, for example, to have their companies issue shares with limited voting rights, or to set up 'cascade' companies and get stock market listing for both parent and daughter companies (when the holding in the daughter company was often the parent company's only asset). This has made it possible for the family to maintain control over the whole line of companies solely by owning the majority of the parent company's voting stock.

Secondly, the existence of Mediobanca – a merchant bank (for a long time the only one in Italy) jointly controlled by the foremost private entrepreneurs and the main state-owned banks – has made huge financial resources available to the owner families and allowed them to survive hard times.

For the owners of these family businesses and for the country's economic authorities, the operations and growth of these firms pose a series of very special ethical and economic questions. For example:

- Is it right to hire a son or daughter of the entrepreneur (governor-shareholder) and speed them to the very top of the career ladder without subjecting them to any process of appraisal, even when there are non-family senior managers in the company with better qualifications and skills?

- Is it right to keep the company's growth rate down – with obvious negative effects on employment and on prosperity in the places where the firm is located – in order to retain control of the majority of the firm's capital?

- Is it right to bring in and maintain a system of laws which helps owner families to maintain control over the firms they own, even if this clearly paves the way for the accumulation of huge personal fortunes and for the formation of power bases with enormous possibilities for conditioning the social and economic life of the country?

These are important questions that concern a particular type of capitalism (family-based capitalism) but they are only specific aspects of the problems previously considered in relation to all types of governor-shareholders.

In addressing issues relating to responsibility and rights of ownership, it is worth giving a preliminary brief outline of one of the possible models of relations between governor-shareholder and firm.

In Italy – and so particularly in cases of family-based capitalism – the behaviour of governor-shareholders can frequently be attributed to an approach which subordinates development of the firm to their own interests. In cases of this kind the governor-shareholder of a family business maintains that he and he alone has the right to decide what happens to the firm. He or one of his ancestors founded the firm by conceiving an entrepreneurial idea, providing the necessary capital and performing the role of entrepreneur and sometimes manager too. He therefore believes nobody is entitled to challenge his right to use the firm to achieve his own and his family's ends – for example appointing his son as managing director, despite his lack of knowledge and ability.

Business ethics studies offer a number of principles and theories that can help to assess the case of governor-shareholders who, on the basis of their right of ownership, claim the right to subordinate the interests of the company to their own ends.

In the first place, ethical theories recognize an important difference between rights of ownership: there are so-called 'natural' rights of ownership over assets and resources which belong to an individual in a natural situation devoid of social interaction, and there are so-called 'conventional' rights of ownership over the same assets or resources within a framework of social interaction, in which the value or benefits obtainable from use or consumption of said assets and resources depends on the social co-operation of other individuals.[14] Ownership of a firm's capital is obviously classified among conventional rights of ownership.

Justification for natural rights can be provided by person's work. Locke wrote:

> Each individual is the owner of his own person, over which no-one else has rights. Work done with his own body and hands is his alone. Whatever man takes from the state in which nature created it, he incorporates his own work and adds to it something that belongs to him, and so takes possession of it. By removing that object from the common condition to which nature allocated it, he has – with his work – added something that rules out the common right of ownership of other men.[15]

Locke puts only two limitations on the exercise of natural rights of ownership: that it does not harm other individuals who, with their own work, wish to take possession of other assets, and that anyone who has taken possession of an asset also assumes responsibility for preserving that asset or, in the case of commodities, for not letting that asset deteriorate.

Natural rights of ownership cannot be justified on the basis of work in the case of conventional rights, according to which benefits obtained are not simply the outcome of one person's work, but are made possible only by social co-operation.

A decision taken by an individual whose autonomy is protected by (conventional) right of ownership must therefore also consider the legitimate claims (legitimate from a moral standpoint, even if not recognized by the law) made by other people who have contributed to producing the benefits obtained. On this basis there can be no moral justification for the behaviour of owners who, solely because they have a conventional right of ownership, think they alone can 'dispose' of the company/asset and of the benefits obtained from it.

Many governor-shareholders admit that the nature of their right of ownership obliges them to acknowledge that other stakeholders in the company are entitled to part of the benefits produced. But they none the less insist on their autonomy to 'dispose' of the company, using the following reasoning to support their claims.[16]

A company can be likened to the sum total of a series of agreements which the various stakeholders – starting from the managers and entire workforce – enter into with the shareholders of the company, establishing at the outset both the service they give and the remuneration they receive for it. The governor-shareholder is instead in an asymmetrical position: although his side of the agreement (supply of capital and entrepreneurial and managerial skills) is pre-defined, what he or she is entitled to receive in return is not, nor is it even guaranteed that s/he will receive remuneration for every period worked. Therefore, since he or she accepts to subordinate his or her remuneration to that of the other stakeholders and because he or she is the essential catalyst for the resources without which firms do not develop, s/he declares his/her entitlement to 'dispose' of the firm once the right of the other stakeholders to receive the agreed remuneration for their contribution has been respected.

It is obvious that this approach cannot be extensively applied to management-controlled firms where no investor-shareholder has the power to impose their own designs and where most senior managers who do have the power to 'rule' the company cannot point to the lack of pre-definition of their remuneration as justification for their actions.

Over the next few years it will be interesting to watch the behaviour of managers of the big pension funds: now that they have invested huge amounts in individual firms and will not find it easy to release them, their situation will get closer to that of governor-shareholders. And the managements of management-controlled firms will find it increasingly hard to justify their role by pointing to the absence of governor-shareholders.

Returning to the line of thought followed by many governor-shareholders, some changes currently in progress could modify the conclusions reached by the governor-shareholders, at least as regards one particular category of corporate stakeholders: the workers.

On one hand we have the higher-quality performance now being demanded of workers, particularly in 'brain-intensive' sectors like research but also more generally in many 'labour-intensive' production activities. The present-day work organization demands from its workers a performance that cannot always be defined at the outset – as in a Taylor type of organization – and that is also heavily dependent on the creative skills and dedication of the individual worker. In these cases the asymmetrical situation created is similar but opposite to the one that applies to governor-shareholders, inasmuch as the workers' remuneration can be established at the outset, but the performance required of them cannot.

On the other hand we have the recent introduction in Italy of labour contracts in which part of the workers' salary is pre-established and part is calculated at the end of the work period on the basis of the company's results. Again following the same logic as for governor-shareholders, in these cases too workers could make rightful claims to 'dispose' of the firm.

These changes could therefore modify the conclusions of the line of thought followed by governor-shareholders, questioning shareholders' exclusive entitlement to 'dispose' of the firm once the other stakeholders have been paid for their services.

For the time being, however, we are tied to the existing situation in which the governor-shareholder thinks he or she is entitled to subordinate the firm to the attainment of his/her personal ends, because s/he is the only party to make his/her own compensation secondary to payment of the other stakeholders. So let us try to analyse the limits and consequences of this line of reasoning.

A first possible limit could be the failure to comply with the moral prerequisites of the agreements which the shareholder enters into with the other stakeholders.[17] An agreement satisfies moral prerequisites when:

- both parties entering into an agreement are fully aware of its consequences;
- neither party intentionally gives the other party a false picture of the situation on which the agreement is based;
- neither party is compelled to enter into the agreement through use of force and/ or coercion;
- the agreement does not bind the parties to commit immoral deeds.

Only if all the requisites are met must the parties feel obliged to fulfil the promised assignment. It is therefore obvious that if the governor-shareholder does not comply with these requisites when he or she enters into agreements with the other stakeholders, his/her moral authority is non-existent because the other parties are justified in not standing by the agreements.

By way of an example, we can take the case of the governor-shareholder of a family business who needs the work skills of particular people outside the family. To convince them to join the firm, he promises them a career path which he knows full well to be already earmarked for members of the family working in the business. In this case the governor-shareholder has no authority to 'expect' compliance with existing agreements since he intentionally presented a false picture of the contractual situation.

A second limit can be found in the reasoning put forward by governor-shareholders: they have to stand by agreements entered into with the other stakeholders and so they have no justification for behaving in a way which might jeopardize the long-term survival of the firm because in this case they might fail to comply with these agreements.

In the case previously cited as an example, the governor-shareholder did not have the right to appoint a son ill-qualified for the job because this could cause corporate performance to deteriorate and thus violate the rights of the other stakeholders to see the agreements complied with.

A third limit, very closely connected with the second, could stem from the consideration that not all a firm's stakeholders are in the same position *vis-à-vis* the firm. According to the well-known theory on stakeholders,[18] within the ambit of a company there are numerous groups of people whose interests are affected by the way in which the company is run and whose decisions in turn affect attainment of the company's goals. But when it comes to relations with the company, not all the stakeholders are in the same situation. The theory differentiates between the company's various stakeholders: in the narrow sense stakeholders are those groups of individuals who are fundamental to the success of the firm and whose interests are profoundly and lastingly influenced by the firm's operations. On this basis, shareholders who invest substantial amounts in the firm's capital and expect dividends in return are to be considered stakeholders in the narrow sense, as are the workers who have developed *ad hoc* work skills to meet the company's needs and who expect pay, job security and other non-monetary rewards. Suppliers and customers who have made specific investments that tie them to the company – and to that company alone – can also become stakeholders in the narrow sense.

For these stakeholders (in the narrow sense) we can say that relations based on reciprocal irreplaceability exist between the company and its stakeholders. Only with the contribution of these stakeholders can the firm produce a surplus of benefits and only in their relations with the firm can these stakeholders obtain a surplus of wealth over and above what the market has to offer them. Each stakeholder (in the narrow sense) therefore takes part in a mutually advantageous co-operative action.

This 'narrow' definition of stakeholder does not apply to investor-shareholders whose capital does not represent an essential resource for the development of the company and who can easily switch their funds to other stocks; nor does it apply to workers for whose skills there are openings on a responsive job market. As the relationship is – for both sides – an essentially replaceable one, it would make little sense to say that it is vital either for the company or for these stakeholders.

Using this theory we can therefore say that claims made by governor-shareholders on the basis of their right of ownership must be balanced against those made by the other stakeholders (in the narrow sense). Otherwise a governor-shareholder will not even obtain the result expected for him/herself: the other stakeholders – who make a determining contribution to the success of the firm and hence to the company's possibility of paying dividends on capital employed – will opt to behave in a self-interested fashion or, even though their withdrawal involves them in some costs, will break off their relationship with the company. In the first case, to reduce this self-interested behaviour, the governor-shareholders will have to increase supervision costs, thereby reducing the company's profits and hence their own earnings; in the second case, they will have to replace the people who have left, incurring costs that will likewise have a negative impact on profits.

In the case mentioned in which a shareholder appointed his inexperienced son to a key position in the firm, we can imagine the possible reactions of some of the stakeholders: their right to work under the direction of a well-qualified person having been denied, the workers may stop caring about their work and reduce their contribution; the most deserving members of senior management may take this appointment as an affront and start to look for another job; and so on. All this may involve the company in additional costs which might even jeopardize its development.

4.5   Conclusion

The distinction between natural and conventional ownership rights and the stakeholders' theory, with identification of stakeholders in the narrow sense, brings us to the conclusion that the autonomy of governor-shareholders that stems from their right of ownership is morally limited at least by the rights of the other stakeholders whose relationship with the company is based on reciprocal irreplaceability.

The governor-shareholder is therefore not morally justified in using the company for his or her own ends, not even considering that his or her own compensation is secondary to that of other stakeholders. As we have seen, from a theoretical moral standpoint, the governor-shareholder obviously has a (conventional) right of ownership but at the same time there must be the consensus of all the stakeholders (in the narrow sense) who help produce the 'co-operative surplus'. It is within the rights of these parties that the company be run to their advantage too, and that the person or persons who control or manage the company take no action that might deprive the company of this 'surplus', nor create conditions that make the production of this surplus less likely.

Our conclusions could also provide a piece of advice for the governor-shareholder who decides to proceed, regardless, with putting his unsuitable son in charge of the company: in this case the shareholder should at the same time – and at no extra cost to the company – hire a senior manager or consultant to work alongside his son, thereby ensuring the appropriate quality of corporate management.

These conclusions open up two other areas of debate, which relate to issues dealt with in depth elsewhere: on the one hand, how to ensure that the interests of all categories of stakeholder (in the narrow sense) are represented and defended. One way is to change the structure of corporate governance bodies, so as to make room – for instance – for parties representing the interests of workers who have developed specific skills to meet the company's needs. As things stand at present, in these bodies one category of stakeholders – the governor-shareholders – undertakes to represent and defend the interests of all the stakeholders. A change to bring in corporate governance bodies in which different categories of stakeholder are actually present would be a highly complex procedure: it would require gradual changes in mentality and in legislation[19] and it would have to satisfy the need for effectiveness and efficiency in corporate decision-making processes.

A second issue is the remuneration of all the stakeholders (in the narrow sense) in the event of corporate losses. It seems logical that, in circumstances of this kind, all the stakeholders (in the narrow sense) should forgo not only their share of the surplus – in any case non-existent – but also, if necessary, part of their contractually established remuneration. This issue too calls for major and complex changes in the mental outlook of the parties involved, above all for those categories of stakeholder not accustomed to taking risks.

The intention of this chapter has been to draw readers' attention to the question of the rights/duties implicit in ownership of a company. It is a topic which, as recent developments in managerial capitalism have also shown, concerns all types of capitalism. Reference has been made to the case of firms subordinated to the interests of governor-shareholders (typical of family businesses) because by analysing this case – which is the most radical interpretation of ownership rights applied to the corporate environment – it has been possible to open up debate on the nature and limits of the right of ownership, while not denying the existence of this right.

Notes

1. 'Business ethics' is taken to mean 'studies which apply philosophical ethics to the analysis and justification of the particular practices and institutions of contemporary societies' (L. Sacconi, *Etica degli affari* (Il Saggiatore, 1991), p. 4.
2. Cf. M. G. Velasquez, *Business Ethics. Concepts and Cases* (Prentice Hall, 1982).
3. Cf. R. T. de George, *Business Ethics* (Macmillan, 1990), p. 173–80.
4. Cf. A. A. Berle and G. Means, *The Modern Corporation and Private Property* (Macmillan, 1932).
5. Cf. M. Albert, 'Capitalisme contre capitalism', in *L'Expansion*, 20 December 1990.
6. IRI and ENI are Italy's two leading financial corporations controlling state holdings.
7. H. H. Segal, *Corporate Makeover. The Reshaping of the American Economy* (1989).
8. H. Mintzberg, *Mintzberg on Management. Inside Our Strange World of Organizations* (Free Press, 1989).
9. The terms are taken from A. Hirschman, *Exit, Voice and Loyalty: Responses to Decline in Firms, Organizations and States* (Harvard University Press, 1970).
10. Segal, *op. cit.*, chapter III.
11. Cf. P. F. Drucker, 'Reckoning with the pension fund revolution', in *Harvard Business Review*, March–April 1991, pp. 106–14.
12. Cf. *Plc UK Survey*, no. 7, 1992.
13. The case is related in Segal, *op. cit.*, pp. 159–61.
14. Sacconi, *op. cit.*, pp. 146ff.
15. J. Locke, Treatise on government.
16. Cf. C. Dematte', 'Le fonti di legittimazione del governo dell'impresa' (Sources of legitimization of company management procedures), in *Economia & Management*, vol. 22, 1991.
17. Cf. Sacconi, *op. cit.*, p. 178.
18. For a presentation of the theory, cf. R. E. Freeman *Strategic Management: A Strategic Approach* (Pitman, 1984).
19. Cf. the proposal for the Fifth Directive adopted by the EC Council on 19 August 1983.

CHAPTER 5

Customers

Eberhard Kuhlmann
Technische Universität Berlin, Germany

5.1   Point of departure: consumer rights in the social market economy

Most democratic states provide their citizens with basic rights or general human rights through a constitution. In the Federal Republic of Germany, the inviolability of a person's dignity and of their home, the right of expressing one's opinion freely and gaining information without difficulties from publicly accessible sources, the right to private property while still serving the common good, are all laid down in the constitution. These and other rights protect human beings and oblige them to behave accordingly. They thus affect the numerous daily actions which we undertake to form our individual lives, as we pursue happiness.

A large part of human behaviour is directed towards achieving goods to satisfy certain needs. This represents the economic way of reaching happiness. Satisfaction of needs for food, clothing, housing, entertainment and education ensures that mind and body can survive and develop. When we gather goods for our individual needs or those of a small group like a family, we act as a *consumer*.

The consumer is able to create some goods him/herself – e.g. preparing a meal. Other goods have to be acquired through transactions. In this case the consumer becomes a *customer* of producers and dealers and has to interact with highly specialized organizations which are superior to him/her in many respects. Not only do agents and producers have better and more information at their disposal, they also have larger economic resources to draw on. Regarding business transactions, this subsequently puts them in the position to increase their advantage at the cost of the buyer. This produces an almost natural power imbalance which could limit the customer's rights while s/he is trying to satisfy his/her needs through consumption.

As in other constitutions, the statutes of the Federal Republic of Germany list two further propositions:

- In the eyes of the law all people are equal.
- Every person is entitled to develop his/her personality freely, provided that no other person's rights are violated.

In other words, everybody can make equal use of the existing rights, as long as other people's rights are respected at the same time. This is the fiction of the equilibrium of power which of course also holds for the relationship between buyer and seller. Similarly, the assumption of a symmetrical distribution of power can also be found in economic theory and legal theory. The model of the perfect market contains the assumption that the buyer maximizes the satisfaction of his/her needs by making decisions without being influenced by others. In fact, civil law assumes that both parties to a contract can make use of this contractual freedom: in drawing up a contract, both the buyer and seller are expected to be able to attain their interests.

We can now draw the following conclusions:

- There are basic rules and theoretical models which demand a balance of power between sellers and buyers. At the same time they protect the buyer from gross disadvantages.
- It cannot be denied that a power imbalance does exist, which is a source of real or potential disadvantage for the buyer.

This gap between fact and fiction has often been criticized during the course of this century (Kuhlmann, 1990: 23–39). US President J. F. Kennedy was the first person to attempt to close the gap systematically. In his message to Congress in 1962 he refers to four 'consumer rights':

1. Right of safety: damages to health and property caused by using faulty or 'dangerous' products should be diminished or prevented.
2. Right to be informed: on the one hand, deception and misleading of customers is to be eliminated by means of more efficient communication and, on the other hand, information is to be offered to support and encourage purchasing decisions.
3. Right to choose: by using an effective competition policy, monopolies are prevented, abuse of market power is reduced and the market stays open to new competitors. In this way a broad range of high-quality goods can be offered at the most favourable prices. Furthermore, contracts should also enable the customer to benefit from his/her right of contractual freedom to maintain his/her interests.
4. Right to be heard: this right ensures the presence of consumer representatives when laws are constituted. Also, possibilities are to be created for the customer to convey complaints and dissatisfactions to sellers of consumer goods.

The rights we are dealing with here are, of course, not formal rights, but rather directives or goals enforcing a policy in favour of consumers. The goals have been achieved in very different manners and levels of intensity, at first in the USA, followed by European countries later.

In different European countries even more 'consumer rights' have been added to the list. The following two deserve special reference:

5. Environmental rights: in a wide sense all human beings are consumers of the natural resources air, water and soil. If these resources are polluted the consumer

will experience a diminution of his/her consumption and life quality. This can be caused, for example, by traffic noise in cities, poor quality of drinking water or food containing harmful chemicals which are due to modern cultivation methods of our agricultural industry.

6. Consumer education rights: specific educational measures are to be taken in general public schools for the purpose of increasing consumers' knowledge, abilities and motivation and thus safeguarding their personal interests.

The following duties of producers and sellers can be derived from the 'consumer rights':

1. Manufactured and offered products must provide a minimum level of security.

2. Supplier communication must not contain any deceiving or misleading information, but rather educate the consumer with regard to important product qualities.

3. Contracts may not be drawn up at the consumer's disadvantage but must enable both parties equally to attain their interests. Furthermore, they should provide the consumer with the right to demand redress for damages.

4. Suppliers should be open to customers' complaints and attend to their problems as well as to reasons for satisfaction and dissatisfaction concerning products and services.

5. The environmental pollution caused by production, distribution, use and waste disposal of goods should be minimized. In addition, all costs should be borne by the persons responsible – no matter whether they are producers, dealers or consumers. Costs of production and disposal, especially, should not be externalized as they then would have to be paid for by the general public of taxpayers and consumers.

6. Not only state authorities but also suppliers of consumer goods can help to educate the consumer by introducing adequate measures. Whoever, for example, offers high-quality goods at a reasonable price does not need to fear a well-informed consumer.

Here again, we are not dealing with duties of producers and sellers in the strict sense, but rather with guidelines on the grounds of which they ought to arrange their market transactions.

The following discussion mostly refers to the situation in Germany. Let us first examine a few important areas of conflict between firms and their customers and then focus on a few strategies of conflict regulation.

5.2 Areas of conflict between firms and their customers

Conflicts between individuals and organizations occur every day and show the following simple structure:

A has a goal (GA) which prevents B from reaching his goal (GB) at the same time.

The classic example of this is salespeople aiming for the highest possible price. It is considered logical, however, for buyers to seek as much product for their money as they can get. Conflicts always end up being conflicts of goals but they are created by different causes:

1. *Goal conflicts* are caused by different aims: seller A demands a high price, buyer B seeks a low one.
2. *Perceptual and prognostic conflicts* result from different perceptions, for instance of the quality of an object, or different predictions about its consequences: seller A considers his product PA to be safe due to the results of quality control; buyer B thinks PA is dangerous because, in her opinion, the whole product range P is potentially dangerous to health.
3. *Resource conflicts* occur when A and B desire different distributions of a jointly used resource: A offers a product, the packaging of which leads to high waste disposal costs. Consequently, the jointly exploited ecological resources – air, soil and water – are affected much more adversely than they would be by a different kind of packaging.

In 1992 a typical conflict arose between suppliers and customers; as a result of negotiations with the Secretary of State for the Environment, producers of consumer goods signed a contract, committing themselves to dispose of their packaging by means of their own recycling system (Dual system). The Secretary of State endeavours to relieve the public waste disposal whilst the suppliers – by offering the voluntary measure – strive towards preventing a greater severity of packaging laws. All companies involved in this recycling system are compelled to participate in its financing. These firms mark their packages with a symbol – the 'Green Dot'. In large-scale advertising campaigns the suppliers claim their recycling system to be an important contribution to environmental protection. Shortly after this recycling system was introduced, representatives of consumer associations, however, objected to several serious imperfections:

1. In order to finance the system, the prices of consumer goods are raised, which essentially means that the system is actually being financed by the consumers.
2. The 'Green Dot' does not lead to a decrease in packaging – particularly not of packages which are most harmful to the environment, as they are composed of many different materials.
3. Since the beginning of 1992, many packages have appeared with a 'Green Dot'. Nevertheless, a large number of them have to be disposed of by the official bodies, all because many regions do not provide the necessary special waste containers.

This example combines the three kinds of conflict expounded above.

The causes of the above-mentioned conflicts are unavoidable and recurrent, so it is important to observe how strong the resulting conflicts are and how they can be solved. The stronger party is often tempted to force through a solution for its benefit. Facing the comparatively weak consumer, sellers are able to make use of their stronger financial potential and their know-how (knowledge or information).

A conflict will only arise if there is a relationship between A and B. Sellers get into contact with their customers by using marketing tools. By examining some of these tools, let us illustrate four typical areas of conflict.

5.2.1   Conflict area: 'media advertising'

If we accept the fact that a customer has a right to be informed, two significant conclusions can be drawn:

- Media advertising should provide the customer with 'correct information' with which s/he can make sensible purchasing decisions.
- Media advertising should not contain any 'deceptive information', as this would mislead the customer and direct him/her towards decisions s/he would not have made with 'correct information'.

What do the terms 'correct' and 'deceptive' information exactly imply?

1.   *Correct information*   An advertisement claims that product P will lead to result X if it is used over a long period of time. Customer B reads the advertisement, buys the product and experiences the true result X. A scientific analysis of the product verifies the result.

2.   *Deceptive information*   After purchasing product P a customer notices that it does not show the promised result X, or only under a condition which the dealer purposely conceals. The customer's experience is again verified by a test.

In Germany deceptive advertising contravenes the 'Law against Unfair Competition' (UWG). The administration of justice speaks of a remarkable case of misleading information if the following occur:

- 10–15 per cent of the people who came into contact with an ad or a spot
- had a subjective idea of the advertised product or service
- which could not withstand later examination.

The facts of misleading really ought to be proven by means of empirical examinations of the real effects of every single case. Due to the high costs and large amount of time required for such examinations, they do not occur. Instead, experts are consulted in court. Supposing, for example, a supplier claimed to have raised his vegetables 'biologically' even though this was demonstrably not the case, he would have to be prepared for his competitors or consumer associations bringing an action against him. The court would then prohibit further advertisement and compel him to make up for damages which he may have caused the competitor. Only in extreme cases of deceptive advertisement are the customers presumed to have suffered damages.

A third case lies between these two easily recognizable extremes:

3. *Potentially misleading information*   An advertisement shows a product in front of a beautiful, untouched, natural landscape. At the same time the information is given that product P is made of only natural materials. Subconsciously customer B gets the impression that P could have a positive effect on his health. The result of consuming P regularly, however, manifests itself in teeth cavities and overweight, caused by the high percentage of sugar and calories contained in the product. Nevertheless the dealer's statements about the materials are true and can be proven.

This last case describes the daily conflict situation which does not violate coded law (opposed to case 2). The following examples will illustrate these two cases.

In their advertisement for a white chocolate called 'Cracky Mountains' the Bahlsen company in Hanover stated that it is permissible to snack on sweets ('Naschen erlaubt'). According to the Berlin Consumer Protection Association this statement carries misleading information, as the consumer could start believing that eating chocolate would have no negative results such as cavities and overweight. A Berlin court prohibited the statement 'Naschen erlaubt' as misleading. The reason for this judgment was that the impression was made that snacking on Cracky Mountains was permitted by way of exception. But, if something is allowed, the customer is almost forced to gain the impression that it will not have any negative consequences (AID, 1992).

In 1991 the Cologne Institute for Applied Research of Consumer Behaviour examined TV commercials in public (ARD, ZDF) and private (RTL+) television programmes. Within three weeks, 1,600 commercials with child actors were gathered. Of these commercials 300 advertised sweets, especially cookies, drops and chocolate which were often claimed to be full of vitamins or highly nutritious. One producer stated that its chocolate was an 'important contribution to a child's nutrition'. It further asserted the most important ingredient to be three-quarters of a litre of milk. A commercial for candy emphasized that the candy 'contained as much calcium as a glass of milk'. The children are addressed directly: 'It is exactly what you need'. Some producers address the parents with information such as 'Sweets your child likes. Vitamins your child needs.' Such information in commercials gives the observer the impression that sweets not only mean no danger to health, but are even physiologically valuable.

The effect of 'potentially misleading advertising' is, above all, based on emotional stimuli and normative statements. Emotional stimuli are communicated, for instance, by pictures, colours, music and odours. Their effect is explained in the theory of 'emotional conditioning'. The image of a Marlboro cigarette is therefore closely attached to the subjective imagination of cowboy adventures, freedom and romance of the great outdoors. Normative statements such as 'Take care of your health! Use X!' lead to the conclusion that X could improve the customer's health.

No evidence of misleading is given with emotional stimuli. Emotional advertising contains no assertions regarding specific demonstrable features of the products and services offered. This also applies to normative statements; in the example mentioned above the supplier does not explicitly say 'X is good for your health!' Furthermore, the administration of justice assumes that a person with average mental abilities can estimate the usual exaggerations and the employed images and other stimuli of advertising realistically; their effect is comparable to the efforts of a tom cat courting a queen.

The example of media advertising demonstrates very well that conflicts are a 'natural part' of economy life and that different people perceive them differently.

Companies advertise in order to increase or stabilize their sales, turnover and profit. The results of advertising are ascertained, among other criteria, in terms of rates of recall or recognition, impact on attitudes and intentions, effects on sales and turnover. In research on advertising effectiveness there is no such measure as 'customer information'. Nevertheless, representatives of consumer associations often demand that advertising should contain a high level of information:

- It should convey information on all product characteristics which are of importance with regard to the customer's purchasing decision, e.g. running costs of household appliances.
- Statements claimed in advertisements ought to be verified by scientific methods of evaluation, e.g. the effectiveness of medicine.
- Ads should be easy to comprehend for all consumers and not cause any false interpretations.

These and similar demands are due to a misunderstanding of the advertising tasks in a social market economy in which more than one independent information system exists. In such economies the task of informing the consumer lies with institutions dealing with comparative product testing or others dealing with consumer counselling. If the advertisement would satisfy all the above-mentioned demands, the consumer would soon be confronted with an 'information overload'; consequently, the flood of presented information would be averted by cognitive defence mechanisms and, in return, the aspired information effect would not be able to develop.

5.2.2 Conflict area: 'product safety'

In order to call a product safe, products for sale must meet certain minimal requirements regarding their quality. The use of unsafe products can lead to the following:

1. damage to body and mind
2. economic damage:
   - by loss of the ability to work
   - by loss of property.

We can only speak of an unsafe product if the damage can be attributed to failures of the product. This term cannot be employed in cases where other influences caused the damage or where the product was incorrectly used.

How to use complex products such as electronic devices or medicine correctly should always be described in the instruction sheet. If a producer sells a defective product, the customer is threatened by damage caused by the product itself: a washing machine no longer runs properly, a piece of furniture is scratched, etc. The customer can avoid this damage if he or she makes use of his or her right of guarantee, which means later improvement (repair) or a new consignment (exchange). A defective product or an incomplete instruction sheet can also lead to consequent damage: the faulty electrical system of a washing machine can cause fire; medicine taken according to false instructions is most likely to damage health. The producer can be sued for damages within the bounds of product liability.

The German appliance safety laws assert that technical devices – including appliances for household use, sports, gardening, crafts and playing – can only appear on the market if they adhere to the generally accepted technical regulations. This is to guarantee the protection of health and property of the user and third persons as much as possible, providing the goods are used properly. The generally acknowledged technical regulations are part of the German Industrial Norms (DIN) and VDE Norms (VDE = Association of German Electrotechnicians). Despite this law, dangerous products continue to appear on the market. In 1990, the company Tchibo was forced to withdraw a certain kind of electrical hair dryer. Due to a fault the hair dryer turned on automatically when it was plugged in, even when the switch was turned off. In two provinces in Germany three of these hair dryers caused fires which led to damages amounting to DM 1000 (*vpk*, 35/1990).

Milupa AG, a producer of baby food, sells instant teas which contain about 90 per cent of sugar. The commercials pointed out that the baby would be content and calm and sleep soundly after drinking instant fennel tea. A plastic bottle with a rubber nipple on top was sold along with the tea in order to enable constant consumption. The permanent use of this tea caused the well-known 'nursing-bottle syndrome' which began to show up at the beginning of the 1980s: the children's teeth were severely affected by caries. After a long lawsuit initiated by the parents affected, the Federal Court (BGH) sued Milupa AG for damages in 1991. According to the BGH the company had not given precise enough information in the instructions about the consequences and possible damage of continual use. The verdict was based on the law regarding product liability which has been in force since 1990. Quite possibly some 100,000 parents of affected children could claim payment for damages. Since February 1992 Milupa no longer sells the plastic bottles (*Spiegel*, 47/1991; *Tagesspiegel*, 22 February 1992).

Products and services will never be able to ensure absolute safety. This will always raise the question of how much safety is considered sensible from the economic point of view. Binding safety rules exert an influence on trading by excluding some offers and giving preference to others. Buyers who prefer taking risks may feel limited in their freedom to choose, as they will no longer be able to require risk-involving but cheaper products. Thus safety norms simultaneously touch both the suppliers' and customers' interests. The benefit of safety norms must therefore be examined in three steps (Kuhlmann, 1990: 177–80):

1.   The first fact to be examined is whether or not damages can be avoided without applying safety norms. Consumers tend to lead their lives in a considerably careless manner – just think of our behaviour while driving a car or skiing downhill. Here the question arises: to what extent could possible damages be avoided by changing our attitudes towards thoughtless behaviour? With regard to some areas, such as use of technical appliances and medicine, there actually is a realistic chance of changing the consumers' behaviour as far as information on and use of the product are concerned. The suppliers can bring about this change by introducing informative labelling, drawing attention to risks and creating instruction sheets. The government can try to evoke changes through consumer education and information. Nevertheless we may assume that these measures will only prevent a few damages to a limited extent.

2.   In case damages cannot be avoided it has to be examined which damages can be carried by whom and to what extent. Serious irreversible damages to health and property are principally intolerable. Damages which are principally tolerable must be examined with regard to their pressure on the economy. Ordinary minor damage can be carried by each consumer. He or she can take out insurance policies for more serious damages (household insurance policies or health insurance). Producers and sellers sometimes pay for part of the unavoidable damages through guarantees or within the bounds of their product liability.

3.   If damages are unavoidable and intolerable it must be examined to what extent they can be reduced by safety norms. Safety norms are no universal remedy and their costs and benefits have to be carefully weighed against each other. For the consumer these costs result in higher prices, a reduced range of products offered and the fact that possible innovations do not appear on the market. Norms are significant obstacles to trade without fixed rates! The consumers' benefits lie in the diminished risk or damage, in lower insurance rates as well as reduced information costs and less uncertainty.

Attention must be paid to the fact that safety norms are the last step of measures to be taken within this hierarchy. The measures of the first two steps grant both suppliers and customers a greater scope of freedom and individual motivation.

5.2.3   Conflict area: 'pricing'

Before purchasing, customers typically try to find the retailer who demands the lowest possible price for a certain article. The consequence of competition in a social market economy is that prices vary widely. At any given time, different retailers demand different prices for the same article and the prices can also change later on. Considering the fact that a private household purchases many thousand different goods and services, it is understandable that the average consumer knows fairly little about prices. Apart from a few frequently purchased articles, he or she is hardly ever able to judge whether a certain price which is fixed for an article at a certain time is adequate – which means fairly low – or inadequate, which means fairly high. The fact that sellers declare their prices to be sensationally low or special offers, makes it harder for consumers to comprehend prices (Kuhlmann, 1990: 231–42).

An empirical examination was conducted to analyse how strongly special offers could objectively be considered as favourable prices (Diller, 1988). They were compared with normal prices which were not especially commented on by the seller. The result showed that 30 per cent of the special offers turned out to be more expensive and 13 per cent meant only a reduction of between 1 and 5 per cent. The average reduction of all special offers amounted to 5 per cent. Surprisingly, more than two-thirds of the special offers were sold at a more favourable price two weeks later.

Unemployment, illness, bad planning and thoughtless expense force many consumers to avail themselves of more credit than they can redeem with their normal income. We call this 'heavy indebtedness': in such a situation, a customer no longer receives credit from normal banks, but from credit institutions which demand high interest and negotiate very unfavourable terms. This can lead to a loss of one's whole property and life-long debts. The contract, however, can be declared null and void if it was based on a profiteering credit business. This is the case when the average interest rate, which is fixed by the German Federal Bank, has been exceeded by 90–100 per cent and further unfavourable conditions have been agreed upon. The contract is also illegal when a subjective condition is added to those mentioned above. The credit institution could have misused the customer's inexperience or weak will, as often occurs with foreigners or elderly persons.

A 24-year-old married man reports: 'I did not see clearly through the whole situation. A loan was already being recovered by a debt-collecting agency. I had also already sworn an oath of disclosure. I had to pay for various insurance policies and the nursery school. Above all, I owed DM 46,000 to 27 different banks and private customers. Because of the rent arrears the landlord gave me notice for my old apartment.' (Reiter, 1991: 225) This man reveals great deficits of knowledge and proves that he is incapable of planning rationally and economically. Granting him further credit would plunge him into worse economic chaos, as he would only receive 'help' from an expensive credit agency.

The never-ending basic conflict between suppliers and customers finds expression in the argument over the heights of prices. If the suppliers have a dominant position in the market they are not subject to any pressure of competition and can exploit and misuse their market power by demanding exorbitant prices. A price is called 'exorbitant' if it is considerably higher than a fictive price fixed on the basis of a functioning market – in other words a competitive market.

On the grounds of U 22 of the German 'Law against Limitations to Competition' the Bundeskartellamt (Federal Anti-Trust Office) can prohibit abuse of dominant market positions. If this abuse leads to considerably exorbitant prices the Bundeskartellamt can insist on price reductions. The following 'Valium-Librium' case makes clear that the calculation of the fictive competitive price is connected with quite a few problems. In the named case, the company Hoffmann-La Roche was accused of demanding highly excessive prices for Valium and Librium in spite of their dominant position in the German market regarding both drugs. The Dutch market was chosen for comparison, where the same articles were sold at much more favourable prices. Hoffmann-La Roche argued they were forced to cover high costs of – often even superfluous – research and development investments. As a result of the action brought by the Bundeskartellamt, the Berlin Chamber Court at first charged price reductions of 40 per cent for Valium and 35 per cent for Librium which were reduced again later to 35 and 24 per cent. During further proceedings the Federal Court decided that abuse of a dominant market situation was only the case if the competitive price were being considerably exceeded by at least 25 per cent. Hoffmann-La Roche then did not have to reduce their prices. According to the Federal Court the prices demanded in the Netherlands were not suitable for comparison.

This case leads to the following conclusions: a pioneer developing and introducing new products on a market should be granted a temporary monopoly benefit for their audacity. However, imitators should be given the chance to enter the same market and to reduce monopoly prices and benefits by making cheaper offers. Over the years this actually happened on the tranquillizer market. Workable competition is doubtlessly the best means to achieve the lowest possible prices.

5.2.4   Conflict area: 'terms of contract'

Most consumers have little knowledge of law. Therefore they neither pay attention to the conditions of the contracts they are signing, nor are they capable of using the rights that pertain to them (Kuhlmann, 1990: 199–202). Hardly any customers read the sellers' General Terms carefully. Later on, they are often surprised that the guarantee is not as favourable as it appeared to be when they read the contract superficially in the beginning.

The German subsidiary of the car manufacturing company Peugeot had a sales brochure in which a warrant repair of the bodywork of the car was promised if it rusted on the inside within six years after the date of purchase. This statement was also part of the General Terms and Conditions. Peugeot had concealed, however, that the guarantee was only valid on the condition that the car owner had his car specially serviced twice in a garage under contract with Peugeot. The two visits had to be two years apart and the customer had to carry the full price which would amount to about DM 250 to DM 300. This condition was mentioned in the guarantee booklet which was delivered with the car after the purchase. The Berlin Consumer Protection Association (VSV) then brought legal action against Peugeot. The verdict of the court prohibited this kind of advertising as misleading. Peugeot did not appeal and changed their advertising concept completely (*vpk*, 20/1988).

Hospitals, too, have General Terms and Conditions which define the rights and duties of the hospital and its patients. As in many other public concerns, the customer's rights are strongly limited here. If a person is severely ill, they hardly have any other choice: they sign the contract in front of them without reading it carefully.

A very ill woman was taken to hospital and upon arriving asked to sign a contract which was printed in very small letters and was three and a half pages long. The woman expressed the wish to be treated as a private patient. According to the terms of the contract, the hospital could withdraw from liability for part of the medical treatment for private patients. The paragraph containing this stipulation was on the last page of the contract, number 13 out of 15. The woman died because of malpractice during the anaesthesia. In its verdict the Oberlandesgericht KÖLN declared the paragraph on exclusion of liability invalid. The seriously ill woman had been overwhelmed by the contract. Patients must be informed of such paragraphs ahead of time and be fully capable of comprehending them (*vpk*, 14/1990).

5.3   Strategies of conflict regulation

In section 5.2 we acquainted ourselves with a few areas of conflict which arise between producers and sellers on the one hand and consumers as their customers on the other hand. Many of these conflicts occur every day and are not very striking. Others, however, are extraordinarily intense and meaningful for the customer. As there is a great difference of power between the seller and the buyer, conflicts often result in limitations of consumer rights, as described above.

During a normal business transaction, each side is usually equally strong; that means buyer and seller take an equal interest in their advantages. Only a satisfied customer is a loyal buyer, as he or she sees that his or her needs are satisfied through market transactions. This balance of interests can also be maintained by different strategies of conflict regulation which are divided into the following:

- strategies to avoid conflict and
- strategies to solve conflicts.

Both of these basic strategies complement each other, as only some conflicts can be avoided in advance. Conflicts which still arise have to be solved later on.

One should also mention that there are areas where customers achieve their interests to the disadvantage of the seller. Thefts and insurance fraud are good examples which occur often enough. These, however, are criminal phenomena which we shall not dwell on any further at this point.

5.3.1 Business strategies of self-regulation

Let us begin our examination of business strategies of self-regulation of conflicts by dividing them into two types: self-discipline of business firms and self-control of industries. The strategies of self-regulation reflect the prevailing business moral with all its predominant norms (Steinmann and Löhr, 1992: 7–14).

Self-discipline of business firms
When managers apply certain norms, this can be related to two complexes of causes:

1. The norms are internalized, i.e. they have been learned and are a fundamental part of the mind. Norms are especially learned during primary socialization in the family, but also in secondary socialization at school, university, church, in political parties and in enterprises where managers are and were employed. The person applying internalized norms is often not aware of them. He or she thus does not think about their costs and benefits.

2. Norms are employed like tools, when the benefit achieved by their application clearly outweighs the costs. One benefit of using norms can be that the customer's approval of a company and its goods and services increases. These customers then become loyal and heavy buyers and possibly are prepared to accept higher prices. This benefit manifests itself directly in the increasing turnover and profit. One could speak of an indirect benefit if the company's image improved in the eyes of important

groups of stakeholders due to the perceived application of norms. The company's reputation grows in the eyes of politicians, journalists, trade unions and bank managers, etc. This triggers a sequence of long-term positive effects on turnover, costs and profit. Norms which are employed as tools are usually put down in written form and called ethical guidelines or codes of practice (Richardson and Morris, 1988).

A company's moral code is reflected by its customers' reactions. Some companies do not do more for their customers than they absolutely have to, as laid down by contractual agreements or by law. Others create consumer departments which deal systematically with customer complaints, discontent and ideas.

The Migros alliance of associations supplies goods for twelve regional Swiss Migros retail associations. Having founded a consumer department which supports the customer's economic interests as well as health concerns and ecological questions for all Migros companies, the managing department has an employee in charge of consumer problems. All enquiries and complaints of Migros customers are examined and settled by the consumer department. In the past, 40 per cent of the consumer requests were complaints, 70 per cent of which referred to products, advertising and selling policy. Almost 60 per cent of the consumer requests were enquiries and recommendations which, for example, drew attention to problems concerning ecology or nourishment.

Special care is devoted to making sure that each question is answered. Complaints caused by a consignment of faulty products, for example, are settled in a satisfactory manner. Complaints, suggestions and enquiries contain valuable information for a company, which can be used for improvement of products, packaging, advertising and distribution. In their weekly magazine (circulation over 1 million) the Migros company once a month publishes a supplement which provides important information and support for the consumer. Thanks to the consumer department, many successful improvements have been made for the benefit of the consumer, as the following examples illustrate (Holliger, 1985):

- Food and non-food products show both an expiry date as well as the last possible selling date.
- The amount of sugar, fat and salt in food has been reduced.
- Instructions were changed to be more comprehensible.
- Dangerous products were found and replaced by safe ones.
- Small packages were introduced for small households.
- Clauses which diminished customers' rights were eliminated from guarantee conditions for electric devices and clocks.

Self-control of industries
Almost all employers' associations try to achieve self-control through the industries which they represent. They act this way, in order to reach the following goals:

- To protect honest companies against unfair competitors.
- To maintain or improve the industry's image.
- To protect customers and to create a demand for the industry's products and services.
- To forestall state regulations, especially measures of law.

This last aim is losing importance within the European Community as the EC administration is apt to replace voluntary measures by compulsory EC legal directives.

Voluntary regulations show both advantages and disadvantages. Some of the advantages are:

- A faster adaption to changing conditions in industry is possible when not restricted to laws.
- The quality of the adjustment to specific conditions of an industry is better.
- Voluntary participation of the member firms of the branch prevents destructive behaviour and secures the efficiency of self-regulation.

Some of the disadvantages are:

- Informal behaviour of an industry is hard to generalize and codify.
- Member firms are rather inclined to agree to non-binding and mild regulations than to obligatory demanding standards.
- Not all companies of a certain branch are members of the association. Consequently they are not forced to adhere to the regulations.
- Violations of rules are often hard to punish.

The codes of conduct should be able to eradicate the most important reasons for complaints and dissatisfaction of the customer. They should be widely spread among all member firms and be applied with conviction. In order to do so, the firms must know the rules and how to apply them. Furthermore, an effective arbitration board is required (Richardson and Morris, 1988).

The German Advertising Council (DWR) was founded in 1972 by the Head Association of Advertising, which is also called the Central Association of Advertising (ZAW). The DWR is composed of ten members which belong to associations of the ZAW and has three fields of activity (Nickel, 1989):

1. It works out codes of conduct to prevent faulty developments in publicity and to improve advertising for the benefit of the consumers.
2. It deals with violations against codes of conduct.
3. It informs publicity associations and the public about its work as well as developments of political measures concerning advertising.

Codes of conduct are generally based on the 'International codes of conduct for commercial practice'. They were brought out by the International Chamber of

Commerce (CCI) in collaboration with the ZAW. The following examples offer an illustration of the content of these rules:

- Commercials are not to offend codes of ethics, neither by text nor by picture, and are not to abuse the consumer's confidence or lack of knowledge.
- Advertising should not mislead the consumer by making allusions or unclear statements, concealing facts or claiming exaggerated facts.
- Advertising is to be distinguished clearly from editorial contributions.
- Advertising should not take advantage of children's and adolescents' credulity and lack of experience.

Furthermore, there are other special rules for advertising 'critical' products and services like medicine, alcoholic drinks (liquor), cigarettes and tobacco as well as loans and capital investments. The DWR has added a few more details to the rules composed by the ICC. In 1990, the DWR received 261 complaints, 129 of which were transformed into rules (Jahrbuch DWR, 1991). The two following examples of 1991 illustrate those decisions (Spruchpraxis Deutscher Werberat, 1990):

1.   One commercial showed adolescents sitting around drinking wine. The spot was underlined with the slogan 'Adolescence has also discovered how good wine tastes', to advertise the liquor. DWR objected to this ad, as it violated the codes of conduct regarding advertisement for liquor by inviting youths to consume alcohol.

2.   'No more wrinkles!' – this slogan was advertising a certain cosmetic. The DWR contested this ad, too, as it gave the misleading impression that wrinkles could be completely eliminated, a claim which could not be supported by science.

In the UK there exists a regulation procedure for the advertising industry which is comparable to the actions of the DWR. The executive committee of the Advertising Standards Agency is composed of nine members of which only three belong to the advertising industry. The other six belong to other social groups, so that groups representing the public interest are taking part in decisions.

5.3.2   Public strategies of regulation

'Soft law'

'Soft law' forms a growing 'grey' area between obligatory legal norms and the non-controlled sphere of trade (Reich and Smith, 1984). By soft law we mean codes of conduct or standards which are not laid down by law. These codes are formed by an administrative body which is also in charge of supervising laws and regulations (Tala, 1987). On the grounds of governmental guidelines the administration negotiates the content of codes of conduct with representatives of the suppliers – namely the corresponding associations. The consent of all persons affected – namely the associations representing them – facilitates the enforcement of the codes of conduct and minimizes the expenses of surveillance. Due to a legal obligation the Office of Fair Trading (OFT) in Great Britain has negotiated codes of conduct with various economic associations in order to settle rules concerning all business practices of the association members. In Sweden negotiations concerning information standards were carried through by the national office of consumer policy, thereby determining minimal demands as to the wording of advertisements and informative product descriptions. 'Soft law' contains the following three principles of regulation (Tala, 1987):

1. Joint negotiation and approval.
2. Development of rules and regulations by collaboration between state offices and market parties.
3. Offices and associations supervise adherence to rules jointly and equally, and deal with cases of violation against rules.

The advantages and disadvantages of soft law are similar to those explained in 'Self-control of industries' above.

Law and jurisdiction

It has always been the goal to limit the seller's power in the consumer's interest through law and administrative measures. In each European country there are laws referring to the whole scope of the seller's marketing tools – advertising, labelling, product qualities and safety, contracting and pricing, to name only a few. When laws are adhered to through court and administrative bodies, relationships between firms and their customers are regulated in manifold ways. Where managers do not have moral standards or do not apply them, consumer rights cannot be realized efficiently by governmental regulation.

One of the advantages of the law-based supervision of suppliers through courts and supervisory offices lies in the fact that it applies to all persons who are protected by these laws. Opposed to the advantages there are a number of disadvantages caused by supervision and the enforcement of legal norms (Kuhlmann, 1990: 89–90):

1. Laws often consist of generally worded clauses which each lawyer interprets according to the specific case. Only few lawyers have economic expertise; many of them are dependent on the information of 'experts' who also have different levels of expertise and individual attitudes. Judgments are therefore hard to predict and the insecurity of affected persons is a priori very high.

2. Due to an insufficient number of courts, proceedings are often postponed and of considerable length.

3. State regulations induce suppliers to develop strategies which bypass and evade the regulations. Consequently, laws and regulations are altered. This bears the danger of an infinite sequence of state interventions and thus a resulting limitation of competition.

Laws and judicial or administrational supervision lose their menacing effect if suppliers estimate the costs of a sentencing to be much lower than the benefit resulting from law violation.

5. The span of control of supervisory boards is often much greater than their capacity of control. This means that the probability of being caught violating a norm is not high enough to encourage all suppliers to be law-abiding.
6. Neither consumers nor lawyers know all consumer rights sufficiently enough to use them for themselves.
7. Consequences arising from the enforcement of laws and regulations can often only be incompletely predicted. Many examples show that regulating interventions support the interests of consumers from one point of view, but harm them from another point of view. For instance, higher legal safety standards in some cases lead to higher costs, reduce the innovation rate in the market and represent a barrier for new suppliers accessing the market.
8. State regulations mostly have reactive effects – apart from preventive administrative control, as for example authorization of medicine by the Federal Health Office. Often the horse has already bolted before the stable door was locked, as far as enacting new laws or charges for redress for damages by court authorities are concerned. Laws and regulations, as well as their enforcement, are very cost-intensive measures to solve conflicts between suppliers and customers.

5.4   Consumer policy

Relationships between companies and their customers can also be created by activating the consumer – who represents the other side of the market. A sophisticated, active consumer can perceive his or her rights and fulfil his or her interests better. Let us name a few measures which help to strengthen the consumer (Kuhlmann, 1990: 265–410).

Consumer education at schools which should raise the consumers' abilities and motivation to pursue their own interests. The most important goals are as follows:

1. Improvement of the general ability of making decisions; recognition of needs, ability of gaining information and weighing alternatives and consideration of the consuming effects reflected in the community as a whole.

2. Strengthening of abilities to run a household; planning of income and expenses, property and debts; knowledge about certain qualities of goods and methods of household production and waste disposal.

3. Increase in the efficiency of market behaviour: use of sources of consumer information and counselling, qualification towards effective purchasing behaviour, knowledge and appliance of consumer rights and understanding of supplier behaviour and general market rules.

Empirical examinations prove that so far only little effectiveness has been achieved, i.e. few goals have been reached. The reasons for this include – among others – unapproachable methods, too short lesson periods and teachers who are not educated adequately. Furthermore, within the whole process of consumer socialization, education plays only a small part: parents, brothers and sisters and peers as well as supplier communication have a much stronger influence which is often opposed to the goals of consumer education.

Consumer counselling forms an approach to support individual consumers or small groups with solutions to the problems by means of individual advice. According to the kinds of problems different people require counselling regarding products and appliances, credit and debit, energy and environment as well as counselling on legal matters, budget, nourishment, housing and renting – to mention only the most important subjects. As enquirers have to approach the counselling organization, the clients mostly belong to the group of active consumers whose income and education lie above the statistical average rates. The success of counselling is mainly dependent on the counsellors and their tools but also on the enquirer him/herself.

A successful counsellor should:

- provide specialist expertise;
- express him/herself in a comprehensible manner;
- not only give advice on how to act but also ascertain the enquirer's needs and problems;
- have a manifold selection of influencing strategies handy.

The tools include encyclopaedias, test magazines and – to a great extent – databases within computer-assisted information systems. At this point we reach a critical bottleneck of counselling with regard to its success, as the consumer has to implement the received information on how to solve the problem him/herself. For example, if someone knows that he has the right of guarantee and also knows how to proceed, he will not always necessarily transform his knowledge into action.

Consumer information furnishes large groups of consumers with information in order to judge products and services. The most important measure of consumer information is to compare goods in tests and diffuse the results through mass media such as magazines, newspapers, radio broadcasting and television. This kind of consumer information has been for several decades the most successful part of consumer policy all over Europe. The process of setting up information can be outlined as follows:

1. Choice of objects to be tested. Important criteria for choosing an object are the importance of the objects regarding health and fortune, the amount of money required for a single expense or the amount of total expense in a year, the relevant lack of information of the consumers, the number of users, the complexity of the good, the ecological importance and the innovative speed of the market.

2. The criteria for examination must be measurable by objectified methods and, at

the same time, should comply with the consumers' needs of information. Important criteria are, e.g., normal functioning, safety, durability, operation, adherence to legal requirements, possibility of repair, customer service, resale value and environment-friendliness.

3. The form of representation and formatting of the test results are of immense importance with regard to the effectiveness of information policy. Only few consumer experts will be prepared to study extensive test diagrams. Preferably, this information should be presented in proportionate form, as in 'marks out of 10'.

4. Also, if the media spread the information, this has a strong influence on the success of the measures taken. Test companies' magazines are subscribed to and read by only fairly few active consumers. In order to increase the reach it is important to make sure that simplified versions of the test results are also spread by other forms of mass media. Another important factor is the private communication between the consumers themselves.

The overall influence of consumer information is reflected by direct and indirect effects. The direct effect is easy to understand: a person reads about the results of a test and therefore buys the cheapest product rated 'good'. An indirect effect develops from supplier reactions: producers improve products which were rated 'bad' and draw special attention to high-class products in advertisements. Salespeople eliminate poor goods from their assortment and enforce sales of the good and excellent ones. This way the average level of quality improves in the whole market, from which all consumers benefit.

Consumer elucidation emphasizes three main goals:

1. *Abstinence*: a certain behaviour is supposed to be given up or the intensity decreased, e.g. smoking or use of medicine.
2. *Prevention*: a certain behaviour is to be prevented right from the beginning, e.g. addiction of youths to cigarettes and alcohol.
3. *Adoption*: consumers should adopt new forms of behaviour, e.g. purchasing reusable packages instead of one-off packages or using special containers for waste disposal.

Mass media and individual counselling are used to reach these goals. If the scientific findings of the theory of communication and adoption are used for planning and carrying out these campaigns, moderate success is guaranteed.

For the past few years important basic conditions for consumer policy have been changing or getting worse. In quite a few EC states and even in Brussels itself financial means for measures concerning consumer policy have been reduced or frozen. Elderly consumers who experienced shortages after the war are interested in problems dealing with favourable offers of high-quality goods. Most younger consumers take a sufficient general supply of conventional goods for granted. They consider a deterioration in elemental living conditions to be a problem, e.g. pollution, housing scarcity, traffic chaos in cities, supply of health services. Consumer policy will have to see to these needs more extensively to raise its standing.

We have to realize, though, that these measures of consumer policy are not developed very far. The power between buyers and sellers is not balanced. This is also the case when sellers are guided by effective competition in a functioning market economy in such a way that they check each other and limit each other's potential.

5.5 Concluding remarks

Conflicts are an inherent part of the relationship between suppliers and customers. This basic conflict cannot be eliminated. Shared ethical norms, combined with self-discipline, offer the most efficient way to balance conflicts of interest between suppliers and consumers. To the extent that this ideal is not reached, there must be resort to the less efficient solution represented by law and regulation.

References

AID, *Verbraucherdienst*, Bonn, 37, 1992.

Diller, Hermann, 'Das Preiswissen von Konsumenten', *Marketing ZFP*, 10, 1988, 17–24.

Holliger, Eugénie, 'Die Abteilung für Konsumentenfragen beim Migros-Genossenschafts-Bund Zürich', in Hansen, Ursula and Schoenheit, Ingo (eds.), *Verbraucherabteilungen in privaten und öffentlichen Unternehmen* (Frankfurt: Campus, 1985), 296–302.

Jahrbuch Deutscher Werberat (Bonn: Edition ZAW, 1991).

Kuhlmann, Eberhard, *Verbraucherpolitik* (Munich: Vahlen, 1990).

Nickel, Volker, *Werbung in Grenzen* (Bonn: Edition ZAW, 1989), 10th edition.

Reich, Norbert and Smith, Lesley Jane (eds.), 'Implementing the consumer–supplier dialogue through soft law?', *Journal of Consumer Policy*, vol. 7, 2, 1984, a complete special issue on soft law.

Reiter, Gerhard, *Kritische Lebensereignisse und Verschuldungs-karrieren von Verbrauchern* (Berlin: Duncker & Humblot, 1991).

Richardson, William and Morris, David, 'Towards more effective consumer market-place interventions – a model for the improvement of O.F.T. Codes of Practice', *Journal of Consumer Policy*, 11, 1988, 315–34.

Spiegel, Der, Hamburg, 47/1991.

Spruchpraxis Deutscher Werberat (Bonn: Edition ZAW, 1990), 6th edition.

Steinmann, Horst and Löhr, Albert, *Grundlagen der Unternehmensethik* (Stuttgart: Poeschel, 1992).

Tala, Jyrki, 'Soft law as a method for consumer protection and consumer influence. A review with special reference to Nordic experiences', *Journal of Consumer Policy*, 10, 1987, 341–61.

Tagesspiegel, Der, Berlin, 22 February 1992.

vpk = *Verbraucherpolitische Korrespondenz* (Bonn: Arbeitsgemeinschaft der Verbraucherverbände e. V.).

CHAPTER 6

Business, law and regulation: ethical issues

Antonio Argandoña

IESE, International Graduate School of Management,
University of Navarra, Spain

In the first weeks of January 1993, the dealers in Mercabarna, the food wholesale central market in Barcelona, saw an increasing movement of foreign trucks loaded with vegetables, many of them coming from The Netherlands. Spain is a country naturally endowed with Mediterranean crops, whereas the Dutch must resort to greenhouses to obtain cheap vegetables. Nevertheless, Dutch foodstuffs were invading the Spanish markets, as soon as the regulations and barriers to the free circulation of goods and services were dismantled by the Single European Market on 1 January 1993. The Spanish farmers and dealers immediately understood that the competitive conditions in their markets had changed. Many of them had already prepared for the new competition; others did so after the invasion; and others preferred to ask the government for more protection. But the erection of new trade barriers was no longer feasible: since 1993 business opportunities, profits and life have changed for many Europeans.

This chapter deals with some ethical problems that arise between the state and businesses as a result of law and regulations. The first part attempts to justify the existence of the state, the moral duties it imposes on businesses, why the firms must obey the law and the ethical challenges that this duty poses for companies. The second deals in more detail with the ethical problems of a special form of relation between the state and businesses, i.e. regulation.

6.1 Business and the state

If economists are to be believed, economic freedom is the normal setting for business, because the lack of restrictions guarantees an optimal allocation of resources, under certain conditions. Nevertheless, real economic life is certainly not characterized by unrestricted freedom. And this is good for companies: if the law of the jungle prevails, business disappears. Moreover, governments like to have power and influence. And many lobbies or groups of interests succeed in getting regulations for their own benefit, even if they damage consumers and competitors. Finally, in many cases ideology prevents such liberty in the name of alleged superior principles.

124

Law and regulations are, then, an important part of the background of business. They restrict the set of possible actions and decisions and lay charges and costs (e.g. taxes) upon them, using the coercive power of the state, and they also protect companies, reduce uncertainty and offer opportunities to them. This poses problems for businesses, as they try to know and observe the law, but also to profit from it, avoid its charges, adapt themselves to the legal and regulatory environment, to change it (if possible), and use it as a shield or as a weapon against other economic agents. And all this contributes to shaping their goals, strategies, structures and policies. A change in the legal background has important consequences for companies in every function and activity (including business ethics). We are interested here in the ethical problems which regulation poses for businesses, focusing first on law, discussing the ethical arguments for the existence of laws and then the ethical problems they pose for companies.

6.2   Ethics and the legal framework of business

6.2.1   Why law?

What is the *raison d'être* of law? Is it an arbitrary imposition of power that free people may morally oppose? Or is it something society needs and which reasonable people must obey? What are the ethical foundations of law? And what should be the ethical attitude of business towards law? Here we must make a detour and comment briefly on the philosophical and ethical justification for the existence of law before discussing its implications for business ethics.

Sociability is one of the basic features of persons, implying their need to live in society – first, to survive, but above all as a prerequisite for personal development. Human beings join collective bodies, ranging from the family and the local community to the nation and the world society, including companies, religious and civic organizations, voluntary associations, and so on. All of these spheres of association, natural or voluntary, share in common the creation of rights and duties that govern both individuals and groups and which require some type of organization, protection and defence: in short, an institutional and legal framework.

The state is the institution defined by means of a legal order, which exercises the authority and power to facilitate the development of citizens and the goals of society, the so-called 'common good'. The government is the representative of the state and the visible manifestation of its authority and power. We are referring to government at all levels (central, regional and local) and functions (executive, legislative and judicial, as well as administrative).

The first task of the state is to establish and develop the legal and institutional framework within which (economic) life operates. Moreover, it provides services for society; it collects taxes and other levies, in order to cover its expenditures, maintain economic stability and redistribute income; it makes transfers and buys goods and services, etc.; it is a customer of companies, often their supplier as well, and not infrequently their owner, adviser and controller. And, as the government is not a physical person, its relationships with citizens are articulated through complex organizational and administrative structures (parliament, government, magistracy, civil service, etc.) and are mediated by legislators, senior executives, civil servants, advisory bodies, political parties, etc.

In particular, the market economy and the world of business would be inconceivable without that institutional and legal framework, which guarantees the rights and duties of economic agents and sets forth the 'rules of the game': for example, it defines property rights, their content, how they are given, their limitations, how they are transferred, their relationship with the rights and duties of other individuals or groups, how disputes are settled, etc.

The state creates and legitimates the law. Coercive power cannot be continually exercised; the authority of the state must be accepted and this requires a legal order based in turn on ethical foundations: the acceptance of certain principles and the embodiment of certain values. Thus, the state is founded on law and ethics and is bound by both, since the state's power is not (or should not be) absolute or arbitrary but subject to a legal and moral order.

The previous paragraphs suggest that there is a role for the state, a role not only compatible with freedom, justice, the dignity of persons and other ethical values, but necessary for the social achievements of the members of society. Nevertheless, real life frequently does not fit in with this principle, as there are many instances of arbitrary, unjust, discriminatory and immoral decisions or actions of governments. This notwithstanding, we cannot disregard the role of the state as ruler of the society, and we must obey its (just) laws.

6.2.2   What is law?

In a wide sense, the law is a rational declaration of will made by the appropriate authority to order behaviour in society towards the goals of society, the common good. This means that a piece of legislation must be obeyed from the ethical point of view if it has the following characteristics:

1.   It is a *rational* act, i.e. it excludes the legislator's arbitrary will as the origin of law. From the point of view of ethics, an arbitrary act is not a law and companies or individuals are not compelled to obey it (but don't forget that the state holds the power of coercion to impose obedience even of despotic or irrational precepts).

2.   It is ordered towards the *achievement of society's goal* – the common good – and different laws will address different aspects of this purpose. In that case, the law must be just: provisions made for the sole and unjust benefit of the legislator or of a faction are therefore excluded (although there may be just laws advocated by a particular interest). An act that does not (directly or indirectly) serve the common good cannot be laid upon the companies or the individuals.

3.   It has a *normative* content, a 'must be', not merely a desire, a purpose or an intention. Guidelines or suggestions do not have the ethical strength of law (this is the case, for example, with voluntary import restraints or guidelines on the increase of wages or prices).

4.   It is *coercive*, because it is based on the state's power to impose some behaviours and prohibit others by means of corresponding sanctions. But the law must be observed not because of fear, but because of ethical persuasion. This poses the ethical problem of resistance to unjust laws (for example, laws that discriminate against minorities due to race, religion or ideas).

5.   Because it is just, law must be *general*, addressing a group, not an individual, and *non-discriminatory*. On occasions, this may give rise to a conflict between the general rule and what is just for a particular case (so that a law cannot be enforced on a particular citizen or firm, in certain circumstances).

6.   Nevertheless, the law must be *permanent*, even though it is brought into being with the intention of having a temporary validity. Therefore, it remains in force until it is repealed. Hence, the non-retroactiveness of laws: citizens cannot be required to adapt their behaviour to a law that has not yet been passed.

7.   It must be enacted *in the proper manner* by means of a set of procedural requirements, as it must be known by all those it addresses (it is for this reason that ignorance of a law does not excuse its non-fulfilment).

8.   It is an act of the *competent authority*, specified in each country's legal order.

Moreover, the law must conform to other conditions:

1.   It cannot be a *totalitarian* imposition, in the name of ideology, class, race or political power, but must respect the person's dignity, freedom and fundamental rights. If it restricts his or her freedom or rights it is so that they may be developed in an ordered fashion, together with the freedom and rights of other citizens.

2.   Law is *necessary* to regulate life in society, but not sufficient. The legislator cannot (and should not) intervene in all facets of life.

3.   The content of civil law must be *dynamic*, matching the evolution of knowledge and circumstances.

4.   It is not necessary that laws be accepted by the citizens, nor that they are the will of the majority.

The plurality of legal settings in Europe

In a multi-cultural arena composed of different nationalities (although with pretensions to unity), as in Europe, one observes a variety, not just of specific laws, but of legal frameworks. The Continental system considers justice as a network of abstract statements whose source is to be found in laws and which form a coherent whole specific for each country. The Anglo-Saxon system, on the other hand, asserts that justice is not the body of laws, but that laws are basically a source of knowledge on justice. For the Continentals, laws are a higher criterion of justice and have an intrinsic validity, while the Anglo-Saxons consider that laws may lose validity and disappear, without any need for a positive act of repeal. Laws, for the former, delimit individual rights while, for the latter, the rights are primary and any law that does not recognize them does not deserve to be called a law.

However, from the ethical viewpoint, the function of the law is the same in both systems: both have standards of behaviour, expressed either in a formal code or in common law, and specified in detail or left to the free interpretation of the judges. And these are the rules that citizens must obey.

6.3   Does *legal* mean *moral*?

Ethics is a practical science that directs humanity's actions towards the achievement of its goal. All human actions contribute in one way or another, positively or negatively, to this purpose; therefore, all are subject to ethics, even if they are not subject to law. Hence, moral criteria are much more far-reaching than the contents of laws: not all human behaviour can be subject to law (it cannot order or prohibit, for example, a person's internal acts, like thinking, desiring, loving or hating, nor many external acts). Therefore, it may be legal to pour toxic waste into a river if it is not prohibited by a law, but it may also be immoral.

Moreover, laws change (sometimes arbitrarily) and it does not seem reasonable that moral criteria should change in the same way. And it is easy to find examples of contradictory laws which, if legality means morality, would require incompatible moral behaviour.

Even more, laws themselves must be governed by moral criteria, which gives rise to the classic distinction between just and unjust laws. Thus, a law that violates a person's dignity (sanctioning slavery, for example) is not just and therefore cannot be accepted and observed.

It can reasonably be concluded, then, that law cannot be the ultimate criterion of morality. But obedience to the law may be an ethical duty: and this brings us to the central issue of this section of the chapter.

6.4   Why obey the law?

We are therefore led to the conclusion that a just law, that meets the conditions stated above, must be observed, not for merely practical reasons (to avoid punishment, for example) but also for moral reasons: there is an ethical obligation to observe it. Philosophical reasons can be given for this (law orders behaviour towards the common good of society and it is the duty of all citizens to further this common good) and also practical ones (because of the harm that would be done to society if the law were not observed). Thus, to drive on the right or left is a practical criterion, not an ethical one; however, once the sense has been specified in a law, common good requires that everyone respects this rule so that, now, it is no longer a debatable practical criterion but an ethical one.

The obligatory nature of the law should be interpreted in a fairly strict sense: it is always assumed that laws must be observed, so the possible reasons why a law cannot be ethically enforced in a particular case should be carefully assessed. A detailed moral analysis of the law and its circumstances is necessary in order to decide if this precept is morally binding or not.

The observance of law is objectively an ethical action, although it may not necessarily be so subjectively: a citizen who pays her taxes with great reluctance, for fear of punishment, produces the result desired by the legislator but does not improve as a person, because it is the intention that governs the personal results of ethical actions. And it is also desirable that citizens not only formally observe laws but voluntarily follow them insofar as laws contribute to the common good of society. As Aristotle said, one of the purposes of law is to 'educate citizens in virtue, by knowing the means that lead to virtue and the essential end of the most worthy life' (*Politics*: IV, 13). Legality is satisfied with the result, while morality operates on the agent's intention who, by behaving in accordance with the law, learns to act not only legally but also ethically. So, then, observance of law does not detract from the individual's freedom and dignity.

Multi-nationals and the ethical problems posed by the variety of national laws

The existence of different laws in different countries does not alter the moral duty to obey the law – not because of the rule of thumb 'When in Rome, do as the Romans do', but by an ethical principle that obliges people and organizations to contribute positively to the good of the society they operate in, and this good is represented in part (not wholly) by the laws.

Moral problems are often raised in multi-national or transnational companies: which law should they obey, when the legislation of the headquarters' country is not the same as that of the subsidiary's? This question can be solved by the distinction between legality and morality. If the legislation of the country a firm is operating in is different, but is just, it must be followed because, by so doing, one contributes to that country's common good. If there is no law, or if it is not in accordance with moral criteria, one must always follow the moral criteria.

Let us take an example: what must companies do if environmental legislation is more strict in Germany than in Portugal? Namely this: German and Portuguese companies operating in Germany must observe German legislation, if it is not unjust, even though it is more strict than the Portuguese. And German and Portuguese companies operating in Portugal must observe Portuguese legislation, except when, due to its greater permissiveness, they consider in all conscience that they should not observe it, in which case they should follow their moral criterion (which may or may not match German legislation).

An interesting moral dilemma arises when a company operating in a country with high environmental standards must compete with another company producing in a country with loose (but not necessarily unethical) environmental requirements, so that the first one has a competitive disadvantage. This case demands harmonization of legislation, as is intended in the European Single Market.

6.5   Conclusions on law and business ethics

Companies do not operate in a vacuum but within an extensive legal and institutional framework that facilitates (or hinders) their activity. Institutions such as the family, democracy, private ownership, contracts, taxes or wages comprise the medium within which business activity is carried out, and through which it is governed by the rules, regulations, codes, uses and customs created by a society in the course of its history. Within this legal and institutional framework, the state plays an important role as representative of society and the embodiment of authority. The first task of the state is to define the legal framework which will give consistency and legality to such institutions, norms and regulations.

The state thus has the power to pass laws that, if they meet certain conditions, are also morally binding. Law is necessary to attain the common good of society and of its members. Companies must contribute to this good, and this is why they must obey the law. So, the obedience to laws is a part of the moral behaviour of a company but not identical with it. Ethics is above law and is also the source of the power of the law to oblige morally.

Laws are not something sacred, as Latin culture sometimes pretends: they are no more (and no less) than an instrument at the service of the common good of society. They are not an obstacle that must be knocked down, jumped over or bypassed. They should be respected as a condition for the proper functioning of society, and even as a condition for personal freedom. (This notwithstanding, it must be recognized that in practice many laws may be defective or even immoral, and therefore not compelling.)

6.6   The regulation of business

Regulation is a body of general rules or specific actions imposed by the government which interfere directly with the mechanism for resource allocation in the market or indirectly, by changing the decisions of consumers, suppliers, workers and companies. From the point of view of a firm a regulation is a specific interference (coercive but sometimes simply in the form of recommendations) by the government or a regulatory agency in its affairs outside the realm of market transactions.

Governments have been regulating economic activity for a very long time. However, since the 1970s there has been a series of changes in the way this regulation is carried out, the consequences of which we are perceiving now:

1. Governments and experts are more sceptical about regulation, so that *deregulation* is now the watchword. This means making more room for the market (and for ethics as a condition for the performance of markets).

2. Instead of regulating *structure* (for example, the number of firms competing in a market, or their relative size, as in anti-trust policy), governments tend to regulate *behaviour* (for example, preventing entry barriers from being raised against new potential competitors). So, more confidence is placed in companies (and more legal, social and ethical responsibility).

3. Regulations extend to a large number of new fields (environment, health and safety at work, consumer protection, product safety, etc.); they are more functional than industrial; less aimed at competition and more at quality of life. This is also positive from the point of view of business ethics.

4. There has been a strong movement towards privatization of public companies as a form of deregulation. At the same time, this movement is accompanied by re-regulation, that matches the incentives of the new private owner to the requirements of economics and ethics (if, for example, the basic telephone service is privatized, the rights of users and suppliers of other services, the so-called 'value-added services', to use the basic network in fair and competitive conditions must be clearly established).

5. Although regulation is justified when there is a market failure (a situation in which the free play of market forces does not produce the social optimum), the existence of state failures is also admitted. Regulation is not a panacea.

6. Therefore, governments must carefully study each problem before defining which would be the most suitable regulation (if regulation is indeed necessary). And they also must search for alternatives to regulation, such as the so-called 'competitive regulation mechanisms', like competitive franchises or licences (competitive bidding among the possible suppliers of a good or service under monopoly conditions); or competition between regulatory offices; or reliance on the market whenever possible (a 'pollution market', for example, that defines rights to ownership and economic incentives that encourage more appropriate behaviours in each case), etc. Once more this means more freedom and moral responsibility for business.

7. Nowadays, the existence of two extreme strategies towards regulation is recognized. On the one hand, there is the 'adversarial approach', or 'regulation + litigation' (the state establishes regulations and takes legal action against those that do not observe them); on the other, there is the 'co-operative approach', or 'negotiation + incentives' (which seeks to obtain the co-operation of all the parties involved – users or consumers, producers, government, etc. – in the search for information, the design of the regulation, its implementation, the sanctions, etc.). These incentives also have an ethical appeal, both because they are more effective and less costly, and because of the greater freedom given to the agents involved, the greater degree of co-operation, the appeal to companies' sense of responsibility, etc.

Diversity or harmonization of regulations within the European Community

The economic unification process begun with the Common Market and continued with the Single Market and the Economic and Monetary Union project, with a possible Political Union as ultimate goal, implies major changes in the regulatory environment of the various member countries of the European Community (EC) and also of those countries that may join the EC in the future. What are the ethical implications of this process?

At national level, there arises the need to adapt a large number of regulations, with significant economic and moral effects. Assuming that all the changes are justified from the economic viewpoint (which is not the case), governments must also consider the costs and benefits they will impose on their citizens. Many of these changes will benefit some citizens and harm others, which is not a hindrance if these changes are expected to bring about an improvement of the common good: increased competition (which will lead to lower costs and prices and greater efficiency), access to new markets, safer and better-quality products and services, a greater freedom in the circulation of goods, services, capital and people, etc. Thus, from the ethical viewpoint, the above-mentioned changes should be considered as being positive.

Governments should also give thought to the inevitable losers from these changes. The question is not to prevent there being any losers at all, but suitable adjustment measures should be provided (for example, an advance warning period – but not economic aid, which is not permitted by the European Commission). In short, the intention is that companies should have the same possibilities of competing within the EC, regardless of their nationality; therefore, governments should facilitate the adjustment to this situation.

A typical case could be the regulation of product quality, safety and hygiene. National governments must accept foreign products and services that meet the conditions established in their home country. Consequently, all the governments will foreseeably set minimum conditions (which is the aim pursued by EC legislation) so that the products are sufficiently safe for use by consumers, but without imposing excessively restrictive conditions for domestic companies or discriminating arbitrarily against products from other member countries.

At the same time, governments should also avoid regulating against products from non-member countries: competition should be free within the EC but also for products coming from outside. A typical case is provided by the regulation of airlines or road transport. The evidence on the deregulation of these industries in the United States and the United Kingdom shows that it results in lower costs and prices, greater economic efficiency, more competition, greater choice for users, wage moderation (in industries that are protected from competition, wages 'swallow up' a big part of the benefits of protection), etc. The effect on quality of service is not clear, although the evidence from North American airlines suggests that small towns have not been neglected, nor have there been more accidents, and that customers' needs are better catered for, although at the cost of greater airport congestion and delayed flights. It therefore seems that the result is encouraging, in spite of which the EC is still reluctant to liberalize, probably because of the loss of control by national airlines this would involve and lobbying by the affected companies.

To adapt national legislation to EC rules is not a simple process. Often, it is not simply a question of ordering or prohibiting something: for example, in the process of adapting environmental legislation, countries must change their production structure and the products with which they will be able to compete in the future, redesign equipment, alter processes, etc. Thus, any change of regulations must be cautious, but should not be omitted: at present, many regulations serve only to protect existing, dirty industries and hinder the advent of new, cleaner ones.

6.7   Why regulation?

Economists usually argue that, under certain conditions, the free market provides an efficient allocation of resources and the greatest possible growth of output, given the endowment of factors (land, labour, capital, etc.) and their ownership, the technology available, the state of knowledge, etc. If this is so, there is no economic justification for public regulation, except when one or more conditions are not fulfilled. Hence, in practice, the economic justification of regulation is usually based on one of the following arguments, which we will utilize to develop the forms of regulation and to introduce a broad set of ethical issues related to it (the specific issues of the regulated companies will be discussed further on).

6.7.1   Market power

The typical case discussed under the heading of market power is natural monopoly when, given the size of the market, the existence of a single supplier guarantees the lowest costs. If, for example, each distributor of gas, telephone services, water or electricity had to build and maintain its own network, the cost of the service would be much greater than with a single supplier. However, if there is only one supplier, it may charge a monopoly price, higher than that which would prevail in competitive conditions. Thus, natural monopolies give rise to economic inefficiency – resulting from prices that are too high and from production that is too low – and to an ethical problem, because the monopolist obtains extra profits at the expense of consumers.

The regulation of natural monopolies seeks to establish a price that is closer to that which would be obtained in competitive conditions. Several solutions have been traditionally applied, all of which have their drawbacks:

1. *Public ownership of the monopoly company*. This gives rise to efficiency and morality problems, due to the lack of incentives to produce a quality good or service at the lowest possible price and incorporating technical advances.

2. *Pricing by the regulatory agency*. The problem here is that it is difficult to define efficient and just pricing criteria. If, for example, public transport tariffs are too low, they will penalize the factors used in production or endanger the quality of the service, the introduction of innovations and even the survival of the firm. And if they are too high, the economic and ethical problems of the monopoly recur.

3. The prices set by the agency often include some type of *subsidy*, for example for the extension of the telephone network to rural areas. But the technical and moral problems increase dramatically when there are cross-subsidies: when, for example, a monopoly is granted for a low operating cost, city centre bus line on condition that the company offers a low-price service on other, peripheral, high-cost lines. Apart from the inefficiency in the use of resources, it is equivalent to taxing the users of the former line in favour of the users of the latter, a practice which is morally questionable.

4. In services that operate a network (telephone, water, electricity or railroad) it is common that competition be encouraged by having the network operated by *different suppliers* (several railroad companies, for example), while maintaining the ownership of the network (the railway lines and stations) as a regulated public service. This case raises ethical problems concerning the different treatment given to different users and in guaranteeing free access to all – even to potential future competitors – against the interests of those already existing.

5. Another solution is the *competitive licence*: the monopolist must periodically compete with other potential suppliers to win the licence that will enable it to operate the service during a further period of time. This also raises moral issues, because the price charged is a monopoly price (even though the extraordinary profit is collected by the government through the bidding). There is also the possibility that the potential competitors reach an agreement to fix a low bidding price or to unfairly exclude other competitors.

6. When the monopoly is not natural but due to collusion, a cartel, artificial entry barriers, customs tariffs, or protectionism, the solution is not to regulate the market but to put an end to this situation by *anti-trust* actions, *reducing tariffs*, or *facilitating the entry of competitors*. But if the advantage to the company is the result of its innovative superiority or greater efficiency, then the wisest thing to do is not intervene.

6.7.2 External effects

External effects occur when the actions of an economic agent affect other agents without there being a direct market transaction between them. For example, when a plant pollutes the atmosphere or a river, or when its trucks congest the roads, it is passing on to others a cost that should be borne by it alone. Or, in the opposite case (*positive externalities*), when a company carries out research or staff training programmes, it is indirectly improving the scientific and technical level of the other firms, which do not pay for it.

The actions to be carried out to correct external effects will depend on the type of effect produced:

1. If there is a problem of *congestion* (of lines, roads, radio or TV wavelengths, etc.), the number of suppliers can be restricted (for example, by distributing a limited number of radio frequencies), but not without causing a number of technical and moral problems, such as maintaining competition and establishing equitable criteria for rationing the scarce resource. Another possibility is to use the competitive licence mentioned above. Or the right to use the service (the right of users to connect to a congested or congestable network) can be regulated. In other situations, taxes can be used, such as those levied on the buying or using of automobiles or on fuel consumption to reduce traffic congestion.

2. There is an interesting kind of external effect based on *confidence*. For example, if the customers of a bank question its capacity to return the funds deposited in it, they may start a rush to withdraw those funds, which will undoubtedly place the bank in a situation of illiquidity (and the problem may spread to other banks). The solution here involves the implementation of regulations oriented to restore confidence: cash and solvency ratios, the central bank acting as a lender of last resort, deposit insurance, minimum capital, etc. A moral and economic problem related to this type of solution is the risk of the regulations being too strict, because the authorities prefer security to efficiency. It may also lead to undesirable behaviours (for example, if there is a generous deposit insurance, it is possible that a bank's administrators may undertake operations that are excessively risky).

3. Another type of external effect is that which gives rise to the obtainment of a *licence or permit* (normally accompanied by the payment of a fee) for certain activities, such as digging ditches in streets for laying electricity or telephone lines, or

occupying land to lay a railway line or erect telegraph posts. A licence opens the door to a privilege, so that new ethical questions may arise.

4. As we have already stated, there are *positive* external effects that it may be desirable to encourage. Thus, the state may grant a temporary monopoly to work a patent in order to create an economic incentive to research; or it may grant the monopoly to run a motorway for a certain period of time, enabling the construction costs to be recovered, etc. In these cases, there is an extra economic incentive to fulfil some of the social responsibilities of the firm.

External effects always have important ethical implications, because of the consequences that the actions of a company may have on other people. It is a part of the moral responsibility of firms to take into account these effects, although there may be no easy ways to implement this responsibility.

6.7.3   *Internal effects*

The so-called 'internal effects' are costs or benefits within an economic transaction that do not form part of the agreement. There are many examples of these effects: a good or service with a quality below that agreed or expected, or that is not safe or hygienic, etc. A frequent internal effect is related to the lack of information: before entrusting our case to a doctor or lawyer, we wish to know if he or she is competent, and before buying a medicine we wish to make sure that it has no harmful effects, etc.

The lack of information, or its asymmetrical distribution among economic agents, is again a problem with economic and moral implications. It can be corrected by measures that affect the product or service, such as the standardization of contracts (common in transportation, financial services, insurance, etc.) and the establishment of standards governing the good or service, its production process or its distribution (for example, those concerning the quality, safety or hygiene of goods, and the standards of behaviour accepted in certain professional services, like doctors, lawyers, financial intermediaries, etc.).

There are also regulations concerning the inputs (qualifications of professionals, use of dyes or preservatives in foods), the final service (the coverage of an insurance policy or the establishment of conditions of carriage), a result (maximum authorized emission of pollutants), some permitted or prohibited operations (for example, by a bank), conditions of safety and health at work, working hours, the granting of licences or the required membership of a professional association to perform certain activities, the requirement of certifications (financial ratings, classification of hotels or campsites), the performance of tests (to examine a professional's qualifications, the contents of a product, the strength of a material, the properties and effects of a medicine, etc.), or the involvement of specialists in an operation (property agents), etc.

The moral problems raised by these regulations vary considerably. For example, compliance with a standard does not necessarily guarantee quality, and the possession of a qualification does not guarantee the necessary knowledge (once more, legality does not mean morality); standards can be used as entry barriers to reduce competition; the normalization of contracts can encourage abuses of the lack of knowledge of less experienced customers, etc.

Sometimes the regulations imply the disclosure of certain information for the benefit of the customer (for example, that the attending professional has a degree in medicine, or that the drug purchased has passed certain prior tests). On occasions, the contents of the regulation concern the provision of this information (the contents and expiry date of a packaged food, its manufacturer, its price, etc.). Other examples are the financial and economic information that must be provided by companies listed on the stock exchange.

A specific ethical and economic problem raised by the non-internalization of certain costs is that of occupational diseases and accidents. It may be difficult for the worker to obtain information about the risk he or she is incurring; hence, his/her inability to take suitable protective measures (which, in any case, cannot be taken unaided, if the company does not take them). As it is expensive for firms to establish internal prevention and protection standards, they often prefer to pay compensation for damages. However, this implies that safety and health will never be an internal affair but an external cost, and so measures will not be taken to solve the problem. And at the same time the person's dignity – the basis of all ethics – is forgotten.

Also, the information on occupational diseases and hazards will be inadequate if firms are given no incentive to compile it and make it known to their workers. The problem lies in that workers are often unaware of the nature of the products they are handling or of the hazards they pose, and it is not in the company's interest to provide this information, as it would mean higher safety standards, demands for higher pay to cover the risks and higher claims by workers suffering from disease. However, for labour relations based on justice to exist, this information is vital, in the same way that the worker's dignity demands that s/he be informed of his/her occupational hazards.

6.7.4   Other arguments

If a certain distribution of income or wealth does not seem to be fair, measures may be taken to correct it either directly (through taxation, subsidies to basic needs, education, health, housing, etc.) or indirectly (by correcting the supposed causes of this unjust distribution, by means of obligatory education, minimum wage, unemployment insurance, etc.).

Redistributive policies have a clear ethics component (positive, but perhaps also negative, when what is sought is the unjust benefit of a group or when the results of the regulation are ethically undesirable). They contain an interesting combination of economic and moral effects, which must be separated into their individual components in each case. For example, a minimum wage policy usually increases the income of some unskilled workers but with the likely result of less of them being employed, or fewer jobs being available for new entrants to the labour market. In the same manner, generous unemployment insurance enables an unemployed worker to look for a new job without anxiety but also allows the loafer to enjoy a long period of income without working. Finally, rent freezing usually improves the tenants' standard of living, but at the cost of the income of the owners of the dwellings (and also leads to the disappearance of rented housing from the market, to the detriment of future potential tenants). These are ethical issues for the policy-makers, but also for businesses, at least as they affect their social responsibility.

There are also other arguments for regulation: protecting employment or incipient industries, defending sovereignty or national security, redressing the balance of payments, etc. Not all of them are equally convincing. It could also be added that regulation is not necessarily the best procedure for solving these problems (and, from the ethical viewpoint, the first thing that must be demanded from a regulation is that it be efficient, i.e. that it achieves its purpose at a reasonable social cost, justly shared out).

6.8   Are there ethical foundations for regulation?

The first question posed by regulation refers to its very morality: can the state dictate rules that imply a limitation on the freedom of action of businesses? The answer, as we have seen, is in the affirmative: since the state is responsible for the common good of society, it can (and must) regulate, even though companies wish to regulate for themselves, because companies are not always able to identify the problem with objectivity and design the best solution. For example, there are 'free rider' problems: if a group of companies voluntarily accept a regulation, an economic incentive is created for any one of them to follow another type of behaviour and benefit from doing so, at least in the short term. Therefore, the state must support regulations with its coercive power. Also, the state must represent those who do not have a voice to be heard (for example, future generations).

However, this duty must be exercised with particular care because economic science and empirical evidence very often show that regulation may be unnecessary and even counterproductive. This does not mean that the state should not regulate but that it should act with particular prudence, strength and equanimity.

Is there a direct moral justification for regulations? Specifically, may regulations correct ethical failures? The possibility is appealing but disputable. Let us consider an example. It seems to be just that two users of the same telephone network pay the same rates, whether they are near the telephone exchange building or far away from it. But the private and social costs of serving the client who is further away are greater. Should the user who is nearer pay a higher price that subsidizes the user who is further away? What criterion of justice should be used in this case: the same price for everyone, or a price that is proportionate to the cost? Furthermore, economic science suggests that cross-subsidies are not efficient and that, if it is considered desirable to price below cost in some cases, it is preferable to establish a subsidy financed by a general tax and not, as in the case considered, by a 'tax' levied on the low-cost user through a high price. Economic regulations must have solid economic foundations, not only loose ethical motivations.

Nevertheless, there are also examples of regulations that seem to be substitutes for ethical rules. For example, would legislation on pollution be necessary if companies would always respect the environment? But the ethical rules are general ('do not harm the environment', or 'do not harm the environment if possible') and the companies need more concrete rules with which to operate. What is 'harm' to the environment? Is every damage undesirable, however little it may be? Moreover, ethical companies may not know what is good or bad for the environment, or how to avoid the damage. Therefore, there is a role for regulation even if people always try to behave ethically.

So ethics and regulation are not equivalent. They may be complementary (companies that try to be ethical need regulations to guarantee success), sometimes unrelated, and even substitutes (if people would always behave ethically a number of regulations would be redundant).

But to regulate is to interfere with market mechanisms which are justified by reason of economic efficacy. This implies a generic presupposition against regulations, because they limit the economic agents' freedom, impose a cost or loss, and perhaps limit economic efficiency. When, then, are specific regulations acceptable?

6.9   When is a regulation ethically obligatory?

Here, we apply the general principles of the morality of law (as regulation is basically the specific development or application of the right to legislate).

1.   *A problem must exist* which, from the technical (economic) viewpoint, demands a regulation. It cannot be the result of arbitrariness, caprice, ideology or particular interests.

Often, a bad regulation is merely the result of an insufficient definition of the problem. For example, the question is sometimes raised of prohibiting the sale of low-quality products (in developed countries, because of the standard of living acquired, and in developing countries because, it is argued, it is immoral to sell there what it would not be moral to sell in more developed countries). Apart from the fact that this is usually an argument used to reduce the competition from cheap products, it contains an ambiguity *ab initio*. If by low-quality product one means, for example, a simple, cheap car, then there is no economic or ethical argument against it; not all cars have to be a BMW or a Rolls. However, if by low quality we mean defective manufacture or an unsafe product, then there are ethical objections to their sale in any country.

2.   Regulation must be *the most suitable solution* (or, at least, sufficiently suitable). Here, policy-makers must be realistic, rejecting the 'best solution possible', which may

be too expensive, but also a 'sufficient' regulation that does not go far enough. What makes a 'reasonably' safe car or an 'acceptable' emission of pollutants will depend in each case on the society's values and on the reasonable foreseeable effects of regulation.

Governments must also avoid excess regulation. For example, the conditions imposed on US nuclear power plants after the Three Mile Island accident (1979) were excessive and motivated more by the desire of the regulatory agency to protect itself against criticism in the event of possible future failures than by a reasonable study of what was necessary in each case.

3.   *The regulation must be general*, applicable to all those who are in the same situation, and non-discriminating.

4.   *It must be concrete*, so that it can be implemented without ambiguities, as far as possible. For example, an advertisement can be forbidden because it deceives the consumer, because it is based on an untrue argument, or because the product is harmful, but not on the basis of arguments such as that 'it rests on non-rational persuasion', or that it 'gives rise to unviable consumption models' (which, however, can be used to argue an ethical case – not a legal case – against that advertising).

5.   As regulation has negative effects on freedom, competition, costs, prices, etc., it must *meet some conditions* for it to be called ethical. For example, it would have to observe the impartiality principle (the regulation will not attribute unjustified benefits or harm to any person or group) and the proportionality principle (the harm done by the regulation is in proportion to the benefits obtained from it). It must also be remembered that a specific regulation may obstruct competition (becoming an entry barrier for future competitors), require other regulations (to set the price of a basic necessity is the first step towards reducing its supply, which will require further regulatory measures to correct it), change the motivations of the economic agents (such as the incentive to work of unemployed people covered by a generous unemployment insurance), introduce significant costs (bureaucracy, licences, delays, etc.) and produce many other effects whose economic and ethical consequences must be duly examined.

Another important point is the political process inherent in regulation: the proliferation of regulatory agencies, the creation of lobbies, the possibility of unethical behaviours in order to obtain a regulation or the protection from a regulation (for example, bribes), the attempts to retain a regulation even when it is no longer necessary (because there are always parties interested in its continued existence), etc.

In short, the regulating body will no doubt have to proceed with due caution in order to match the desired goal with effects that are not always desired. It must listen to the regulated parties, who are the ones who know best their problems, but using its own criteria so as not to accept unquestionably their biased arguments. It must listen to the experts, although adapting their recommendations to the specific situation. It must apply imagination and fortitude; put to one side popular solutions in the search for effective and reasonable-cost solutions (a limit to the maximum allowable pollution by a factory is a simple and attractive solution but is usually very inefficient). And the regulator must do all this while negotiating with political forces, lobbies, those who will lose and those who will gain.

6. Finally, the regulation must be applied equally to all the affected parties. Otherwise, the common good, which the regulation is precisely designed to serve, is harmed, and an injustice is committed.

Gambling in Europe

> As Conservative members of parliament gathered at Westminster last November [1990] to elect a successor to Margaret Thatcher as leader of their party and the government, a camera crew from Italian television was covering the event from the headquarters of Ladbrokes, the UK's largest betting shop operator. The Italians' interest was engaged by Ladbrokes offering odds on such a serious battle as if it were just another contest at Rome's Campanelle race course. ('The odds against harmony', *International Management*, October 1991, 89)

Like many other sectors, gambling has also spread through Europe, so that the European Commission has been studying the possibility of harmonizing its regulation.

Gambling and gaming differ only in that the experience and ability of the player are not relevant in the latter. Both have raised ethical problems for centuries. Sometimes they have been accused of immorality because of the prevailing motivation – profit. Probably they deserve a wider judgement: they are not essentially immoral activities (save in certain cases), although they may have undesirable effects (time-wasting, addiction, quarrels, vengeances, poverty, the temptation to change the conditions of the game or to use unethical means, etc.). In those cases it is necessary to apply the ethical rules of an action with both good and bad effects.

The ethical problem must also be analysed taking into account the culture, temperament, style of life and regulations of the country. In France, for example, casinos have been legal since 1907 in spa towns, but remain banned within a radius of 60 kilometres of Paris. In Denmark they were legalized very recently, to discourage Danes from travelling to Germany to bet. The French and British are fond of horse-race betting, but Spaniards are not. In England there is no national lottery, as there is in the other countries (probably because of the opposition of football-pools operators).

Governments regulate gambling and betting very strictly, for public order and control reasons, but also because they obtain huge financial revenue from those industries. And this is the cause of several contradictions: for example, in Portugal,

Spain, France, Italy and Greece casinos are legalized as a tourist attraction, although 80 per cent of their customers are nationals. In The Netherlands the government tolerates the illegal private casinos. They are also illegal in Belgium, but the Treasury officials control them, for revenue reasons. In Spain the addiction of young people to legal slot machines worries specialized psychiatrists.

But a case could be made for a European-wide regulation of gaming and gambling. The freedom of movement of people and services calls into question the existence of legal monopolies, like that of Pari-Mutuel Urbain in horse-race betting in France, in contrast to the freedom of business in other countries (in addition to the fiscal and financial advantages the French government has given to Pari-Mutuel, against the EC criterion of free competition). Moreover, national lotteries (the great majority being publicly owned or managed) oppose the entry of foreign lotteries into their own country. Finally, technological progress and the deregulation of financial markets make it easy to operate in a foreign country, seeking the highest profits. However, the European Commission does not seem to be interested in the regulation of such a complex sector.

6.10   Ethical problems of regulation: the point of view of business

Companies may be affected by a regulation before taking decisions (for example, before starting the production of a drug subject to restrictions as regards content, tests, advertising, etc.) or when the decision is being implemented (when, for example, after a certain period of time selling a domestic appliance, it is made subject to new safety requirements). From the ethical viewpoint, both situations should be given the same treatment, although implementation may be much more difficult in the second case.

It is therefore common that when a new regulation is issued, companies react first by avoiding or ignoring it (pretending that the regulation does not exist) or opposing it (trying to change the regulation, requesting an exemption, or a lengthy adjustment period, or subsidies to implement it). Later on, they will decide to fall into line with the new regulation, although perhaps with little enthusiasm. Only truly ethical companies will quickly pass these stages to assume their responsibilities, which include accepting the need for the regulation, making the internal adjustments that might be necessary and co-operating actively with the authorities, so that they turn into an opportunity what initially seemed to be a threat (and obviously this does not prevent objection to regulations, when necessary).

It is very difficult to summarize the ethical problems with which a regulated company can be faced, as the situations may vary considerably. Here, we will mention only some of these problems, briefly explaining the criteria that are applicable in each case.

1.   A just regulation is morally obligatory for all the parties affected by it. The force of this obligation will depend on the type of regulation, its scope and effects, and the nature of the problem: it is not equally reprehensible to omit the composition of a packaged food as to discharge toxic products into a river. But a company trying always to behave ethically must obey every regulation with a sense of moral duty. Even though some experts hold that business ethics is concerned only with results, not with intentions, motivations or attitudes, this criterion seems to be more fit for law or regulation than for ethics.

2.   A regulation may sometimes not be morally binding. For example, if the managers of a company are convinced that the safety standards for a product are counterproductive, they may not observe these standards. Obviously, the argument that extra costs will be caused or profits (even large profits) will be lost is not sufficient to side-step the regulation. Nevertheless, when the damage produced by not observing a regulation is very small and the trouble caused by observing it is very harmful, the moral criterion that 'no one can be forced to do the impossible' (nor even the very difficult, if the reason is good enough) can be applied.

The moral decision of disobeying a regulation requires more than general arguments (such as 'governments always do things worse than the market') or circumstantial evidence (like 'on such and such occasions, the government was wrong') but a true conviction, after a careful analysis of the specific regulation, the circumstances and the situation of the company (including in many cases reference to an expert or a moralist). Even more: if the managers of a company believe that the regulation is unjust (discriminating, clearly inefficient, or enforced without any regard for the rules of law), then they *must not* obey the regulation, as this would amount to doing something bad (although legal).

3.   The absence of a regulation does not justify unethical behaviour. It cannot be pretended that all possible behaviours should be covered by a regulation. Consequently, above and beyond regulations (and their loopholes) one must observe the rules of ethics.

An interesting example is the shipment of toxic wastes to Third World countries, where there is no law prohibiting their dumping. The argument that this provides those countries with the opportunity of making a profit is false, as the social costs of the dumping will probably be far greater than the benefits received.

4.   Must the regulation be applied at the lowest level possible and strictly according to the letter of the law, or should it be observed in a wide sense and in accordance with the spirit of the law? If the aim is to avoid legal conflicts, then minimal compliance may be sufficient, but if the desire is to act ethically, then the criterion must be to promote the common good. This implies observing the spirit rather than the letter and to comply with the regulation in a broad sense (but this does not mean that extra moral duties be laid upon the company: if, for example, the law requires that certain additives or colouring contained in a food product be stated

on the package, then, even from a moral viewpoint, it will be sufficient to do only that).

5. The existence of a regulation cannot be used as an alibi for unethical behaviour. Therefore, it is not ethically correct to scrupulously comply with a regulation when this means breaking a rule of ethics. To follow the legal instructions regarding the dosage of a drug when there are good reasons for thinking that this dosage is harmful is by no means morally acceptable behaviour.

6. A difficult problem is raised by the obligation to observe a just regulation when competitors do not obey it, which places the reliable company at a disadvantage: if it observes all the regulations on protection of the environment, safety at work, tax payments, etc., its costs may be excessively high, particularly in certain unethical circles, and it may lose competitiveness. What should it do?

It is not possible to give an answer to this question without first knowing the circumstances of the case: whether it can report its unethical competitors to the authorities or to the press, whether it can negotiate with them the joint implementation of the regulations, what would be the effects of not observing each regulation, and how difficult is the competitive situation. In any case, it seems reasonable to conclude: (a) that the obligation to observe all regulations remains valid, as a general rule; (b) the rules concerning the morality of an action with both good and bad effects must be applied to this particular situation; and (c) in many cases, the dilemma may be solved by a higher authority (a producers' association, the government, the European Commission, etc.).

It is a fact of experience that many ethical dilemmas are only the consequence of bad decisions taken in the past. The managers that know that new legislation on environmental protection is to be passed and do not prepare the company for the new rules are to be blamed if in the future they are caught in the false dilemma of polluting or closing down the firm.

It is also a fact of experience that a little ingenuity and initiative may help to solve many ethical dilemmas. For example, how can many companies (multi-nationals, for example) pay taxes in countries where tax evasion is the norm, without endangering their profits? The answer is difficult to understand for people who cannot conceive making business without breaking the fiscal law (this is a dilemma for them). But managers of ethical firms count on paying taxes from the beginning and prepare their plans so that being fiscally correct is not a burden but an advantage.

7. Precisely because regulations must be respected by everyone in an industry to be effective provides one more argument in favour of the presumption that regulations must be observed: because they give rise to an external effect (a public good) that is beneficial to everyone. And although every participant in the industry may have an incentive not to observe the regulations (the free rider effect), in the final analysis their observance benefits everyone (which is the reason why they are accompanied by a certain degree of coercion).

This is the case, for example, in the pharmaceutical industry: given the nature of the products, it is important for the entire industry that the image of high-quality, safe products be maintained. This explains why Johnson & Johnson immediately withdrew Tylenol from the market when it received threats of poisoning the product, and the greater protection it incorporated subsequently in the packaging of its products, which enhanced the quality image of the company, and of the industry as a whole.

8.   What should one do when there is a conflict between regulations? For example, when a national or supranational agency issues standards that conflict with those of a regional or local agency, or when a multi-national company must cope with requirements in the foreign country in which it operates that are different from those in its home country. The distinction between legality and morality will be helpful in this case: if the company follows an ethical criterion of care for the common good, it will consider the various regulations as (partial) indicators of this common good, not as definitive criteria.

Consider, for example, the case of the United States Foreign Corrupt Practices Act that has sometimes been presented as an example of legislation in one country that contradicts cultures and regulations (or, more exactly, the lack of regulations) in other countries. From an ethical viewpoint, the problem is simple: a company must not use methods of corruption in any country, whatever the legislation of that country or its home country may say on the matter. And if there are sometimes reasons for utilizing ethically questionable methods (for example, to accept an extortion, but never offer a bribe), there are ethical rules for resolving the dilemma (which, in this case, would perhaps be more flexible than the above-stated Act).

Let's sum up the previous paragraphs:

1.   Take regulations seriously, if you try to be ethical in business.
2.   Make positive efforts to obey regulations in spirit and in a wide sense.
3.   Take regulations not just as tedious duties, but as business opportunities.
4.   Do not feel obliged to obey regulations when there are serious reasons to believe that they are not compelling in a specific case (but be careful when appraising these reasons).
5.   Finally, always put ethics above regulations as a guide to your behaviour.

The right to privacy versus direct marketing

Every person has the right to privacy: the right not to have his or her personal details disclosed. But as a social being, s/he also has the duty to disclose information to other people, and the right to know other persons' data that are of interest to him/her. The problem is where to draw the boundaries between the right to privacy and the right to information, and what to do when this information is used for arguable goals (blackmail, extortion, etc.).

The restrictive European position on the right to privacy contrasts with the more liberal American position, when confronted with the supply of data for direct marketing purposes. Thus a conflict arose as a result of the European Commission's Draft Umbrella Directive on Data Protection which, according to the American firms in the sector, would harm their commercial activities in Europe (and, in the long run, in the United States too). The projected Directive on Data Protection would mean:

> (1) Data use is prohibited without authorization of the subject (consumer).
> (2) Data subjects must be personally notified to whom information has been passed and for what purpose. (3) Data subjects can claim compensation if data is 'misused and causes damage'. (4) European Community data can only be transferred out of the European Community if the receiving country can guarantee the same level of protection. (N. di Talamo, 'Private secrets', *Direct Marketing*, April 1991, 42).

And point (4) means that the USA must pass legislation as restrictive as Europe's. According to the American Direct Marketing Association (DMA), the protection provided by the Draft Directive is excessive and seriously damages direct marketing, but its European counterparts are less concerned because less developed techniques and methods are used here. The Americans defend the free use of databases where it is not inappropriate ('illegal', 'immoral'), but the Europeans are more worried about the nuisance of mass unwanted mail. The nuisance disappears when the potential customers state a priori the use they want to be made of their data, but useful advertising information may be lost that, with a broader criterion, could be sent to them.

The European Direct Marketing Association (EDMA) proposes an alternative solution: the interested person (consumer) would authorize the direct marketing use of his or her data, but with the right to the suspension of that use at his or her request.

Consumer protection European-style

The protection of the consumer from damage caused by the products he or she buys, uses or consumes has economic, legal and ethical consequences. Unlike the seller, the buyer may not know the good in detail – its quality and strength, or the possible risks of using it. He or she is thus at a disadvantage, so that the seller has the duty to provide the buyer with the relevant information and increasingly to guarantee that the good has the features implicit in the contract.

The European Commission's Directive 7/88 compels the member states to adapt their laws on product liability to European standards. This means that a supranational law is imposed on the national legislators in order to extend consumer protection to the whole Community with common provisions. The Directive concerns only the intended outcome of the legislation, the member countries being free to search for the best way to attain it. This is an important step in the harmonization of consumer protection regulation inside the EC, with the aim of guaranteeing to consumers that the goods they buy, either produced or imported into the EC, comply with some specified safety standards, and that there is always one person or firm about whom to complain in case of a defective good.

In the past, consumer protection was based first on the law of contracts (a sale contract recognizes the buyer's rights on the quality and characteristics of the product, so that their non-fulfilment gives rise to the right to compensation), and later on general laws about negligence damages (this recognizes the duty of the seller to guarantee the safety of the product, but the consumer should prove the damage, the negligence of the manufacturer and the causal link between the negligence and the damage). The Directive mentioned goes beyond this protection when it states that 'the producer will be liable for damage caused by a defect in his product' (art. 1), even if there were not negligence in its manufacturing or handling, and although the manufacturer can prove that the product was not known to cause the damage now attributed to it when it was first put into circulation (art. 7).

'A product is defective when it does not provide the safety which a person is entitled to expect, taking all circumstances into account including: (a) the presentation of the product; (b) the use to which it could reasonably be expected to be put; and (c) the time when the product was put into circulation.' (art. 6) This includes defects of design as well as of manufacturing and handling, and also the warnings the manufacturer must make on the risks in using the product. The liability takes in the manufacturer of the good, of its parts and raw materials and 'any person who by putting his name, trademark, or other distinguishing feature on the product presents himself as its producer' (art. 3), and also the importers of products from outside the European Community.

The Directive is an important step forward in developing the social responsibility of manufacturers, importers and dealers in relation to the goods they produce and sell.

6.11   Ethical problems of regulation: the relationships between the regulatory agency and the regulated company

Interesting ethical problems are frequently raised in the relationships between regulator and regulated. Here are some examples:

1.   It is desirable that a relationship of fair co-operation be created between the regulatory agency and the regulated company, enabling the latter to provide information, offer solutions, and point out the drawbacks of the norms proposed. It may be in its interest to do so, if both the agency and the regulated firm wish to achieve the common good (although there is no shortage of cases in which this supposition is not reasonable).

This co-operation will not be an easy task, as both parties may have opposite interests (at least in the short term) and mistrust each other. It is part of the ethical will of managers to foster this attitude and to bring it into the culture of the company. Nevertheless, we cannot forget that there is a legitimate discrepancy of interests between regulator and regulated, as well as different points of view about what is good for the company and for society, so that this co-operation has obvious limits.

2.   The regulated company usually has more information than the regulator. This may give rise to a biased flow of information or the capture of the regulatory agency by the regulated firm; the further this is removed from the principle of co-operation in the achievement of the common good, the more reproachable it will be, from the moral viewpoint.

3.   Ethical (and organizational) problems are often raised regarding the control of the process, when the regulated company's managers are faced with several external sources of control (regulatory agency, government and judges) in addition to the internal ones (board of directors and shareholders) and the presence of other stakeholders. This very plurality of controls can reduce the managers' freedom of decision and resulting responsibility.

4.   Can the regulated company try to change the regulation? Obviously yes, if it considers that it is unnecessary, inefficient, arbitrary or unjust, or if it thinks that the same goal could be achieved using more effective and cheaper means. It could be a very good act, morally speaking, but also a reprehensible one, if it is done with hidden intentions (to drive a competitor out of business, to establish entry barriers for new competitors, or to gain more pricing power, etc.) or using illicit means (falsification or non-disclosure of information, bribery, false accusations, etc.).

5.   Regulations will have inevitable redistributive effects. Saving cases of blatant injustice, the agency should not mitigate these effects because of the protests generated by them, because the market can usually solve by itself the 'disastrous effects' that industry normally fears from a regulation. For example, when steps were taken to reduce the use of CFCs, the affected companies responded that they had no suitable replacements. However, faced with the necessity to comply with the regulation, they put their research machinery into motion and soon found them.

6.   Regulations may also change the relationships among competitors, or among clients and suppliers, etc. This opens new opportunities and risks for companies, and poses new ethical challenges. For example, a firm whose prices are fixed by a regulatory agency may take it for granted that the agency takes care of the quality of the goods and services, or of the introduction of innovations. But this is more than may be expected of a regulatory agency. The existence of regulation, then, cannot free the company from its duties towards the consumers (unless the regulation makes it very difficult for the company to attend to these duties).

Here is another interesting case in the changing relationships between suppliers and clients: the owner of a telephone network must rent the use of the network to suppliers of value-added services, but in doing so it may discriminate in favour of certain users against others (or even in favour of the network's owner itself if it is also a supplier of those services). It then needs high ethical standards to act with justice in a case in which the pursuit of short-term profits would advise immoral behaviour.

A different case of tax evasion

Tax fraud, concealment and evasion are serious social ills, which in some societies reach scandalous proportions, from the point of view of social ethics, and produce important social ills, that run from depriving the state of the resources to which it has a right in order to fulfil its role in the pursuit of the common good, to unfair comparative burdens on honest citizens, or the encouragement of social imitation processes that generalize immoral conduct.

In 1991 a new case was discovered in Spain that posed special ethical problems. A number of big companies were accused of using false invoices to avoid payment of value-added tax (VAT), and several companies were discovered whose principal and even only business was to write out those false invoices, charging a price for this 'service'. The ethical problem arose in that the main motivation of the accused companies was not VAT evasion, but the need to justify important payments that could not be justified before the auditors by other means, because these payments were made to political parties in order to win public work and public procurement contracts.

The ethical dilemma lay in the fact that the companies had to pay a certain percentage of the amount of the public contract to the political party, not for immorally winning a contract by illegal means, but just for being awarded a contract that they won fairly. It was, then, a case of extortion, but a very special one in that it was an indirect contribution to public, semi-official corruption.

Greed versus health

In January and February 1991 more than 200 persons were poisoned in several parts of Spain by the consumption of cows' liver treated with chlembuterol. This is an anabolic steroid that increases the appetite and sleeplessness of the cattle, and so the profits of the stockbreeder. Poisoning with chlembuterol is not normally serious, but can be in some cases.

The economic reasons for using chlembuterol are obvious: more flesh, less fat, better appearance of the food, more rapid growth of the cattle and more profits. In Spain, as in the other countries of the EC, the use of chlembuterol is forbidden (although in the United States it is permitted in very low doses), and this prohibition is well known by the producers of feeding stuffs, the cattle dealers and the veterinary surgeons.

So, there is no other justification than greed for the use of chlembuterol (except in the case of some respiratory diseases).

This is a case of illegal and unethical behaviour that endangers the health of the consumers and disobeys the law, with no positive result other than higher profits. The chlembuterol case in Spain revealed the existence of a network of laboratories and plants manufacturing feeding stuffs with illegal drugs. The case served to increase the awareness of consumers of the quality of food, to set the health authorities to work more seriously on their control responsibilities, and to persuade the cattle dealers of the need to act jointly to defend themselves against the greedy and unethical members of their profession.

6.12   Self-regulation

Regulation is a necessary process but it is also expensive, often inflexible, and inefficient. It has therefore been proposed to replace it by self-regulation, a process by which the company itself, or an association of firms, takes responsibility for establishing criteria, setting rules and enforcing them. Self-regulatory bodies are common in the professions, in which an ethical committee takes care of the complaints of the clients and of the members of the profession, or even acts on its own initiative to maintain standards and to develop new norms when circumstances require it. And the same occurs in firms, industries and sectors where reputation is an important asset, and where the costs and consequences of distrust and litigation may be high.

When a company or a whole industry uses certain internal criteria to set limits on some of its actions, in the absence of any regulation imposed from outside (or beyond that regulation), it could be applying ethical criteria or not. The association of advertising agencies that decides to apply strict truthfulness criteria in its business, in the absence of any law that so requires (or beyond the law), may be doing so in compliance with the moral duties of its members, but also for aesthetic or cultural reasons, or to avoid official intervention, or for reasons of public relations.

The main economic justification for collective self-regulation is to reduce transaction and agreement costs. If someone wishes to object to an advertisement that is untruthful or morally offensive, he or she can take legal action, but it is time-consuming and expensive. It may be simpler and cheaper, and less irksome for the claimant, if the offending advertiser and the media appear before a private court created by the leading advertisers, the media and the advertising agencies, which will give a quick decision. The authority of this self-regulating agency or body will depend on the agreement reached by the parties interested in self-regulation. Insofar as it is in their interest to promote their good name, flawless advertisements and good-quality work, they will be the first to want these agreements to be put into practice, and in a way so that nobody can act as a free rider.

That is how self-regulation works. Its effectiveness will consequently depend on the institution of simple, cheap, efficient and unanimously accepted mechanisms, accompanied, if necessary, by coercive measures, either through the same association or because the government backs the decisions taken by the self-regulating body.

This brings us to a very common problem in ethics: the lack of co-ordination between the actions of a group of agents and those of each individual agent (somewhat similar to the prisoner's dilemma). Each advertising agency, for example, considers that untruthful advertisements are harmful because they make the public view all advertisements with scepticism and all agencies with distrust. Therefore, if all observed this moral rule, all would readily accept it. However, there is then the incentive for one firm to break this rule, sheltering under the good name of the whole but benefiting from its own lack of truthfulness. Hence the interest in the existence of a regulation that prevents this and, if it is too expensive, a self-regulating body.

Self-regulation raises a number of other interesting questions: how does one attain and enforce the agreement? Should minimum criteria be established or should one set requirements that exceed those of currently existing or possible future regulations? Should they be confirmed by an appropriate authority? Self-regulation also runs the risk of nullifying its efficacy and becoming a mere instrument for confabulation between member companies for less noble ends.

Self-regulation is more and more common in individual companies or groups of firms. Companies expound in ethical codes, statements of principles or letters of intention the ethical goals they desire to attain in their business, either inside the firm (with respect to managers, workers and shareholders) or with outside stakeholders (clients, suppliers, financial institutions, local communities and the state), and the means to achieve them. The codes usually contain a statement of goals (and/or the so-called 'mission' of the company), the basic ethical principles and the specific means to be applied, and a certain specification of those goals and means in several areas of special interest. Often they include norms about how to proceed in case of ethical complaints, the procedures to solve conflicts, etc.

An ethical code is usually a means to attain many different objectives: to engage the managers in the fulfilment of the company's ethical duties; to motivate its managers and employees to comply with their duties towards the other members of the company and towards outsiders (suppliers, customers, local community, etc.); to define these duties in a precise way; to contribute to the creation of a culture in the company; to homogenize different cultures in the firm (for example, after a takeover); to create an image of responsibility, credibility and excellence; to improve the professional attitude of managers and employees; to raise the performance of the workers and to prevent opportunistic attitudes; to provide criteria for times of emergency or crisis; to reduce uncertainties on the expected behaviour of the firm and of its employees; to motivate the clients and suppliers to also act ethically in their dealings with the company; and many others.

Due to this long list of potential benefits, an ethical code may be an opportunity for a company to build moral capital and to improve ethical behaviour in the company and in its community, and also to get financial or economic benefits. But the company may also use the code to attain short-term profits, exploiting a reputation for morality that does not correspond with the truth. Therefore, the existence of an ethical code is not necessarily a guarantee of moral attitudes, nor is the existence of external regulations an assurance of moral behaviours.

There are two different ways to warrant the ethical results of a code. The first one is to 'oblige' the company to behave always according to the rules of the code: for example, referring ethical affairs to a superior body in the company, or creating an internal authority specialized in ethical affairs, or giving full powers to an ombudsman or ethical director, or submitting the company to an ethical audit, etc., so that any opportunistic behaviour be penalized. Nevertheless, all these measures cannot guarantee that the company and its managers and employees will always behave ethically.

The second way to support a code is through the reputation of always being a moral corporation or, at least, of having customary moral behaviour. This reputation goes beyond a mere exercise of public relations, because a person (or a company) is morally well regarded when his or her convictions and values are not only compatible with ethics, but based on them; when his or her behaviour not only abides by the rules of ethics, but attempts to obey them with excellence; when s/he does not wash his/her hands of the behaviour of other persons, but tries to help them to improve their ethical level, while respecting their freedom.

So, a company may have a strong ethical reputation, gained day by day through the efforts of its managers and employees (even if some of them are not fully ethical), and its errors will not damage its reputation if it recognizes them, apologizes for them and makes amends for them. In this case, the ethical code is backed by the moral capital of the company, i.e. by the attitudes of managers and employees ethically trained, committed and motivated.

An ethical code is, then, a manifestation of morality and a means to attain it. Following are several features of a good code:

1. It is not necessarily the result of a consensus of those involved in it, but must be accepted by them (because nobody can be obliged to act against their conscience).
2. It should contain clear and well-founded ethical rules.
3. It must be internally consistent, and also coherent with the mission, the goals, the strategy and the policies of the company.
4. A good code cannot be all-inclusive nor too detailed.
5. It must balance rights and duties, and internal and external stakeholders.
6. It should provide for exceptions (giving also the moral criteria to focus on them).
7. The code must deal with the mechanisms of conflict resolution in the interpretation and application of its rules.
8. It must be respectful of the freedom of persons.
9. It cannot be a means of indoctrination.
10. The omissions in a code are more important than its precepts.
11. And its application must be easy and inexpensive.

To sum up, an ethical code is not a panacea, but a useful instrument, especially if it reveals a demanding moral climate in the company and if it is directed to foster it.

6.13   Conclusion: ethics, or regulations, or both, or neither?

Regulation is an expensive and often inefficient process. If everyone were to behave morally, regulation would still be necessary, but much diminished. Ethics is not a replacement for regulation. Ethics fulfils a function that is much higher than regulation: it guides people towards their goal, it makes them 'better' people, and this is far beyond the possibilities of regulation. With or without regulation, people need ethics, and so do companies.

Ethics must also be part of the observance of regulations: to obey regulations for fear of punishment may achieve the desired external results but will not improve people. To obey regulations because by so doing one contributes to the common good – that is ethics. The external results may be the same, but the internal ones (the process of learning and improving oneself) also count.

Ethics goes beyond regulations because regulations cannot reach everywhere (and, if they do, it makes the situation worse, because they destroy the economic agents' initiative and freedom).

It is true that some regulations would not be necessary if we were all ethical (it would not be necessary to prohibit and persecute prostitution or pollution or discrimination on the grounds of race or religion). However, this should not lead us to fall into utopian beliefs: regulation will always be necessary, at least for that minority (sometimes, large majority) who would prefer to act otherwise. And, in any case, someone has to decide whether we drive on the right or the left.

However, it is true that a more ethical society would have less regulations, less conflicts and less observance costs. The fact that people learn from their own actions and those of others leads us into a chain of negative effects, when behaviours start to become immoral: because there are thieves, we must spend part of our income on measures to protect and defend ourselves and pay higher taxes to maintain police, judges and prisons. If this should lead us to protest at the lack of freedom and the reduction of after-tax income and induce us to adopt more individualistic and less co-operative behaviours, then we would be giving one more turn to the screw of immorality, which would soon manifest itself in the form of new social and private costs (for example, higher social security contributions to pay for more old people's homes because their families will no longer accept them).

So, my conclusion is that regulation is good and necessary, but ethics is, simply, indispensable and urgent.

CHAPTER 7

Business and community

Luk Bouckaert[1]

*Katholieke Universiteit Leuven, Centrum voor Economie en
Ethiek, Belgium*

The relation between business and community is a complex one because of the vague
and different meanings of the term 'community'. In one sense the term community
refers to such distinctive social and territorial units as hamlets, villages, towns, cities
and metropolitan areas. Most of the sociological empirical research on community
works within the delineation of this positive definition of community. In the words
of Poplin (1972: 9): 'The term community refers to the places in which people
maintain their homes, earn their livings, rear their children, and, in general carry on
most of their life activities'. Community as a social unit refers to what Marcel Mauss
calls a 'phénomène social total' or what Königs describes as 'a global society on a
local basis'. These definitions suggest that community remains a more or less large
local and social unit in which men co-operate in order to live their economic, social
and cultural life together (Königs, 1968: 25).

Following this definition we can restrict our analysis to the interaction between
the firm and its global social environment which forms a complex and organic unity.
In fact a firm is a subpart of such a global network system. A community is not based
on one single purpose or function but on the integration of different functions and
on a sense of co-operation. To analyse the relation between business and community
means therefore to pay attention to the network of interaction within the social
system: the interaction between business, family life, school and training, social
activities, local culture and political structure. The dimension of the community one
focuses upon will depend on the dimension of the firm. Small businesses are integrated
in a local community while multi-nationals operate within the much looser system of
an international community.

But the term community has other meanings too. In present economic and
political theory community often refers to a specific model of social co-ordination
that can be distinguished from market or state regulation. We have to discuss its
features and its relevance for business ethics today. Another more normative and
ethical approach will define community by referring to feelings, values and personal
relations. In discussing their idea of community Minar and Greer (1969: IX) tell us
that 'it expresses our vague yearnings for a commonality of desire, a communion with

those around us, an extension of the bonds of kin and friend to all those who share a common fate with us'. The 'search for community' is a quest for conviviality, fraternity and co-operation. Every social group which internalizes these values will call itself a community. The term is often used for religious, moral or academic groups. But today the terms 'economic community' or 'business community' are not unusual and some authors as Etzioni (1988), Boswell (1990) or Selznick (1992) introduce the term community with its normative connotations in the field of economics and business.

So the theme 'business and community' can lead us to several types of analysis and reflection according to the different meanings of community. Although each definition of community has its own focus, they are not mutually exclusive. So the first thing to do is to clarify the concept 'community', and to see how the different meanings relate to each other and what their relevance for management and business ethics is. Therefore, in the first part of our contribution, we will design a more general and theoretical perspective rather than tackle specific issues. This theoretical framework does not fit completely in the conventional 'stakeholders approach' in business ethics. We call it therefore a 'community-oriented perspective'. The main difference is that in a community-oriented perspective the community is much more than just a stakeholder like any other. It is a comprehensive environment of which the firm is part and member. So the relation is one not only of social contract but much more of internalization and symbiosis. The second part is devoted to empirical applications. We will discuss a case of regional development in Belgium, the importance of culture in management and the process of communitarization in Europe.

7.1   A community-oriented perspective

7.1.1   *Community as a co-ordination principle*

Market, state and community
Market, state and community can be seen as three ideal types of social co-ordination. In a first approach these ideal types are used to differentiate three types of institutional order in society: the economic, the political and the socio-cultural sphere. Market regulation, which lies at the core of the economic order, can be characterized by the price mechanism and by free exchange relations. State or political regulation is organized by law and through relations of legal coercion. Community or moral regulation operates by the internalization of values and through relations of trust and co-operation. The community regulation is primarily anchored in the socio-cultural sphere. Institutions such as families, schools, churches, cultural and social non-profit organizations are the basic communities to learn and to internalize values.

Although there is a privileged link between the ideal types of co-ordination and the three institutional spheres, this does not mean that the link is exclusive. One of the characteristics of our present society is a strong mutual penetration of different institutional spheres and the mixture of different co-ordination principles. The demand for ethics in business and economics is a result of this intensified interaction. It has to do with the discovery of moral self-regulation as an important form of economic co-ordination in a context of uncertainty and high transaction costs.

Economists such as F. Perroux (1963) and K. Boulding (1968; 1970) have done some pioneering but mostly forgotten work in articulating the tripartite system of co-ordination. An interesting consequence of the tripartite distinction is the view that social co-ordination is not restricted to the traditional opposition and relation between market and government. In the present literature there seems to be a growing interest in the tripartite distinction (Hamlin, 1986; Miller, 1990) and in the proliferation of mixed forms (for a survey see Thompson *et al.*, 1991). A demarcation line between the three models of co-ordination can be drawn by clustering some of the key-concepts used in the literature (Table 7.1).

Relations between economics, politics and ethics

The term 'community' in Table 7.1 is defined as a specific model of co-ordination in contrast with the market and the state. But as we have said in our introduction, community refers primarily to a local unit within a global system of interaction. From the global point of view, we pay attention to the type of relation between the economic, political and communitarian (socio-cultural/moral) forms of life. Whenever the relation and the proportion between the three co-ordinating systems changes substantially, we get a completely different society and even a different definition of the subsystems of economic, political and moral life[2]. Possible types of relation between market, state and community are hierarchy, autonomy, reduction or symbiosis. To each of these models corresponds a specific type of social structure, social science, ideology and praxis. We are especially interested in the symbiotic relation as it can explain the present interest in economic and business ethics. But let us first have a look at the other models.

In the pre-modern writings of Aristotle, for instance, we find a consistent model of hierarchical ordering: ethics as the good life of the community has to inform politics which in his vision is a higher activity than economics. To keep economic activity in its instrumental and subordinate position, it must be restricted to its function of

Table 7.1   Demarcation concepts between the models of social co-ordination

market	state	community
free exchange	social contract	ethos
exchange	law	gift
preferences	rights	values
autonomy	hierarchy	network
price	authority	trust
competition	control	co-operation
production	distribution	participation
economics	politics	ethics

fulfilling basic family needs. To extend economics (the ekonomikè technè) to profit activities and money accumulation (the chrèmatistikè technè) is unnatural and immoral because it leads to the inversion of the natural hierarchy between ethics, politics and economics. The dynamics of money accumulation, according to Aristotle, has no limits in itself and will in the end use politics and ethics for its own expansion. Therefore he made an ethical argument for the prohibition of interest as a form of immoral money-making. Although the Aristotelian approach to ethics is revitalized today by all kind of communitarian theories, it does not mean that Aristotle's model of hierarchy is taken as a paradigm for the global relation. The plea for an Aristotelian orientation of business ethics (Koslowski 1988; Solomon, 1992) does not entail the subordination of economics to politics and a return to a pre-industrial and patriarchical household economy. What is searched for is the application of Aristotle's concept of an ethical and political community to the realm of business. This is in fact a non-Aristotelian use of an Aristotelian concept.

Modern society no longer follows the hierarchical relation between ethics, politics and economics. A process of differentiation and autonomy of the three spheres characterizes modern institutions and reflects itself in the disintegration of Aristotle's integrative 'moral science' into different, moral-free and autonomous disciplines. Each sphere and each scientific discipline has its own logic and protects its autonomy by immunizing itself against the influence of other spheres and disciplines. This process of differentiation explains why economics and ethics have become worlds apart.

The autonomy of the different spheres does not imply that there are no relations at all. In fact, there will be a kind of external input–output exchange. Each sphere depends on the input of the other to realize its final purpose. For instance, the functioning of a market is impossible without some forms of political regulation and public services (e.g. property rights, anti-trust laws, public infrastructure, correction for market failures, etc.). The same can be said about ethics. A market economy needs a cultural ethos expressed in values such as freedom, entrepreneurial spirit, trust and honesty in contractual relations, intellectual competence, service in the relations with consumers, co-operation and solidarity in the workplace, etc. The source of this ethics lies to a large extent outside the firm and the marketplace. Indeed, forming or failing to form values is mostly realized through our participation in family life, school education, national culture, religious life, cultural and caring activities. So there is a real input of moral and intellectual values from the socio-cultural sector into economics. The economic sector in turn is a necessary condition for the other spheres in society. The financial surplus created by economic activity is the basis for political programmes of distributive justice and for sponsoring socio-cultural activities. But all these input–output relations, however important they may be, do not affect but rather enhance the autonomy.

A third possibility is the reductionist model which means that one of the institutional spheres tries to control the other. In a system of state communism economic and cultural life is controlled quasi-completely by the political sphere. Fundamentalist groups strive to co-ordinate and regulate social life from the point of view of a traditional and religious ethos. In a capitalist society there is a tendency to organize society as much as possible through the logic of the market. A theoretical reflection of this tendency can be found in a lot of economic theories of politics which reduce politics to a market process where political programmes are bought for votes and power. Also cultural and moral activities such as family life, marriage, jurisprudence, religion can be analysed and interpreted as phenomena of rational choice or as the result of supply-and-demand conditions in a market. This tendency to explain all social activity as a kind of economic activity is, from an analytical point of view, very successful in a society where the economic logic in fact dominates the other types of rationality. Although critics of capitalism are convinced that our industrial society is dominated by such a reductionist logic, we believe that our society is characterized by another type of interaction which we denote as a *symbiotic* logic.

The model of symbiosis

One of the characteristics of today is the deconstruction of all types of well-ordered and stable systems. New forms of intensive interaction and flexible combination come into life. They transform the world into networks of flexible and creative structures, changing in a partly unpredictable way our institutions and disciplines. This rather anarchical process of 'creative destruction' is often mentioned as a feature of post-modern society. This does not mean that there is no ordering but that the ordering cannot be understood and controlled from a master point of view. There is no ultimate and foundational theoretical principle (or set of independent principles) to order and determine the totality and its parts. Therefore big technocratic or ideological constructions are treated with suspicion because they try to fix and control reality from an outsider set of principles. The idea of a network may be a concept that escapes the temptation of absolute control and is more sensitive to relations of mutual dependence and influence. We will use the metaphor of symbiosis to clarify this process of interaction.

Symbiosis is a technical term in life sciences. It is a process where two organisms of different kinds live on or in each other to their mutual benefit. As a metaphor it can be used for all kinds of relationships in which institutions, persons, activities or principles exist in a way of close interaction and mutual benefit. How does it work in the case of economics, politics and ethics? The three principles of co-ordination, primarily linked with one of the three institutional spheres, penetrate in the other spheres. The original logic of one sphere, being transferred into another sphere, introduces metaphorical ways of thinking, changes practices and creates new institutional forms. To visualize this internalization of different forms of co-ordination within each institutional sphere, we bring them together in a matrix (Table 7.2).

The result of the logic of symbiosis is a proliferation of plural forms (Bradach and Eccles, 1989) in the economic, political and socio-cultural institutions. This plurality of forms is also reflected in the way economics and ethics as social disciplines find new applications outside their own institutional domain. Today economists are

Table 7.2 Symbiosis of economics, politics and ethics

Regulations	Institutions		
	Economic (business)	Political (state)	Ethical (socio-cultural)
economic (market, preferences)	economic market	political market	non-profit market
political (social, contract, rights)[3]	economic democracy (rights of stakeholders)	political democracy (rights of citizenship)	moral democracy (human rights)
ethical (community, values)	economic community (business ethics)	political community (ethics of justice)	moral community (ethics of solidarity)

writing about economics of trust, economics of marriage, economics of democracy, economics of justice, etc. while at the same time ethicists are interested in political ethics, business ethics and all kinds of applied ethics. The point is that good applied ethics is not merely an outsider application of moral principles on a practical field of action, but the discovery of a moral dimension which is constitutive and operative inside the action field. Albert Löhr, in his fundamental book *Unternehmensethik und Betriebwirtschaftslehre* (1991), points out how business ethics can only become a scientific discipline if the methodological basis for a new alliance between theory and praxis is clearly worked out (see also Etzioni, 1988; Ulrich, 1990).

In this internalized form of interaction institutions are transformed into multi-dimensional organizations. A firm, for instance, can be analysed at the same time as (1) a profit-maximizing organization operating in a more or less competitive environment, (2) a social contract defining the rights and duties of different stakeholders, and (3) a community sharing a common mission and value system. This tripartite definition of the firm means that an enterprise combines the three models of social co-ordination. It is an economic, political and moral institution. Reducing the firm to one of these dimensions is lessening its capability to respond to a growing demand for values and service expressing the symbiosis of different aspects of life. Another argument for a multi-dimensional concept of the firm can be found in the analysis of successful regional development as presented in the next point.

The symbiotic logic is also striking today in the political sphere. Political activity, especially within a democratic system, is always linked with the conquest of the electoral market. But this does not mean, as is supposed in a reductionist approach, that politics is only another way of doing economics. Good politicians may be more than just power-maximizers in an electoral market. At best they may be inspired by some statesmanship or by some moral sense of justice. They may even renounce power in order to speak out for their convictions as a dissident. So there is a need not only for a political and an economic but also for a moral theory of politics.

To take another example from the cultural sphere: the core activity of a university consists in creating a community, morally committed to the search for truth and new forms of theoretical and reflective insight. But the management of a university is not based on the moral and cultural tradition of truth-seeking but rather on the economic view that universities are like firms which must be competitive in the socio-cultural market of intellectual products and services to get their financial resources. So the logic of the market is not absent in the organization of universities and may even be a serious threat to their cultural mission. Even the idea of internal market structures between faculties is an element of modern university management. The political principle of co-ordination in turn is visible in the protection of the rights of all the participants, especially those of the students who have the right of good education and intellectual emancipation. The university as a place of 'Herrschaftsfreie Dialog' (Habermas) is a form of democracy.

7.1.2   Community as a value system

Network structure and symbiosis can be operative just as well in a criminal organization as in a good society. They are concepts that pay attention to the process of interaction but not so much to the substantial and normative meaning of the shared values.[4] The literature about business culture usually stresses this formal and procedural aspect. It teaches us how to communicate, how to stimulate, how to manage a value system but not what kind of values should be communicated or stimulated. The content of the value system is left to the subjective preferences of the stakeholders.

A more substantial approach will look for some value content which is not only the result of the interaction between stakeholders but which as a historical and ethical structure informs the content of this interaction. This substantial approach is more in line with Continental European philosophy and sociology and differs from the social contract models which induce all ethical meanings and values from the preferences of autonomous and negotiating stakeholders.

The substantial normative structure has two aspects. The first is a social one. Value systems are rooted within existing communities and practices. Those communities may be families, religious or national groups. We will limit ourselves in this section to the national community. Such a community is the result of a complex process of a (partly) shared linguistic, ethnic, cultural and social history in a territory. A socio-cultural unity has often (but not always) been the foundation for, or a striving towards, a political unity – the nation-state. Belonging to such a national community has a deep impact on the formation of our preferences and on our lifestyle. The impact may be inadvertent but is nevertheless real and selective. When a national or cultural identity is threatened (or subjectively felt as being threatened), some very strong emotional, aggressive and racist reactions can awake and push away all kind of rational arguments. But national and cultural identity is not only a source of aggressive reaction, it is a source of cultural difference and character. This is an important point for business, especially in Europe. The internalization of cultural differences in the management structure, in marketing and in the quality of the output is an important way for a firm to become integrated in a region or a local market.

History teaches us that the sensitivity to cultural differences has its ups and downs but never disappears. It is in fact a long-term asset for an enterprise. To illustrate this impact of national identity on management style and structure, we will present in the next part the large-scale study of Hofstede on cultural differences in management.

The socio-cultural anchorage of values is not a guarantee for an ethical community. The shared feelings and aims must be justified by some ideal or standard of moral rationality and justice. But the inescapable question linked with this ethical justification in a pluralistic society is the one which MacIntyre expresses in the title of his book, *Whose Justice? Which rationality?* (1988). What is the normative content of the moral ideal and who will define this content? The difficulty in answering this question often functions as an excuse or an alibi to accept ethical relativism.

An important test for the ethical quality of the communitarian values is the question of the range of the community. What are the privileged units of solidarity and community? Community feelings may be very strong but restricted to one's own corporation, social group, country, region, etc. If the analysis of the sources of community stops at an exploration of the socio-psychological roots, we do not touch the question of ethical justification. In order to open the ethical debate on community, we can reflect on some well-known sociological notions of community proposed by Tönnies and Durkheim.

The natural community

A classical reference in the community literature is the work of the German sociologist Tönnies, *Gemeinschaft und Gesellschaft* (1887). His distinction between community (Gemeinschaft) and society (Gesellschaft) rests on his view of two types of human will: the natural will and the rational will. A community (Gemeinschaft) formed by natural will is based on a social unity of emotions and affections. The social unity is pre-existent to the individuals and informs their behaviour. Family ties, neighbourhood, collective propriety can produce this type of emotional unity and natural commitment. The logic of society (Gesellschaft) is a different one. The individuals are prior to the unity. The relations are rational, contractual and based on mutual profit. With the growth of mercantile city life and industrialization in the West, there would be, according to Tönnies, a progressive shift from natural community to rational society.

Tönnies' concept of community, with his subjective and affective connotations, is often used as a kind of moral ideal contrasted with the individualism and the anonymity of modern mass societies (Poplin, 1972: 6). Members of a community have a deep sense of belonging to a meaningful group which gives them identity, security and a normative anchorage. Modern conditions of life are characterized by the loss of this natural communitarian feeling of membership. Rationalism and constructivism in modern society are causes of the disintegration of traditional ties of solidarity. But the traditional community ideal is not dead. The revival of traditionalism and nationalism, the rehabilitation of local cultures, the success of sects, the stress on family values and communitarian ethic – all these phenomena can be interpreted equally well as a resistance to the complete domination of modern rationality.

The organic community

A second meaning of 'community' has been given by the French sociologist Durkheim in his book *The Division of Labour in Society* (1893). His definition of community/ solidarity is not inspired by traditionalism nor is it based on the modern logic of contract and exchange. It rests on the conviction that modern societies produce a new type of solidarity as the result of the organic division of labour. He called this new type 'organic solidarity'. Traditional communities are homogeneous in character, stimulate conformity and protect the 'collective conscience' by a strong repressive law. The individual has to think and to act in conformity with the way 'one' (the group, everybody) thinks or acts. Their solidarity is, according to Durkheim, a mechanical solidarity. Modern societies on the contrary are based on the interdependence of specialized functions. They stimulate differentiation and are more interested in civil law which regulates the relations between individuals and autonomous groups in society. The law is more oriented towards 'restitution' than towards punitive and repressive sanctions. The evolution of society is, according to Durkheim, a process of transformation from mechanical into organic solidarity. This process was seen by him as a moral progress because it fostered relationships of trust, co-operation and moral responsibility.

One can easily link the actual theories of participative management and the view of enterprises as collective and mission-oriented actors with Durkheim's organic conception of community. Durkheim has defended corporatism as the most suitable form of business organization.[5] Analogous efforts were present in British guild socialism, in co-operation movements and in Christian social thinking (Boswell, 1990). But Durkheim's manifesto for corporations as public institutions has also been misused in a different ideological context. Instead of being an expression of 'libertarian solidarism' the programme of 'corporatism' was introduced in and adapted to the ideological programmes of authoritarianism (Salazar) and fascism (Mussolini and Franco). This historical misuse of Durkheim's and similar programmes of organic solidarity makes it clear that organic community as such is not sufficient as expression of a moral society.

The ethical community

Although the notions of natural and organic community have a moral potential, they do not fully express our moral intuitions about solidarity and community. A natural community is a source of spontaneous co-operation but at the same time it may suppress individual liberty and creativity in an unacceptable way. Organic solidarity with its focus on complementary division of labour creates ties of functional co-operation but it says nothing about those who are marginalized or excluded from the functional network. Natural and organic solidarity do not necessarily secure the principle of respect for every human being as a person because they may identify the person with his or her natural origin or with his or her function in an organic system. A 'we-feeling' which is only rooted in natural ties or in functional co-operation has in itself an ambiguous dynamic of exclusion.

The dynamic of exclusion is in itself not immoral. Social identity always implies relative forms of exclusion. Through integration in natural and organic communities people get a sense of uniqueness and specific commitment without which a moral society is abstract. The self is not a faceless point of moral dignity equal to other points of moral dignity, it is always a socially embedded or 'encumbered' self (Sandel, 1982). But exclusion and selection become morally unacceptable when they violate the rights of other people or deprive them of the real possibility to participate in a form of human and social life. Therefore the natural and organic forms of community must be tested on their openness and respect for the intrinsic value of every human being. An ethical view on community defines the value of the person not on a natural or functional basis but as universal and unconditional.

A formal test for ethical solidarity and community has been formulated by Kant's well-known Categorical Imperative. This Imperative requires that our particular forms of solidarity should not contradict the principles of universality and dignity of the person. The Declaration of Human Rights can be seen as a more concrete and elaborated version of the Kantian claim to universality. But the formal approach in those ethics of right always falls short of our original intentions of solidarity. The reason is that actual human relations emerge in a context of unequal power. In such a context community is not only a question of formal equality of rights but is a matter of transforming relations of unequal power into relations of co-operation and participation.[6]

Ethical community refers not only to a shared set of formal rights but to a process of transformation. Solidarity means primarily a transfer of rights, power, knowledge, responsibility from those who have to those who have not in order to create a community of equal rights and free exchange. In this sense community implies a form of gift and requires altruism. This fundamental or deep altruism has nothing to do with paternalistic attitudes which make people dependent on the goodwill of others. This kind of deep altruism is a precondition of a free society (Bouckaert and Bouckaert, 1992).[7] Freedom is a gift before it is a right or a basis for exchange. Once more, we have to consider gift relations as a specific type of social co-ordination which is required to realize a political community of equal rights and an economic community of free exchange.[8]

Can the 'ethical community' be a good metaphor to think about business and industrial relations? Business literature mostly looks upon the firm as a goal-directed system where profit and output maximization are the most vital objectives. This view leads to the managerial obsession of engineering all functions and operations in the firm. Keeley (1988) proposes to replace this organistic image by the social contract metaphor which puts free negotiation at the centre of the firm. In this view the role of management is to mediate among the various interests and demands of the stakeholders. Selznick (1992) goes a step further in his effort to formulate a theory of moral institutions. Although a firm has clearly an economic mission – to produce goods and services in a profitable way – the point is to interpret and to realize this mission as a moral and social good for the community on a long-term basis. The content of social responsibility cannot be defined as a compromise between different groups but as a kind of public philosophy, as a social and moral project. Within such a project the firm transforms itself from a closed towards a responsible system. In this way the economic motive gets a social and moral dimension.

> Rather than ask what groups have a claim, we ask what values should be protected and enhanced. This functional theory of corporate social responsibility shifts attention from the demands of constituencies to the requirements of institutional well-being and integrity. Group claims would no longer be treated as irreducible and self-justifying, an approach which encourages political bargaining and compromise; instead, the mission of the corporation would be expanded to reflect its true role in the community. This expansion emphasizes the substance of corporate responsibility, that is, what is objectively required to sustain an effective work force, to do justice in the workplace, to care for the environment, and to meet changing economic and social needs. Responsibility runs to the social function, not to a constituency. This interpretation of corporate social responsibility is a summons to high politics, not low politics. Obligations are defined by a public philosophy, by a theory of the enterprise and of its place in the community, not by the raw play of power. Only with the aid of such a theory can we design institutions capable of fulfilling their social responsibilities in self preserving ways. Only thus can we create a corporate conscience. (Selznick, 1992: 361)

7.1.3   Community-oriented management

If community as a co-ordination principle and as a set of substantial values is a constitutive part of the firm, what are the implications for management? We will stress three principles. A community-oriented management implies (1) the importance of integral analysis, (2) the institutionalization of moral commitment and (3) a sensitivity to cultural differences.

Management and integral analysis
The metaphor of symbiosis tells us that social reality functions on the basis of interdependence, mutual interaction and all forms of reciprocal influence. All types of system analysis are accustomed to work with similar notions and end with a plea for synergy. But the point made clear by the matrix of economics, politics and ethics is a specific kind of synergy. Every problem must be analysed from a point of view where the interaction of economic, political and moral rationality comes to the front. To this type of integral analysis corresponds a new type of management where the search for synergy between economics, politics and ethics is the key factor. We will discuss further a case of regional development as an illustration. Let us take here a more concrete problem of business ethics – bribery.

As an economic problem bribery can be seen as a price to pay for a preferential treatment, a kind of service. The decision whether or not to pay the price will be the result of a cost-benefit analysis. Short- and long-term benefits and costs in terms of output, profit, employment, public relations, market strategy, etc. will be considered. Should the balance be positive, this gives the actor an efficiency argument to pay the bribery. But this unrestrained logic of efficiency opens the way for a type of economy where the rules of law are only instrumental to the corporate objectives and are no longer seen as the expression of the common good or the rights of persons. Paying bribery, therefore, is much more than an economic decision – it is a political activity, because it is a subversive way to change the rules of the economic game and to transform the system of free exchange and free competition into a system of unfair and invisible manipulation. Bribery makes relations between competitors asymmetric and unequal. A search for influence and hidden power instead of efficiency becomes the dominating strategy. Because the logic of bribery is based on a preferential treatment that does not respect the law which constitutes the economic order, it is at the same time a political and an economic disruption. But some social systems may be organized on different rules and expectations. Not every social system accepts the logic of the market as a free and anonymous play of supply and demand. A society may subordinate market relations to personal relations and community affections, which are expressed in gift-giving activity. What is seen as a bribery in a modern economy may be interpreted as a gift in a pre-modern context. Gifts are necessary to create trust and personal affection, which are pre-conditions to enter into a relation of exchange. Without a cultural analysis it is impossible to make the distinction between bribery and gifts. Bribery in a modern context is a perversion of the moral meaning of gifts because bribery is a way to undermine trust in order to realize an economic gain. But when do gifts become bribery? Only a situational analysis focusing on the mixture of economic, political and cultural meanings will give a good insight and a satisfactory answer.

Management and moral commitment

A lot of business literature sees 'participative management' as an important means to motivate people and to give them some feeling of personal responsibility for the realization of the objectives of the firm. This is a strong argument to develop human resource management (HRM) techniques. But the argument is purely instrumental and based on economic rationality. The temptation to treat persons as manipulable resources is not far away. This ambiguity in the argument undermines the moral reliability of HRM or other forms of 'human relations' management. The ambiguity may even lead to counterproductive results. The alternative is not a neglect of the economic function of human relations policy but a recognition of the moral roots of HRM. This recognition implies not only a personal but also a corporate commitment to some basic values such as, e.g., respect for the dignity and the rights of every person, respect for the culture of the community and respect for the sustainability of nature. This respect means that persons, communities and nature are viewed not only as instrumental but also as intrinsic values. Although intrinsic values are open-ended and can be interpreted in different ways, this does not mean that they are meaningless – rather, they ask for another type of clarification and management than the rational theory of management can afford.

The difference between rational management (based on the operational means–end rationality) and value management (based on the search for a common value commitment) is well illustrated by Selznick's distinction between governing and managing an organization. He writes in *The Moral Commonwealth*:

> In taking community as a model, we must make a distinction between management and governance. 'Management' suggests rational, efficiency-minded, goal-driven organization. This is the realm of administrative rather than political decisions. Ends are characteristically taken as given, and every act is justified by the contribution it makes to those ends. All else is distraction. . . . To govern is to accept responsibility for *the whole life* of the institution. This is a burden quite different from the rational co-ordination of specialized activities. Governance takes account of all the interests that affect the viability, competence, and moral character of an enterprise. The strategies of governance are basically political. . . . A vital aspect of governance is that it has *the care* of a community or a quasi-community. People subject to managerial direction may be thought of as interchangeable, deployable, expendable units, to be used or discarded as efficiency may require. They are not objects of care or of moral concern. In government, on the contrary, leaders (or systems) have a basic commitment to the participants as *persons* and to groups as vehicles of legitimate interests. Such a commitment is diffuse and open-ended, not narrowly defined. . . . *The broader the organization's goals, the more leeway it has in defining its mission, the more requirements there are for winning co-operation, the more fully the lives of participants are lived within it, the more important does governance become.* Each of those conditions brings the organization closer to the model of community and therefore makes the model more useful as a guide to policy. (Selznick, 1992: 290–1).

Management and cultural sensitivity

The re-evaluation of tradition and natural community is not without importance for economics and business. Because economic thinking and practice are deeply embedded in modern rational philosophy and science, they have often neglected the meaning of local culture and community. Especially in the Third World, a dual economic structure is the visible result of this neglect: alongside the formal modern economy exists a hidden informal community and economy. Instead of integrating elements of local culture, multi-national businesses have often caused the destruction of traditional ways of living, production and distribution. The value system within the informal economy is different and often hostile to the value system in the formal economy (Latouche, 1986; Verhelst, 1990). Instead of co-operating, both forms of economies are obstructing each other with a lot of negative external effects and unsuccessful projects as a result. Development economics has to reconsider the relation between informal and formal economies. Third World projects should be based on the premise that local cultures have the potential to develop. Instead of eliminating tradition by modern concepts, a selective use of modern ideas must activate the local development. The South–North Network Cultures and Development is an initiative to promote this new approach of development.[9]

But cultural sensitivity is not only important for Third World countries. We will see in the next part how, according to the enquiries of Hofstede, cultural differences play a role in management all over the world. We may expect that in the future cultural differences may play an even more important role. Along with a type of cosmopolitan and standardized world culture promoted by multi-national companies and their marketing strategies, there is a growing search for cultural identity and diversity. This search for cultural and symbolic meaning in goods and services will create new markets and new types of enterprise. This evolution can be compared with the process of 'greening' the economy which has created a completely new sensibility in the market. In order to produce and distribute symbolic meanings instead of material things, management has to widen its horizons. The engineering way of thinking must be complemented by a cultural and moral way of feeling. Management may not be reduced to a technical operation. It is primarily a cultural and moral activity realized with the help of technical knowledge. Therefore, studying history and literature which develops the cultural imagination and sensibility may be as fundamental as studying mathematical models which develop the art of deductive reasoning. A substantial increase in women in managerial functions may foster this cultural sensitivity.

7.2 Community in practice: case studies

7.2.1 The success of synergy and symbiosis: the case of PLATO

Regional development is a good case to illustrate the logic of community as a system of networking and symbiosis. Regional development has been and still is a major concern for all European governments. During the 1950s and 1960s, the growth pole theory[10] suggested that the best way to develop a region was by attracting large (foreign) companies, who would function as attractors, lifting the entire region in their growth. The major body of measures consisted therefore in the provision of investment credits, capital bonus payments and support for infrastructural provisions. This policy was criticized in the 1980s. It became clear that large companies did not integrate well in a particular region. As a result departure sometimes came as quickly as arrival. Therefore another policy matured, stressing the need to develop a region from within. While the first policy clearly followed a top-down strategy, with a governmental body introducing measures and hoping the rest would follow suit, the new policy chose a bottom-up approach, helping existing and especially small firms well rooted in the region to develop. During the 1980s network analysis came into prominence (see Bergman *et al.*, 1991; Caselli, 1991). Networks were looked upon as institutional devices to increase flexibility, to create forms of synergy and to reduce uncertainty. According to Thompson: 'The key feature of networks that they all address is the way co-operation and trust are formed and sustained within networks. In contrast to either hierarchy or market, networks co-ordinate through less formal, more egalitarian and cooperative means' (Thompson *et al.*, 1991: 171; Donckels and Courtmans, 1990).

In this context we present a Belgian example of such a network strategy, labelled PLATO. The target of this initiative is to help SMEs (small and medium enterprises) with clear growth potential by supplying them with professional advice from big companies. Expansion is the target, professionalism in management the instrument.

PLATO started in 1988 as part of a broader strategic plan for regional development: Strategic Plan Kempen (SPK). The Kempen is a relatively poor region situated in the north-east of Flanders, a region also with sustained high unemployment figures (12.1 per cent). This has made it an EC-recognized development area and PLATO an EC-sponsored pilot project. The name PLATO is a somewhat far-fetched acronym presenting us, however, with the basic notions of this particular action: Peterschap (godparenthood) – Leerplan (syllabus) – Arrondissement (district) – Turnhout (the major village of the Kempen) – Ondernemingen (enterprises). The link with the philosopher Plato can be made in two directions. The authors of SPK link their term 'strategic' with Plato's dialectic method. This method distinguishes between two modes of thinking: the synopsis (synthesis) and the diareisis (analysis). A strategic plan should follow two phases corresponding to these two modes. First there is an in-depth analysis of the problem, unfolding it in all its aspects; afterwards comes a synthetic moment, piecing together the diverse features of the problem at hand in a global plan. A second, more appropriate way to link philosophy and regional development can be found in Plato's educational method, the maieutic.[11] In his dialogue *Meno* Socrates proves his conviction that knowledge is already within humans, through a dialogue with a slave whom he helps to discover geometric laws only by asking him some well-directed questions, awakening the already present ideas. Just as Socrates trusted Meno, the developers of the PLATO project believe in the capacity of their own region, and especially of its businesspeople. All they need is some professional help in the development of their own projects – the ideas are there, they only have to be awakened in their full consequences. A concrete description of the project will clarify this approach.

The Strategic Plan

Let us take a closer look at SPK, the encompassing project. For SPK the long-term target is simply 'to make the district of Turnhout one of the leading regions in Europe, a region where it is pleasant to live, to work and to relax'. SPK is a joint initiative of seven groups: the organization of employers, trade unions, local and national governmental bodies and the farmers' organization. The explicit intention was that the entire community should be represented in the development of a plan, with impact on the entire region. The word 'strategic' was explicitly chosen to picture the global approach and consequently SPK consists not only of PLATO but of several other groups of projects. There is a strategic tourism and recreation plan, an unemployment plan, a welfare and well-being plan, an agriculture and forestry plan, an environment plan – and that is only part of the list. Some of these initiatives are organized on a permanent basis, e.g. the employers' plan PLATO, but others disappear quickly, to make way for other projects. The planners are realistic enough to know that they cannot control all aspects of society. They rather react on some clear-cut problems, and organize an *ad hoc* study group responsible for drawing out a plan capable of handling the problem at hand. Once the set of projects formulated to reach the target is finished, the cell disappears and time and energy becomes available to look at another problem. This gives a flexible form of regional development.

PLATO: co-operation of big and small enterprises

Every PLATO project has, apart from the organizing governmental bodies, two parties involved. On the one hand there is a group of large local companies who are asked to release part-time one or two executives who will be given the 'godparenthood' over a group of SMEs. In order to do their counselling job successfully, the executives get about 70 hours of training in the specific problems of SMEs. Meanwhile a group of entrepreneurs of growth-directed SMEs is chosen, and split into several small groups. They will get two years' training and counselling in close co-operation with their 'godparents'. Three types of activities are organized:

1. Individual counselling of an SME manager by his or her godparent.
2. Monthly sessions for each small group of SME managers, co-ordinated by their godparents. Discussions are organized on topics selected by the SME managers themselves.
3. Plenary seminars where more general topics are presented by external speakers and where the whole group can meet.

The entire project works on a voluntary basis. What drives the participants? For the managers of the SMEs the answer is clear: free professional advice gives them the possibility of growing success. The godparents frequently look upon their task as a way of broadening the scope of their activities which are normally very specialized; also, the promotion opportunities for executives taking part in the project increase. For the big companies participation creates goodwill in the region or can be used as an indirect form of outplacement in a crisis period. In some cases there is a direct economic interest. In order to increase their flexibility big companies prefer partnerships with autonomously organized firms instead of building up the typical vertically integrated firm. Helping SMEs and thereby creating performing supply companies in their own neighbourhood, is one way to reach this target. For the government, the last partner involved, this project should mainly tackle high unemployment problems in a permanent way and without the delicate complications involved when big firms start to perform badly and demand subsidies. The motivation is in fact a combination of corporate self-interest, political aims and social emancipation of the region. At any rate, the result has a surplus in the sense of networking a community. This becomes clear when we take a closer look at the first PLATO project.

Started in 1988, a group of 100 SME managers were brought together with their godparents. In the monthly sessions the task of the godparents is partly that of a professional adviser, but also and more prominently so that of a moderator. Problems thrown up in a session are in fact mainly solved by the trainees themselves, e.g. a manager troubled with motivating his personnel is introduced by the godparent to another participant who has had this type of problem before. And even in the personal counselling part of the project, many problems are solved by directing the manager involved to other persons with similar difficulties. Because of the length of the project (two years), interactions are not a once-only event but can grow into regular contacts on a base of trust and true interest. This is in fact the main target of the project: the creation of a social network. PLATO taught managers to present their problems to others, to talk about it. The organizers of PLATO hoped that they would continue doing so after the two years of professional advice ended. Only then could the professionalism in management expand and this in turn was looked upon as a business-cycle-insensitive achievement and the best guarantee for sustained growth.

That there was in fact the urge to prolong the contacts is shown by the reactions of the businessmen involved at the end of the two-year PLATO. Though it was not intended, the pressure of the participants to go on meeting each other was so great that another project had to be developed, labelled PLATO CONTINU, and giving the framework to continue the built-up contacts. In this sense SMEs in the region got networked and used the synergetic effects of this interaction in what proved to be an economically successful way (employment, turnover and investment all grew at a speed well above the Belgian average). For the big companies involved, the project was sometimes a discovery of local firms who could be of direct interest for their own economic activities. It also intensified their contacts with the region and thereby created a better rooting of the company involved. For two years they played the role of big brother – not in the sense of Orwell, as an all-controlling body, but in the family sense as a person you can lean on and who will give a helping hand when trouble shows up: not the big brother that despises and forbids any personal initiative, but rather the big brother who enjoys the inventive games of his younger friend. In this way PLATO changed the region in a qualitative way by creating a climate of trust and confidence among businesspeople, a crucial factor to make economic life prosper. The increased number of starters is an indication that the change in atmosphere was effectively felt.

The remarkable success of the first project gave birth to several others. By now 300 SMEs and 17 big companies in the Kempen take part in a PLATO project, while several other regions in Belgium follow the same strategy. In Arhus (Denmark) a PLATO project is currently running and numerous other European regions showed interest – Coïmbra (Portugal), Noord-Brabant (The Netherlands), Portsmouth (England), Sevilla (Spain) and Cork (Ireland). All this makes PLATO a successful initiative.

7.2.2   Hofstede's inquiry into cultural differences in management

Our second case illustrates the importance of cultural sensitivity in management. To what extent do management practices and corporate cultures reflect national cultures? Or to reverse the question: how do national cultures determine management styles and business organizations? To get an answer the Dutch anthropologist and sociologist G. Hofstede organized during 1967–73 a series of surveys among IBM personnel in about 50 countries (excluding Eastern Europe and the former Soviet

Union).[12] Although there are always some methodological problems and limits to inductive generalizations, Hofstede's inquiry is a strong argument in favour of a culture-bound theory of management. The premise present in so many business schools and business theories, that there exists a universal or culture-independent theory of management, seems to be falsified by Hofstede's results. This falsification opens new ways for a better understanding and integration of business and community.

Culture is defined by Hofstede as a way of thinking and feeling – and therefore subjective – which partly governs our behaviour on the individual, familial, economic and political levels. It is 'the collective programming of the mind which distinguishes one group or category of people from another' (Hofstede, 1991: 5). This mental program or software of the mind does not contain hereditary elements but is entirely apprehended. Of course such a definition contains an element of circularity because the collectivity is defined by its common mental program, while the collective character of the mental program is defined by its possibility to distinguish groups. This circularity can be removed by defining groups externally, as Hofstede does: it is the nation, or more precisely the individuals who administratively belong to the same country.[13]

Out of his data, Hofstede tried to find by factor analysis some basic cultural patterns in all the differences. He discovered four cultural determinants: hierarchical distance, uncertainty avoidance and freedom, individuality and community, femininity and masculinity. To these dimensions a fifth has later been added on the basis of Asian value research: long- and short-term views. As we will see, Hofstede's results have some important consequences for management style and business organization.

Hierarchical distance

Hierarchical distance or the unequal distribution of power is an essential element in organization and business, according to Hofstede. Important, however, is the subjective experience of these hierarchical relations. Do people accept the present power structure as it stands? Hierarchical distance as measured by the questionnaire is therefore defined as the perception of the degree of inequality in the distribution of power between the one who possesses power and the one who is subordinated to it (Bollinger and Hofstede, 1987: 82). It contains a person's perception of and preferences for a specific type of superior. They could choose among an autocratic chief, a paternalist, a consultative type or a democrat. The autocrat takes his or her decisions rapidly and gives clear orders to his/her inferiors. He or she expects a loyal execution of these orders without resistance. The paternalist chief takes his or her decisions as rapidly as the autocrat, but tries to explain the motives of his/her decisions to his/her subordinate and s/he answers all their questions. The consultative type listens to the executors' advice and opinions before taking a decision. Once decided, s/he expects everybody to co-operate at best, even if his or her advice was not followed. Finally, the democrat gathers the inferiors, confronts them with the problem and accepts a majority-decision rule. The respondents had to indicate which superior they preferred and which type corresponded to their actual superior. Finally, the occurrence of fear when the employee was expressing his or her disagreement with his or her superior was taken into account for the measurement of hierarchical distance. The more individuals prefer a consultative type of leadership and the less frequently people are afraid to express their disagreement with their chief, the lower the hierarchical distance is in society.

According to this index Latin-European (Italy, France, Belgium, Spain, etc.) and Latin-American countries in the neighbourhood of the Caribbean (Mexico, Venezuela, Colombia, etc.) together with black African and Arab countries expose a rather large hierarchical distance. German, Anglo-Saxon and Scandinavian countries are rather non-hierarchic. Asian countries are dispersed all over the sample. Israel and Austria have the lowest hierarchical distance.[14]

Differences in hierarchy have, of course, consequences on the religious, ideological, political and economic levels. In countries with a large hierarchical distance like France, a pointed pyramidal organization, where the number of hierarchical levels exceeds that of flattened pyramidal structures, occurs more frequently than, e.g., in West Germany (Bollinger and Hofstede, 1987: 98–9). This is also reflected in the wage spread between the lowest and highest salary in different enterprises, ranging from 3.7 to 5.5 in France as compared to 2.0 and 2.3 in West Germany in 1974 (Bollinger and Hofstede, 1987: 90).

Uncertainty avoidance and freedom

Mastering a yet unknown future in the most efficient way, is what a major part of the economics of uncertainty is about. Mastering uncertainty, however, is an objective phenomenon whose grip on people's activities differs across cultures according to their relative need – a subjective feeling – for security. This has to do with their perception of the future. As is the case for hierarchical distance, Hofstede also gives a psychological characterization of uncertainty avoidance. Some people feel more uncomfortable than others regarding the mysteries of future. Those who feel more anxious try to establish institutions to resolve this feeling of insecurity. These institutions can be of a technical, juridical or religious (ideological) nature. A less intense need to regulate the future, possibly in an illusory way, corresponds to a greater valuation of liberty. The famous dichotomy between regulation and liberty, repeated innumerable times by famous and less famous economists and philosophers, occurs here once again. The concept of liberty is, however, not opposed to hierarchy in Hofstede's conceptual scheme. It is opposed to the existence of a set of rules alleviating anxiety for future events, while hierarchy is based on the power of persons rather than rules.

In short, uncertainty avoidance is the cultural dimension measuring the degree of tolerance a culture has with respect to disquietude resulting from an unknown future (Bollinger and Hofstede, 1987: 103). The index resumes three questions from the questionnaire. The first refers to the degree of nervousness one experiences during the working hours. This degree of nervousness reflects the general disquietude of society as a whole with respect to the future. The second element of the uncertainty index has to do with career planning. The more people plan to stay for a longer time in the same company (more than five years), the greater the need for security. Finally, when it is generally accepted that the community's rules (in the present case the company's rules) are allowed to be violated if necessary, the need for security is assumed to be less intense.

Latin (American and European) countries, together with Japan, mostly need control of uncertainty. Germany and Arab countries are more or less in the middle. Scandinavian, Anglo-Saxon, South-Eastern Asian and developing countries (like black Africa) feel more for liberty. Contrary to hierarchical distance, uncertainty avoidance seems not to be directly related to a nation's wealth.

Individuality and community

Individualism pertains to societies in which the ties between individuals are loose: everyone is expected to look after himself or herself and his or her immediate family. Collectivism as its opposite pertains to societies in which people from birth onwards are integrated into strong, cohesive in-groups, which throughout people's lifetime continue to protect them in exchange for unquestioning loyalty. (Hofstede, 1991: 51)

Four questions of the survey were selected to construct an index of individuality. Sufficient time for personal and family-life and to live in a family-friendly environment are very important for individualists. An agreeable working environment with people who co-operate and good material conditions were assumed to characterize communitarianly oriented societies. The particular questions used to construct the index do not necessarily capture the essence of individualism or collectivism. They were chosen because they were the most important aspects of this dimension for IBM personnel (Hofstede, 1991: 52).

The picture of national differences can be summarized roughly as follows: the richer a country (in terms of per capita GNP), the more individualistically it is oriented. Of course, other factors, such as the influence of tradition and religion, play a mitigating role and explain why countries such as Japan, Singapore, Hong Kong and Taiwan do not reflect completely the general trend.

This dimension also has important consequences at the enterprise level. First of all the relations between employer and employees in a collectively oriented society originate from the common moral. These relations resemble the former parent–child relation and life in an extended family seems to be extended in the workplace. In individualist cultures, on the contrary, personal interest prevails. Secondly, commercial relations can be established on the basis of an equal treatment of all the partners or on the basis of privilege, as seems to be usual in Arabic countries. Privilege means that commercial pacts have to be preceded by other relations like, for example, friendship. Finally, individualist societies are based on the conflict model, while other cultures need social harmony. In Europe and the United States, conflicts are considered as salutary for everybody.

Femininity and masculinity

The opposition between masculinity and femininity also originates in the difference between social and individual needs. It is closely related to the former factor. However, both dimensions seem to shed light on different aspects of sociability and individuality. The opportunity for high earnings, recognition of your work and the opportunity for promotion and challenging work are important for the masculine side. Femininity refers to a good working relationship with the direct superior, good co-operation with one another, living in a family-friendly area and job security. Two of these items (living area and co-operation) also occurred in the community side of the preceding factor. In the present case, job recognition and job relations are especially opposed to each other, while formerly personal liberty and group adhesion were in question. Some may wonder – especially those who are living in a culture in which sexual differences are not attached to the mentioned differences in a similar fashion – why this dimension was indicated with those names. The explanation is rather simple: IBM personnel showed a remarkable sexual difference, across nationality, in their attitude towards this dimension (Hofstede, 1991: 82).

Japan turns out to be the most masculine country. Among the strong masculine countries one detects further: German countries, Caribbean countries (Venezuela, Mexico and Colombia) and Italy. Next one meets the Anglo-Saxon countries. Arab and Asian countries (except Japan, of course) occupy the middle position. Latin people (other than Italy) and black Africa seem to be feminine cultures. Most feminine are the Scandinavian countries together with The Netherlands.

At the economic level, ecological concern and Third World development aid seem to be more prevalent in feminine cultures, while economic growth is more appreciated by the masculine counterparts. At the enterprise level, the sexual difference seems to be reflected in the job quality. In masculine cultures improving job quality means creating promotion opportunities. Feminine cultures interpret humanizing work as creating an agreeable environment where co-operation thrives. Conflicts are resolved by discussion in feminine cultures, while they are tough and open in masculine countries. In this way one can understand the frequent occurrence of strikes in Anglo-Saxon countries as compared to the prevalence of social consultation in Scandinavian countries.

Management styles

Management styles can be discerned on the basis of a combination of hierarchical distance and individualistic spirit in society. The latter indicates the dependence on different groups to which one belongs, while the former refers to the dependence *vis-à-vis* persons in power. From this, different types of management can be derived. Firstly in developing countries people strongly depend on their clan and family, in which particular persons are entitled to power. These countries combine a great hierarchical distance with a strong feeling of communality. This type also occurs in Japan. Great hierarchical distance is combined with individualism in Latin European countries. Anglo-Saxon, German and Scandinavian countries also expose a good deal of individualism but combine it with only a small hierarchical distance. In Anglo-Saxon countries the initiative to consult comes from the chief while in German and

Scandinavian countries a participatory and democratic style prevails. Exceptions are Austria and Israel, with a high feeling of commonality combined with a low degree of hierarchical distance – this fact was already partly mentioned above.

Such differences have important implications for management methods. A famous method developed in the USA is the so-called 'management by objectives' (MBO) designed by Peter Drucker in his book of 1956, *The Practice of Management*. Such a style requires, however, a possibility to negotiate on the objectives with the superiors (a not too high hierarchical distance), a propensity to take risks (low level of uncertainty avoidance) and a desire for self-realization through tasks (masculinity). These cultural aspects were predominant in the USA but not necessarily in other countries. An adaptation of this management method is therefore required in other countries. For the application of MBO in Germany uncertainty avoidance is too great. To reach a higher level of uncertainty control another style of management was introduced. The decision-making power of the superior was replaced by a more collective and institutionalized agreement on objectives. Such mutually agreed objectives can play the part of a super-ego providing the required feeling of safety. This corresponded to the smaller hierarchical distance in Germany also. This method is called 'management by agreement on objectives'. The precipitate application of MBO in France during the 1960s also caused problems because the high hierarchical distance impeded the internalization of the objectives. A culturally more adapted management style had to be found.

Business organization

Business organizations can be classified according to their type of centralization of power and according to their degree of standardization and formalization of different functions. These aspects suit the present dimensions of hierarchy and uncertainty control. Structuring the enterprise as a market, as is done in Scandinavian and Anglo-Saxon countries, reflects a small hierarchical distance and a weak tendency to avoid uncertainty. Job relations are not centralized and none of the different functions in the factories is standardized. Extended family structure resembling organizations can be found in South-Eastern countries. While relations among individuals are strictly regulated and therefore predictable, working methods are free. The hierarchical distance is higher in such enterprises, but the loose regulation of working methods suits the weak need for mastering the future. Conversely, standardizing the working methods but in a decentralized manner – business as a machine – is typical for Germany. Finally, countries like Japan and France typically have bureaucratic and pyramidal organizations: they combine strong hierarchical relations with an attempt to regulate everything strictly.

The differences in conceptions of industrial democracy can be understood from these cultural dimensions. Informal and spontaneous participation methods are preferred in countries with small hierarchical distance which are not risk-averse. The German Mitbestimmungs model is an experiment in getting control over uncertainty by formalizing the democracy. Where hierarchical distance is great, institutionalization of industrial democracy can only be the work of an enlightened dictator (at the enterprise or political level). But such an imposed democracy risks disappearing together with its inspirer.

Towards an intercultural business ethics

Hofstede has accepted an enormous challenge. Trying to measure cultural differences in an inductive manner is a risky business. Through the lack of any well-developed theory of cultures, a lot of unconsidered theoretical assumptions and normative meanings will enter the scene. The operationalization of concepts such as hierarchical distance, risk avoidance, femininity and individuality cannot be but very selective and based on cultural a prioris. As Hofstede correctly remarks, an inquiry about cultural determinants cannot but be itself culturally determined. Indeed the comparison of a Chinese value survey (composed by Chinese social scientists from Hong Kong and Taiwan) revealed a fifth dimension not detected by the IBM survey: Far Eastern countries are more oriented towards the long term, while Western countries are rather oriented towards the short term. This can be seen from their higher valuation of thrift and perseverance. This dimension is related with the Confucianist attitude in the East. This forgotten factor can contribute towards understanding Far Eastern entre- preneurship and its role in the growth of the 'Five Dragons' (Hong Kong, Taiwan, Japan, South Korea and Singapore). The discovery of the forgotten Confucianist dimension shows the limits of inductive research. Hofstede's method, being imperfect, nevertheless demonstrates very well the thesis that management must integrate cultural differentiation in its theory, strategy and practice.

As a consequence of his inquiry Hofstede foresees a shift of economic towards cultural competition among business corporations. What can be made of this evolution from a normative or ethical point of view? Is a category like competition well suited to define the relations between cultural entities? Such a narrow application of Western categories like competition – and maybe management itself – bears witness, according to a lot of anthropologists (Latouche, 1986; 1989; Verhelst, 1990), to a disrespect for other cultural specifics. Mahieu (1990) illustrates, for example, how in the Ivory Coast the establishment of competitive market relations in an environment where gifts among members of extended families are a central part of what we would call socio-economic relations, had disastrous consequences for the original African communal system of values.

If we want to develop an intercultural business ethics and not just a sociology or psychology of national business cultures, we must be able to go beyond national and corporate cultures. This ethical transgression does not necessarily imply a point of view above all cultures, but at least a possibility to take distance with regard to one's own culture and to place oneself in the position of the other. This attitude of distance and empathy is necessary to engage in a common reflection and dialogue on the truth and the meaning of different cultural presuppositions. The model of the market with its assumptions of cultural relativism and competition is by its own logic not able to create the conditions for an authentic intercultural dialogue and exchange. We need the model of an ethical community to build up within the corporations an institutional framework for intercultural dialogue and exchange.

7.2.3. The story of Europe: from business to community?

As we have seen, the notion of community can be applied to very different groups. It can be applied to the firm itself or to a social and territorial unit, which plays the role of environment or of stakeholder in the firm. This territorial community may be a local network or a region or a nation or even the world as a whole. In this section we will examine in what sense we can apply the notion of community to the case of Europe. As an integrated market Europe creates a new and competitive environment for business; as a political institution it stimulates, constrains and socializes economic freedom; as a multi-cultural space it differentiates the markets and regions. As Europe is at the same time a market, a political structure and a cultural space, we have to analyse again the integrative process in the light of the synergy between economics, politics and culture. The story of Europe demonstrates that the idea of economic integration without sufficient social and cultural integration creates a blind alley. The so-called democratic deficit, the aversion for bureaucratic regulation and the fear of losing cultural identity are the consequences of the present imbalance of European integration. Economic integration asks for an appropriate form of social and cultural integration. The alternative to global integration is in our view the disintegration of Europe into a competitive and aggressive multi-nationalism. This alternative seems to be in conflict with the idea of an ethical community and is not very attractive for business in the long term either.

The history of economic integration in Europe is a good illustration of the strength and the narrowness of an economic theory of social change (Koslowski, 1989: 173–80). The core of this theory is that technological and economic factors are the origin and the ultimate determinants of social change. The political conclusion is that economics is the lever to change society. This general understanding can be integrated equally well in a Marxist theory of social revolution as in a capitalist and reformist theory of social change. Indeed, it seems to be a conviction deeply embedded in EC policies. Even if the aims of European integration were non-economic, the means have always been economic. Maybe there was some doubt within the heads of the founding fathers about the correctness of the idea. But looking back at the history of the European integration in the second part of the twentieth century, we see technological and economic dynamics as the major force to break down some of the national barriers.

Politics by means of economics

At the origin of the actual EC lies the European Coal and Steel Community (ECSC), founded in 1951. It created in the six participating states a common market for two basic products of heavy industry. The founding fathers of the ECSC clearly wanted to realize more than a common market for two products. Coal and steel were basic products for rebuilding Europe. Control over heavy industry had been one of the main causes of the three wars which harassed Europe during the preceding eighty years. By creating a common market for coal and steel, the founders hoped to solve conflicts about the control of major industrial areas (e.g. the Ruhr in Germany) by co-operation and diplomacy instead of violence and war. They were inspired by a European ideal: co-operation would guarantee lasting prosperity and peace. A European arena of peace and welfare would function as an attractive example, bringing about peace and welfare in other parts of the world.

The Cold War incited the member states of the ECSC to think about co-operation for defence matters too. This would necessitate political co-operation as well, bringing about a transmission of national sovereign power to a federative European authority: the European Defence Community (EDC). Strong resistance in France, and a better international atmosphere after the death of Stalin and the end of the Korean war, caused the abrupt end of the EDC project.

In the aftermath of the EDC crisis, the Benelux countries launched the idea of stimulating European integration by a stronger economic integration, in three phases. First of all, a customs union had to be realized. Secondly, a common economic policy had to be developed. This implied a common agricultural policy and the harmonization of economic legislation, in order to create the same conditions for entrepreneurial activity and avoid unfair competition. Finally, the movement of persons, commodities, services and capital had to be made completely free. This project of the Benelux countries led to the Treaty of Rome (1957), by which the European Economic Community (EEC) was founded.

During the 1960s, the European integration movement concentrated on the creation of a common market. Political institutions were created, but their power was limited. There was distrust towards strong institutions, which would take over too much of national sovereignty. The Council of Ministers, for instance, had the power to take decisions; yet the unanimity rule for important matters prevented the replacement of national sovereignty by a supranational power. Anyhow, the creation of a customs union proved to be successful: on 1 January 1968, internal tariffs were abolished and common external tariffs were fixed.

An important aspect of the creation of a common market was agricultural policy. To create fair competition, it was necessary that food prices were the same in the member states, because food prices determine the level of wages. Besides, a common market for agricultural products was an important objective in itself, food being a basic and strategic product.

The further realization of an internal market remained the leading objective of European policy during the 1970s and the 1980s. The necessity of a common economic policy led to the concept of an Economic and Monetary Union (EMU), as a further target. The economic crisis of the 1970s thwarted these plans and only in 1979 did the European Monetary System (EMS), a weaker version of the EMU, become operative.

The idea of the EMU was resumed in 1985 by the Single European Act. Particularly, the aspect of an economic union was pushed forward. The European Commission published a White Paper, setting out some 270 measures to realize the Single Market by the end of 1992. Although the customs union was already realized, there was still a long way to go before the movement of persons, goods, services and capital would be completely free. Legislation concerning product standards, professional qualifications and indirect tax rates still differed strongly among member states. The initiatives of the Commission, based on the White Paper, were aimed at removing these obstacles gradually. The Treaty of Maastricht prolonged Project '1992' by creating the vision of a monetary union by 1 January 1999.

The above survey shows that economic integration is central in the process of European unification. After the debacle of the EDC, full stress was put on the creation of a common market. Readjustments to bring in other aspects of social organization at the same level of integration only took place when the divergence between economic integration and these other aspects became too large. The predominance of economics appears in two-fold fashion: first, integration in other fields is a correction of an imminent imbalance; secondly, as a correction, the integration in other fields never reaches the same pervasion as economic integration.

The search for community

In the field of social policy, the first initiatives were taken only at the beginning of the 1970s. During the 1950s and the 1960s, there was a widespread belief that everyone automatically would benefit from growing welfare in a growing economy. Article 118 of the EEC Treaty mentioned a lot of topics in the social field, on which close co-operation was desirable. But the Commission could only give advice on these topics: it lacked any regulative power. Moreover, for the narrow domain in which regulation was possible, decisions were to be taken unanimously.

During the 1970s, a change in the imposed passivity took place. In 1974, a Programme of Social Action was adopted. Directives concerning redundancy, equal pay of male and female workers, safety and health in the workplace, etc. were enacted. The Commission also wanted to develop programmes to push back the growing unemployment in the EC. Finance for this programme was found in the Social Fund and in the newly established Regional Fund. In the late 1970s, resistance from the British government, among others, prevented further initiatives of the Commission resulting in the adoption of Directives. This was, for instance, the case for the Vredeling Directive, concerning the consultation and information of workers in multi-national corporations, as well as for the project of the European limited liability company.

Social policy received a new impulse in the Single European Act (1985). Article 118A gave the Commission the authority to take initiatives in order to harmonize legislation on working conditions. Moreover, a qualified majority would suffice to enact regulation in this area. Article 118B asks the Commission to stimulate the dialogue between the social partners on the European level. The fact that talks between the social partners started again was a progress, in comparison with the previous period. But this did not result in supranational agreements on working conditions.

The concrete results emerging from the new possibilities created by the Single Act were not very spectacular. Nevertheless the discussion on the necessity of a social dimension in the EC was boosted. People realized that stronger social cohesion would be necessary while the Single Market was being implemented gradually. Several new terms (social dimension, social cohesion, social space) expressed this search for a more social Europe. In 1989 this led to the promulgation of a 'Community Charter of Fundamental Social Rights'. This could have been a landmark in the evolution of European social policy, but the Charter is only a declaration of intent, without any effective legal force. Moreover, the UK did not sign the Charter.

Adversaries of a European social policy often refer to the principle of subsidiarity[15] to defend their position: social policy is a matter for national governments, not for Europe. Most authors admit that a complete harmonization of social legislation is not feasible. Nevertheless, the European institutions and the national governments should co-operate to reach a minimum level of social rights. Minimum standards should take into account national circumstances such as the mean income, the cost of living and the strength of the economy. In that way, rich countries cannot put pressure on poor countries to meet standards with which they cannot comply, nor can poor countries profit from the very low social standards they are used to.

Parallel to the lack of social policy, there is a lack of political power. For a long time, the unanimity rule paralysed decision-making in the Council. The lack of real legislative power of the European Parliament is well known. In the beginning of the 1970s, the European Political Co-operation (EPC) was set up to cover this lack of political guidance. One of the main objectives was to promote co-operation in the field of foreign policy. But typically, this EPC functioned separately from the existing institutional framework of the EC. Only in 1985 did the Single European Act incorporate political co-operation as part of the EC. The Single Act enlarged the competence of the EC: a common environmental policy could be developed and there could be more room for a social policy. These new domains of policy created new executive competence for the Commission; the European Parliament gained some new competence as well. Still, the democratic ideal of a European legislative institution, and a fully fledged European government, was far from realized.

The most underdeveloped field in European integration is culture. The EEC Treaty merely mentions culture. When the EC deals with cultural products, there is a propensity to treat them as economic products for which the same market rules apply. Initiatives to realize a unified market for broadcasting and to abolish a fixed price for books illustrate this conception of cultural products. The same economic bias can be found in the policies of higher education which are mainly defined in terms of the labour market and the competition with the USA and Japan.

Some want the EC not to act in the cultural field at all. However, as the process of economic integration cannot but affect culture and vice versa, this is not a good solution. Instead the EC should develop a global vision on integration, in which social and cultural aspects have their proper place. A proper cultural policy should also enhance the involvement of citizens in the European project. The necessity of a greater involvement of the citizens was mentioned in the Tindemans Report (1975), but a proper cultural policy did not begin before the adoption of the Single European Act (1985). This cultural policy puts the accent on the creation of economic conditions that stimulate cultural development and exchange: technology and infrastructure are subsidized, and there is support of cultural manifestations and educational programmes in the cultural sector. Programmes for the exchange of students have been set up and institutions have been stimulated to co-operate in research and common curricula.

A major problem for a cultural policy is the prevailing EC tradition of harmonization and standardization in the economic field. Contrary to this logic of standardization, a cultural policy requires respect for the diversity of cultures. Rather than trying to create one specific European culture, the EC should create circumstances in which the different European languages and cultures can survive and develop. Only the interaction of initiatives taken at the grassroot level (local, regional or national level), and a European framework that encourages these initiatives, can guarantee that cultural diversity will survive in Europe. A good interpretation of the principle of subsidiarity seems to be crucial here.

The subsidiarity principle – which says that all things that can be done on a lower level of decision and action, must not be taken over by a higher structure of regulation – sets a limit to direct political intervention in cultural matters. It is not the task of the state to control and determine culture. But it may be good politics to create conditions for a rich diversity of cultures and to defend culture against pollution and deterioration.[16]

The relation of politics to cultural diversity and richness may be analogous to the political concern for our ecological environment. Conditions which are undermining the vitality of a culture – relativism, indifference, intolerance, standardization, superficiality – must be discouraged while conditions which are necessary for the conservation and richness of culture – plurality and identity, reflection and imagination, tradition and openness – must be encouraged. Culture is not the result of politics or the product of economics. But as a public good it requires some political regulation and as a scarce good it has some economic value. Beyond this, culture is in its core meaning the creative expression of community values, traditions and imagination. But is there really a shared system of values and traditions which could function as a common resource for European cultural identity and diversity, reflection and imagination?

The European version of morality
Isn't it an illusion to believe in something more than a common market in Europe? Anyhow, nation-specific values and habits will not disappear. In the words of Ester and Halman: 'French people will continue to drink wine, while in Germany they will continue to eat Sauerkraut mit Wurst and the English will continue their typical English breakfast' (quoted in Ashford and Timms, 1992: 4). But cultural values are more than local habits. If languages and national habits will not be 'harmonized', what can be the content of a shared European value system?

One can refer (as was done at the Copenhagen summit in 1973 in a declaration about the European identity) to universal values such as the respect for democracy, human rights, social justice, diversity of cultures, free intellectual dialogue, principles of constitutional state. Today we may also add ecological concern to the list. Those ethical values go beyond national interest although the preference for any one of them may vary in different nations. In fact, ethical values can be seen as a platform for a universal and integral humanism or as the necessary conditions for a world-wide, international community. One may object that because of their universal character those values are not specific enough to define a European identity. And conversely, if those values are typically European, then they cannot be universal. Moreover, the identification of universality with European values is a dangerous mistake which leads to ethnocentrism and imperialism. Although it is true that we may not identify universality and Europeanness, this does not mean that both exclude one another. The objection erroneously assumes that universal values can be completely detached from their historical and particular context. If we give up this supposition, we may be able to formulate at least two arguments in favour of a supranational, universally oriented value system with a European dimension. The first argument is historical, the other more philosophical.

All these ethical or 'universal' values have an historical anchorage in European tradition. This does not mean that these values cannot be rooted within other non-European cultural traditions. On the contrary, some of these values may even have much stronger motivational support within other cultural traditions, as for example the ecological concern in the Indian way of life. But the fact remains that for Europeans the most effective way to internalize these values is to reconstruct them from within the perspectives, arguments, confrontations and not least the failures of their own history. In spite of all national differences, values in Europe have common origins. A few examples are the Greek and the Jewish-Christian traditions; the scholastic synthesis of Latin, Greek and Christian values; the modern cultural programmes of the Renaissance and the Enlightenment; the belief in scientific and technological progress; the liberal and social emancipation ideologies of the nineteenth century; and today, the ecological movement. Through all those traditions and ideological conflicts, the European value system has been constructed and deconstructed and recombined in very different structures and lifestyles. But every new expression is partly built upon elements of the older traditions. This chain of influences gives our values always a particular origin and historical setting, even if they claim universal meaning and truth.

The second argument for an integrated European culture has to do with the multi-cultural character of the world community. How, in the context of the plurality of regions and nations, is a world-wide multi-cultural society possible? The answer will depend on the meaning of this multi-cultural society. A first meaning is suggested by the term itself. Multi-cultural means the mere coexistence of cultures without integration but overarched by a kind of supracultural and neutral cosmopolitanism. In this view, pluralism is at most a synonym for relativism accepting all cultural preferences as equally good. If this is the case, why should there be a dialogue or a search for truth and morality? Why should there be a European version of morality if there is a priori no justification or argument for moral values? As a consequence of this view there would be no intrinsic moral argument for the cultural integration of Europe; however, there could only be an economic argument: cultural integration as a means for the creation of a common market.

But there is another position. We can think of a world community in terms of an *intercultural* society – society being a network of interaction and confrontation between different cultures in their search for morality and truth. As Koslowski points out: 'Die kommende Weltkultur wird plural sein im Sinne einer Weltkultur der Vielheit der Nationalen Kulturen, aber nicht im Sinne einer einheitlich pluralistischen Welteinheitskultur. Die kommende Weltkultur wird Pluralität von sich ihrer identität gewisser Einzelkulturen sein oder sie wird nicht Kultur sein.' (Koslowski, 1989: 188) In the context of an intercultural society, the European version of universality and morality may be one of the voices in the choir of cultures with a potential for dialogue. If we believe that European history and tradition is a particular and rich source for cultural and moral dialogue in the world community, then we have a sufficient argument to foster European cultural integration. Moreover, the necessity for Europe to create within its own national diversity a kind of intercultural dialogue, makes the case of Europe also paradigmatic for the world integration. Europe has in this sense a cultural mission.

The present value system in Europe

Cultural integration does not only presuppose common moral and spiritual traditions but the will of people to invest time and energy in the development of these resources. Do European people want to engage in intercultural dialogue? Is there enough trust and communal spirit? Or are individualism, nationalism, intolerance or materialism so dominant that the conditions for the development of an inspiring cultural context are not yet present? The answer to this question can only come from empirical research on values and attitudes such as, for instance, the studies done by the European Value System Study Group (EVSSG). This Study Group organized in 1981 and in 1990–1 a survey on the basis of a representative sample of nearly 15,000 interviews.

What kind of values do citizens of member states of the EC find important in their lives? Results of the survey have been worked out for different countries.[17] The book by Sheena Ashford and Noel Timms, *What Europe Thinks. A study of Western European values* (1992), contains inter-country comparisons. We get a lot of information about similarities and dissimilarities across the European countries in work ethic, family life, religious belief, moral permissiveness, and political participation. In their conclusion the authors take up the initial question: Is it legitimate to talk of European values at all, or should we focus instead on the divisive nature of the value systems which underpin public thinking in our ten participant countries? Their final answer leaves the question open:

Certainly our findings have revealed many areas in which the national feeling of countries in Western Europe have differed: witness the strong commitment to protecting the environment shown in the Netherlands, the pronounced religiosity of the Irish, or the low levels of national pride expressed in West Germany. In a more general sense a clear distinction can be made between, on the one hand, the countries of Northern Europe where there is extensive support for individualistic values and, on the other hand, the countries of Southern Europe, Northern Ireland and the Irish Republic where religiosity and conventional views are most pronounced. Yet at the same time many areas in the Values Study reveal remarkable similarities in values. A primary commitment to family life is found throughout Europe, countries tend to hold similar views on gender roles, and attitudes to economic issues and the role of the State are broadly the same. Both similarities and differences exist amongst the national Systems of Europe and it is not immediately obvious whether consensus or dissensus prevails. (Ashford and Timms, 1992: 108–9)[18]

This general conclusion is not surprising and does not say much about the chances for a further European integration but neither does it exclude this possibility. In fact a good intercultural dialogue implies a mixture of similarities and dissimilarities. The crucial obstacle to engage in an intercultural exchange lies in the lack of trust in each other or in the fear to lose national identity. Trust is the cement of community relations. The Value Study gives for 1990–1 some interesting indications. The fear of losing cultural identity and national interests as a consequence of European integration must be weighed against the view that a truly unified Europe will protect cultural identity and national economic interests. People were asked to weigh these two viewpoints on a seven-point scale (a low score indicates agreement with the former view, a high score indicates agreement with the latter). The European average of 4.7 suggests that on the whole people prefer the integration of Europe. In each country the balance is pro-European. The least enthusiastic members of the EC are Great Britain (mean score 4.0) and the most enthusiastic country is Italy (mean score 5.3). Age and gender, according to the authors, make little difference to attitudes to the EC, but non-manual workers are a little more positive than manual workers, left-wingers are more positive than those on the political right, while, most dramatically, Roman Catholics are more likely than Protestants to believe in a united Europe.

The issue of trust has been extensively investigated. On the level of individual relations, Europeans have a very high level of complete trust in their families (77 per cent) especially in Britain (92 per cent), Northern Ireland and the Republic of Ireland (92 per cent) while France forms an exception with its comparatively lower position (57 per cent). But trust towards others drops dramatically (33 per cent) and is substituted by a disposition of wariness. The lack of trust may be even more impressive if we look at the analysis of people's trust in institutions. With respect to each institution respondents were asked to state how much confidence they had: a great deal, quite a lot, not very much, none at all. We reproduce here the table of Europe's lack of trust (Table 7.3).

The problem of trust in institutions seems to be a real challenge in Europe. Explaining the lack of trust by referring to a wave of growing individualism may be only part of the truth. Besides individualism also new forms of social sensibility are noticed. In fact, while a claim for equal work rights for young and old or for natives and immigrants is not largely accepted, disapproval of specific injustices such as discrimination against physically handicapped people when jobs are scarce is very high (Ashford and Timms, 1992: 25). A lot of ambiguity is also noticed in the political sphere. Results from the Value Study show that the majority of Europeans are not

Table 7.3 Europe's lack of confidence in institutions

Respondents answering 'not very much' and 'none at all' (%)

	Total	Great Britain	Northern Ireland	Republic of Ireland	Germany	Netherlands	Belgium	France	Italy	Spain	Portugal
Church	49	57	20	28	60	68	50	48	37	47	43
Army	52	19	21	39	60	68	66	42	52	57	57
Education	39	52	34	27	46	34	27	33	51	38	48
Law	50	46	44	52	34	37	55	41	68	53	58
Press	61	86	84	64	66	63	55	60	61	48	63
Trade unions	62	73	76	57	64	46	62	64	66	58	69
Police	34	23	20	14	30	27	49	33	33	42	55
Parliament	55	53	54	49	49	46	57	47	68	56	65
Civil service	58	55	42	40	61	52	57	48	73	62	66
Major companies	47	50	52	47	62	51	49	30	37	50	53
Social security system	45	66	52	41	30	30	32	29	62	60	51
EC	39	51	50	29	52	44	33	24	26	44	41
NATO	52	39	46	40	58	42	43	31	46	72	61

Source: Ashford and Timms (1992: 16)

very interested in politics but on the other hand there is very high support for protest movements (ecology, human rights, anti-apartheid, anti-nuclear, disarmament, women's movement) and a growing participation in the activities of such movements. The same mixture of individualism and moral sensibility is reflected in the work ethic. Certainly, there is the individualist striving for success reflected, for instance, in the clear preference for a performance-related pay system.[19] But on the other side people accept in their work a moral obligation to perform their work diligently, look for social contact in their work, and ask for greater participation in the running of business and industry.

The challenge for business

Can it be that just this mixture of individualism and social participation is one of the keystones of European character?[20] The social market-economy — what is called by Albert (1991) the 'Rhenish' model of capitalism in contrast with the American model of capitalism — is an institutional expression of this European search for balance between individual and community values. But the lack of trust in the prevailing political structures and socio-economic institutions indicates that the European model needs change and reform. This change can go towards a more market-oriented system and approach the American model of capitalism. Or it can lean towards the Japanese business culture based on a strong collective consciousness to promote the firm's long-term objectives. But both of these directions seem to be alien to the European character with its mixture of individualism and social sensibility. Europe has to rebalance its own 'mixed' structure and business culture (Danton de Rouffignac, 1991). The rebuilding of Eastern Europe and the challenge of European integration will be the test cases for the European capability to find a new symbiosis of business and community for the next millennium.

Has the economic mission of business much to do with the cultural challenge of Europe? If it is true that business always internalizes some cultural values of its environment and in its turn changes deeply that cultural environment by the creation of products and services, then business is not an outsider in the process. The making or breaking of Europe's cultural identity is not the exclusive prerogative of the political sphere, nor is it an exclusive task for universities, cultural and religious institutions. European integration will be the result of a good interaction of the three spheres inspired by the search for a shared transnational value perspective.

Notes

1. I would like to thank my colleagues Erik Schokkaert (Leuven), Francis P. McHugh (Cambridge) and Brian Harvey (Manchester) for their helpful suggestions and corrections of the first draft. I am also greatly indebted for the second part of the text (community in practice) to Luc Van Liedekerke, Bart Capéau and Renaat Hanssens, assistants in the 'Centrum voor Economie en Ethiek' at Louvain (Belgium).
2. We accept in this context the holistic premise that the wholeness or more precisely the relation primarily defines the meaning of the parts and not the other way around.

3. We introduced in the scheme democracy as a more concrete form of political regulation. Other forms such as dirigism and authoritarianism may also be seen as expressions of political regulation.

4. This tension between procedural and substantial ethics is one of the issues at stake in the debate between social contract philosophers (Rawls, Nozick, Gauthier, Van Parijs) and communitarians (McIntyre, Sandel, Walzer, Taylor, Rorty).

5. Boswell resumes Durkheim's manifesto for public institutions in six points (Boswell, 1990: 20): (1) New or reformed corporations should provide a wide range of participation and solidarity-enhancing services for the people inside them. (2) The corporations should be national or even international in scope. (3) The corporations would need to be in direct contact with the state, but emphatically not as to be absorbed by it. (4) They should be able to educate their members towards a wider social life and public involvements. (5) They should (and probably anyway would) develop into 'one of the essential bases of our political organization' perhaps even 'the elementary division of the state'. A further implication was (6) an overcoming of the employer/trade union conflict, and the emergence of new or restored forms of self-regulation or associative management of enterprises.

6. Another and more realistic formulation of the moral solidarity rule has been given by the American Catholic Bishops in their Pastoral Letter on justice where they say: 'The fundamental moral criterion for all economic decisions, policies and institutions is this: they must be at the service of all people, especially the poor.' (*Economic Justice for All*, Pastoral Letter on Catholic Social Teaching and the US Economy, Washington, 1986: 12). This formulation is more realistic than the Kantian imperative because it takes into account the real context of unequal power between the rich and the poor. Universality and dignity means therefore not only a sense of formal equality but a preferential concern for the poor or those whose dignity and rights are most threatened.

7. The French economist Kolm has given in his book *La bonne économie* (1984) a theoretical foundation for the full integration of altruism into economics. Another inspiring effort to design a new paradigm integrating economics and ethics is Etzioni's *The Moral Dimension. Toward a New Economics* (1988). But those are not isolated efforts. There is a search for various perspectives to integrate altruistic motives and theories of justice within the framework of economic thinking. This search is accomplished under different names and with different accents, to mention only a few: humanistic economics (Lutz), socio-economics (Etzioni), ethical economy (Koslowski), communitarian economics (Gui, Boswell), normative economics (Sen, Schokkaert), personalistic economics (Maritain, Mounier), economics of the common good (Jordan), etc. All these efforts have in common the premise that ethics is a dimension of economics.

8. The libertarian mistake is to reverse the order and to claim that social contract is the basis of community, that trust is the result of social contract or that free exchange will generate markets for solidarity. This may be true if we live in a world of real equality and symmetry between persons, families, nations, sexes, generations. But this is an imaginary world. The real world is one of unequal power. Transforming the relation of domination into one of co-operation is also a task for government regulation. It is a mission for every organization that tries to appeal to our sense of loyalty and community.

9. The South–North Network Cultures and Development was set up following an international conference held under the auspices of the Commission of the European Communities in 1985 on the role of culture in the Lomé Convention, which associates the twelve countries of the EC with countries from Africa, the Caribbean and the Pacific. From the beginning the South–North Network has been non-confessional and has no specific

links with any political party, yet it is explicitly open to all forms of spirituality. It is an NGO (non-governmental organization). The founders of the South–North Network are people from Latin America, Asia, Africa, North America and Europe, from both the NGO and the academic world. They share a concern about the irrelevance of 'development models' as proposed or even imposed on non-Western societies. They believe that it is imperative to set up both theoretical and practical alternatives and to change certain aspects of development co-operation and NGO partnership. The international co-ordination of the South–North Network Cultures and Development is carried out in Brussels, Belgium. It ensures networking and facilitates communication among all local networks and members. It publishes an international journal (*CULTURES AND DEVELOPMENT – Quid Pro Quo*). It co-ordinates and synthesizes research-action done at continental level. It carries out training, advocacy and consultancy at the international level.

10. The French economist F. Perroux is the father of the growth pole theory with his article of 1955, 'La notion de pôle de croissance'. Perroux's theory was integrated in a broader theory of socio-economic progress where the intertwining relations between social and economic progress were more fully articulated (see Bouckaert, 1973). The later use of the growth pole theory was more exclusively economic-oriented.

11. The Socratic idea of maieutics is also used by Charles McCoy and his colleagues in the Center for Ethics and Social Policy (Berkeley) as a method for moral audits in an enterprise.

12. The results of this inquiry were first published in G. Hofstede, *Culture's consequences: International Differences in Work-Related Values*, Sage Publications, Beverly Hills, 1980. The present summary is based on a French transcription of these results (D. Bollinger and G. Hofstede, *Les Différences Culturelles dans le Management, Comment chaque pays gère-t-il ses hommes?*, Ed. de l'organisations, Paris, 1987), which concentrates on culture's consequences for management. Recently G. Hofstede published a new book, which places the results of the survey in a broader perspective (G. Hofstede, *Cultures and Organizations, Software of the Mind*, McGraw-Hill Book Company, London, 1991).

13. As a consequence of the identification of nation with culture differences in values across different nations are labelled as cultural differences, even if they are rooted in practices and socio-economic relations which are alien to that 'culture', in a broader sense of the word. One can doubt whether the present development of the 'Five Dragons' really is rooted in their culture, even if this development – inevitably, according to Hofstede's own model of culturally determined economic practices – bears traces of that culture.

14. The place of the former can be understood through the presence of the kibbutz movement, the co-operatives which were adored by more than one Western egalitarian in less suspected times. The outstanding non-hierarchical performance of Austria seems puzzling, however (see also Bollinger and Hofstede, 1987: 207–8).

15. The subsidiarity principle is a well-known principle in the catholic social teaching. In *Quadragesimo Anno* (1931, nr. 17) Pope Pius XI defends the principle that what individual people or small communities can do by their own initiative and by their own effort may not be taken away and transferred to a higher or bigger community level.

16. For an overview of the animated discussion between advocates of communitarism and liberalism on this point, see Kymlicka, 1990: 199–237.

17. Greece and Luxemburg did not participate in the inquiry; Denmark only in 1981 and Portugal only in 1991.

18. A factor analysis of the 1981 data revealed consistent patterns in the value preferences across countries (Harding and Phillips, 1986) but this does not say much about the spread

of these patterns in different countries. Therefore, Ashford and Timms use an index of dissimilarity for measuring differences between national responses. Comparing the index of 1981 to the index of 1990, they find little movement towards either convergence or divergence in values. In the Belgian report of the Value Study Delooz and Kerkhofs (Kerkhofs *et al.*, 1992: 287–338) detect a significant shift towards growing tolerance in the index of moral permissivity (measuring tolerance towards abortion, euthanasia, dishonesty, theft, etc.).

19. Seventy-two per cent of people agree that it is fair to pay a more efficient secretary more money while only 22 per cent find it unfair to pay different rates for the same job.
20. Personalism as a Continental social philosophy and ethics (associated with the names of Scheler, Maritain, Mounier, Marcel, Landsberg, Ricoeur and a lot of other European thinkers) is an example of a philosophical effort to clarify this European dialectic of person and community (Bouckaert and Bouckaert, 1992).

Bibliography and further reading

Albert, M., (1991). *Capitalisme contre capitalisme*. Paris, Ed. du Seuil.

Ashford, S. and Timms, N. (1992). *What Europe Thinks. A study of Western European values.* Aldershot, Dartmouth.

Bastijns, T. and Van de Craen, L., *Tussentijdse evaluatie* Plato-Special, SPK, juni 1992.

Bergman, E. M., Maier, G. and Tödtling, F. (1991). *Regions Reconsidered. Economic Networks, Innovation and local development in industrialised countries.* Mansell, London.

Bollinger, D. and Hofstede, G. (1987). *Les Différences culturelles dans le Management. Comment chaque pays gère-t-il ses hommes?, Ed. de l'organisations.* Paris.

Boswell, V. (1990). *Community and the Economy. The theory of public co-operation.* Routledge.

Bouckaert, L. (1973). La pensée économique de François Perroux, in: *Mondes en Développement*, 1, pp. 163–94.

Bouckaert, L., (red.) (1990). *Terugkeer van de ethiek*. Leuven, Acco.

Bouckaert, L. and Bouckaert, G. (eds.) (1992). *Metafysiek en Engagement. Een personalistische visie op gemeenschap en economie.* Acco, Leuven.

Bouckaert, L. and Schokkaert, E. (eds.) (1992). *Winst en waarden. Een ethische agenda voor het Zelfstandig Ondernemen.* Acco, Leuven.

Boulding, K. (1968). *Beyond Economics. Essays on Society, Religion and Ethics.* Michigan.

Boulding, K. (1970). *Economics as a Science*, McGraw-Hill, New York.

Boulding, K. (1973). 'The Economy of Love and Fear'. A preface to *Grant Economics*. California.

Bradach, J. L. and Eccles, R. G. (1989). 'Price, Authority and Trust: from ideal types to plural forms', in: *Annual Review of Sociology*, 1989, 97–118.

Caselli, L. (1991). *From Competition to Co-operation Between Large and Small Companies: a common social responsibility in*, Harvey E. A., 199–211.

Cheal, D. (1988). *The Gift Economy*. London, Routledge.

Danton de Rouffignac, P. (1991). *Europe's New Business Culture.* London, Pitman.

Donckels, R. and Courtmans, A. (1990). 'Big brother is watching over you: the counselling of growing SMEs in Belgium', in *Entrepreneurship & Regional Development*, 2 (1990), 211–23.

Drucker, F. P. (1956). The Practice of Management. London, Heinemann.

Durkheim, E. (1893, 1960). *The Division of Labour in Society.* Glencoe, Free Press, Ill. (translated from the French *De la division du travail social*).

Economic Justice for All. (1986). Pastoral letter on Catholic social teaching and the U.S. economy. National Conference of Catholic Bishops. Washington, D.C.

Etzioni, A. (1988). *The Moral Dimension. Towards a new economics.* New York, Macmillan.

Gui, B. (1987). Eléments pour une définition d'économie communautaire. In: *Notes et Documents*. Rome, Institut Internationale Jacques Maritain, 32–42.

Hamlin, A. P. (1986). *Ethics, Economics and the State.* Brighton, Wheatsheaf Books.

Harding, S., and Phillips, D. (1986). *Contrasting Values in Western Europe.* London, Macmillan.

Harvey, B., Van Luijk, H., Corbetta, G. (1991). *Market, Morality and Company Size.* Kluwer, Dordrecht.

Hermans, W., E. A. (ed.) (1991). *Leidraad bij de geschiedenis van de Europese Integratie.* Alkmaar, Europees Platform voor het Nederlands anderwijs.

Hofstede, G. (1980). *Culture's Consequences: International differences in work-related values.* Sage Publications, Beverly Hills.

Hofstede, G. (1991). *Cultures and Organizations, Software of the Mind.* McGraw-Hill Book Company, London.

Jordan, B. (1989). *The Common Good. Citizenship, Morality and Self-Interest.* Oxford, Basil Blackwell.

Keeley, M. (1988). *A Social-contract Theory of Organizations.* Indiana, University of Notre Dame Press.

Kerkhofs, J., Dobbelaere, K., Voye, L., Bawin-Legros, B. (1991). *De versnelde ommekeer. De waarden van Vlamingen, Walen en Brusselaars in de jaren negentig.* Lannoo, Tielt.

Kolm, S. C. (1984). *La bonne économie. La réciprocité générale.* Paris, P.U.F.

Kolm, S. C. (1986). *L'homme pluridimensionnel. Pour une économie de l'esprit.* Paris, Albin Michel.

Königs, R. (1968). *The Community.* London, Routledge & Kegan Paul (translated from the German *Grundformen der Gesellschaft: Die Gemeinde*, Hamburg).

Koslowski, P. (1988). *Prinzipien der ethischen Ökonomie. Grundlegung der Wirtschaftsethik und der auf die Ökonomie bezogenen Ethik.* Tübingen, J. C. B. Mohr.

Koslowski, P. (1989). *Wirtschaft als Kultur: Wirtschaftskultur und Wirtschaftsethik in der Postmoderne.* Wien, Passagen-Verlag.

Kymlicka, W. (1990). *Contemporary Political Philosophy.* Oxford, Clarendon.

Latouche, S. (1986). *Faut-il refuser le Développement.* Paris, P.U.F.

Latouche, S. (1989). *L'Occidentalisation du monde.* Paris, La Découverte.

Löhr, A. (1991). *Unternehmensethik und Betriebswirtschaftslehre. Untersuchungen zur theoretischen Stützung der Unternehmenspraxis.* M & P Verlag, Stuttgart.

Lutz, M. A. and Lux, K. (1988). *Humanistic Economics: The new challenge.* New York, Bootstrap Press.

McCoy, C. (1985). *Management of Values. The ethical difference in corporate policy and performance.* Marshfield, Massachusetts.

McHugh, F. P. (1988). *Business Ethics. Keyguide to information sources.* New York, Nichols Publishing.

Macintyre, A. (1988). *Whose Justice? Which rationality?* London, Duckworth.

Mahieu, F. R. (1990). *Les Fondements de la crise économique en Afrique; Entre la pression communautaire et le marché international.* Ed. L'Harmattan. Paris, 1990.

Miller, D. (1990). *Market, State and Community. Theoretical foundations of market socialism.* Oxford, Clarendon Press.

Minar, D. W., Greer, S. (1969). *The Concept of Community. Readings with interpretations.* London, Butterworths.

Perroux, F. (1955). 'La notion de pôle de croissance', in *Economie Appliquée*, nr. 4, 1–2, republished in Perroux, F. (1961), *L'Economie du XXe siècle.* P.U.F., Paris.

Perroux, F. (1963). *Economie et Société. Contrainte, échange, don.* Paris, P.U.F.

Perroux, F. (1961). *L'Economie du XXe siècle.* Paris, P.U.F.

Poplin, D. E. (1972). *Communities. A survey of theories and methods of research.* Macmillan, London.

Solomon, R. C. (1992). 'Corporate Roles, Personal Virtues: An Aristotelean Approach to Business Ethics', in *Business Ethics Quarterly*, vol. 2, nr. 3, p. 305–17.

Sandel, M. (1982). *Liberalism and the Limits of Justice.* Cambridge, University Press Cambridge.

Schokkaert, E. (1991). 'Economie en ethiek: een onderzoeksprogramma.' *Tijdschrift voor Economie en Management* (36), nr. 1, 7–16.

Schokkaert, E. (1992). 'The economics of distributive justice, welfare and freedom', in K. Scherer, *Justice: Interdisciplinary Perspectives*, Cambridge, Cambridge University Press.

Selznick (1992). *The Moral Commonwealth. Social theory and the promise of community.* Berkeley, Univ. of California Press.

Sen, A. (1985). 'The moral standing of the market'. *Social Philosophy and Policy*, nr. 2, 1–19.

Sen, A. (1987). *On Ethics and Economics.* Oxford, Basil Blackwell.

Steinmann, H. and Löhr, A. (1989). *Unternehmensethik.* Stuttgart, Poeschel Verlag.

Strategisch Plan Kempen (SPK) (1990). *Visie, een inspirerende kijk op de Kempense toekomst,* trimestrial review, 1–2.

Thompson, G., Frances, J., Levacic, R., Mitchell, J. (eds.) (1991). *Markets, Hierarchies and Networks. The co-ordination of social life.* Sage, London.

Tönnies, F. (1887). *Gemeinschaft und Gesellschaft,* Leipzig, Berlin 1935 (Transl. *Community and Society,* 1957, Michigan State Univ. Press).

Ulrich, P. (Hrsg.) (1990). *Auf der Suche nach einer modernen Wirtschaftsethik. Lernschritte zu einer reflexiven Ökonomie.* Bern.

Van de Meerssche, P. (1990). *Van Jalta tot Malta. Politieke geschiedenis van Europa.* Antwerpen.

Van Luijk, H., *Rights and Interests in a Participatory Market Society,* Paper Fourth Annual Eben Meeting of Business Ethics Research Centres in Europe, Stockholm 18–20 May.

Van Parijs, P. (1991). *Qu'est-ce qu'une société juste?* Paris, Le Seuil.

Verhelst, T. (1990). *No Life without Roots.* London, Zed Books.

Verstraeten, J. and Van Gerwen, J. (1990). *Business & Ethiek. Spelregels voor het Ethisch Ondernemen.* Tielt, Lannoo.

Walzer, M. (1983). *Spheres of Justice. A defence of pluralism and equality.* New York, Basic Books.

Welford, R. and Prescott, K. (1992). *European Business. An issue-based approach.* London, Pitman.

Werhane, P. (1985). *Persons, Rights and Corporations.* Englewood Cliffs, N.J., Prentice Hall.

CHAPTER 8

Environment

Erik Schokkaert and Johan Eyckmans

Katholieke Universiteit Leuven, Centrum voor Economie en Ethiek, Belgium

8.1   Introduction

The deterioration of the natural environment is the most difficult challenge facing the European business world today. Example 1 illustrates some of the main problems. Many people feel that it will only be possible to cope with the environmental problem if one changes drastically the basic structure of the market economy, the technological emphasis in our industrial system and/or the value systems of the citizens. The political world has reacted to this development: the European Commission plays an important role in this process. The resulting broadening of the scope of environmental regulation has increased the pressure on business.

The business world is well aware of the problem. Not only do businessmen realize that their image in the community is threatened, they also realize that there is a big chance that government regulation will further increase during the following years and they fear the resulting interference with their freedom. Moreover, apart from these strategic considerations, businessmen are as sensitive as all other human beings to noise pollution, to the terrible smell of a river, to the sight of a devastated landscape, to health risks following from air pollution.

The growing awareness has led to various actions. 'Green' values are emphasized more and more in marketing strategies. Changes in product design and in production processes are implemented where it is not too costly and where there is a reasonable pressure from the consumer side: the production of washing-powder without phosphates and the banning of CFCs are typical examples. In some cases we can see a deliberate attempt to co-ordinate the efforts by different firms in an industry, the chemical industry being a case in point.

At present, however, these efforts have not been successful in dissipating the general feeling among the public that much more must be done to safeguard the environment. Partial answers are considered to be insufficient. But if we want to go beyond these partial answers, difficult questions cannot be avoided. How much more must be done? How to solve the ethical dilemmas when a better environment necessitates large economic sacrifices? And, more immediately, how to impose the necessary restructuring of decision-making structures? What is the role of business in this effort and what is the necessary scope of government intervention?

Concrete problems can only be solved against the background of an overall strategy. We will first try to sketch such a general background. In section 8.2 we will start from some concrete environmental problems to illustrate the ethical dilemma for a firm faced with conflicting social values. In these cases, an adequate treatment from the point of view of business ethics requires a social-ethical frame of reference. In section 8.3 we will comment on this broader frame of reference. We will try to indicate that some popular and ambitious approaches give a better insight into the important values at stake but are not very helpful when we have to make a choice in a concrete decision problem. The notion of external costs makes it possible to link this broader framework to the questions of business ethics.

In section 8.4 we discuss the relative scope of business and government reactions to the environmental problem. In some cases voluntary agreements and codes may be a better alternative than strict regulation. We will argue that business and business ethics should not restrict themselves to the internal functioning of the enterprises. They also have a crucial role to play in the political debate on the right environmental policies. In this respect we will emphasize in section 8.5 the importance of the European level of decision-making.

The possibilities for environmentally motivated firms are seen more clearly if we take a more dynamic point of view. In this respect, we will discuss in section 8.6 the growth of environmental industries, the emergence of a green market and the importance of R&D activities. Section 8.7 concludes.

1. The state of the environment in the European Community

In 1992 the Commission of the EC published a report on *The State of the Environment in the Community*. Its main conclusion is that, notwithstanding substantial public and private investment efforts, the general state of the environment in the Community shows few indications of improvement. The report focuses in particular on the evolution of air, water and soil quality, on waste management, and finally on a variety of topics like the quality of life, industrial risks and biodiversity. These issues are closely interconnected.

Concerning air quality the report states that Community-wide emissions of sulphur dioxide (held responsible for acid rain), CFCs (held responsible for the hole in the ozone layer) and lead (endangering human health) are indeed stabilizing or even decreasing, but local air quality near highways or in urban areas is not expected to improve given the projected growth of transportation. The main future challenges in atmospheric pollution are, however, of a global nature. In particular global climate change should rank high on the future policy agenda because emissions of greenhouse gases like carbon dioxide, nitrogen oxides, ozone and methane are expected to grow far into the next century if emission restrictions are not implemented soon. In this respect, the report stresses that *the Community must use more effectively its position of moral, economic and political authority to advance international efforts to solve global problems and to promote sustainable development and respect for the global commons* (European Council, *Declaration on the Environment*, Dublin, June 1990).

The quality of groundwater deteriorates rapidly in all member states. In particular the intrusion of micropollutants resulting from widespread use of persistent pesticides (DDT, lindane, atrazine) and the high concentrations of nitrates from nitrogenous chemical fertilizers cause great concern. Almost all major rivers in Europe suffer from eutrophication, i.e. a surplus of nitrogen and phosphorus originating from households and agriculture, and are polluted by heavy metals like mercury and cadmium. Given the quickly rising demand for fresh water, the report explicitly calls for better water resource management, both quantitatively and qualitatively, to break current trends.

The soil has long been neglected in environmental impact surveys. Desertification and soil erosion are expected to lead to lower agricultural yields in the south of the EC, and also in northern member states soil quality degrades as a result of agricultural overexploitation. In densely populated areas of the Community more attention should be paid to rational and well-considered land use respecting the many different environmental functions of the soil. Three main soil pollution priorities are identified: acidification, heavy metals and persistent micropollutants.

Another major environmental problem covered in the Commission's report is waste. On average every European citizen produces annually 327 kg of waste. Landfill (67 per cent) and incineration (25 per cent) are at present the most common forms of municipal waste disposal in the EC but according to the report substantial efforts are required to enhance prevention and recycling of waste. This is the only option to settle the waste problem in a sustainable way. The EC report also indicates that current treatment capacity for industrial and hazardous waste will prove insufficient in the near future, and that substantial investments will be necessary to clean up contaminated sites.

Finally, attention is devoted to the quality of life in the EC, which causes concern especially in the large cities of southern Europe, due to rapid urban population growth. The appropriate management of large industrial risks in response to the accidents in Seveso and Chernobyl and the preservation of biodiversity are also on the agenda. The report warns that economic development should not be pursued at the expense of the rich biological heritage in the peripheral regions of the EC. In all of these cases the report suggests that urgent action and co-ordination at the level of the European Community is required to prevent irreversible damage and to enhance sustainable development.

8.2   Ethical dilemmas for environmentally motivated firms: some examples

Take the case of an environmentally motivated business firm, producing a socially useful and highly desirable product (a pharmaceutical drug, for instance). Its production process leads to the severe pollution of a river, but setting up a cleaner production process would be extremely expensive and would probably lead to the substitution on the market of its own drug by another, cheaper, but less efficient pharmaceutical product. What is the ethically correct line of conduct for this firm?

As in many ethical problems for business, there is here an immediate conflict between ethical values and profit maximization, or between social values and material self-interest. But that is only the easy part of the story. For an ethically motivated firm, it is fairly obvious that material self-interest will have to yield to the social values at stake. The case of the pharmaceutical firm is more complicated, however. Not only is there a conflict between private self-interest and ethical motivation, there is also a conflict between different social values. What is the relative value of clean water versus the increase of physical pain (and perhaps of deaths) as a consequence of the removal of the more efficient drug from the market? The various factors involved may be valued differently by different people. It is not obvious at all that in such a choice situation the decisions taken by the firm itself (even if it is an ethically motivated firm) will reflect what is socially optimal, as judged by the other members of society. Nor is it clear that firms have an exclusive right to decide in such matters of life and death.

A (more negative) real-world example along the same lines is presented in Example 2. This is a Belgian case, where the activities of a firm seriously threaten the health of people living in the neighbourhood. What precautions must be taken by the firm? Or should it be closed altogether? Note that health risk is not an all-or-nothing variable and that closing all firms where there is even a very small risk would entail extreme economic costs. What is the socially acceptable level of such risk? Is it ethically desirable that the firm by its own private decisions determines the risk level for the surrounding community? But, on the other hand, does the surrounding community have the right to enforce the closing down of the firm?

2.   The value of a life: Metallurgie Hoboken-Overpelt

Metallurgie Hoboken-Overpelt (MHO) is a Belgian non-ferrous metal producer with a world-wide established reputation. It specializes in recycling and refining precious metals like gold, silver, copper, lead, zinc, etc. The plant at Hoboken refines some 125,000 tons of lead every year and employs 2,500 people. In the mid-1970s it became clear that the vicinity of this factory was heavily contaminated by lead and cadmium. In 1973 ten cows and horses at pasture near MHO were found dead as a result of lead intoxication. Chemical analysis of soil and grass samples revealed lead concentrations of 900 to 9,000 ppm (parts per million), much higher than the widely accepted maximum of 40 ppm. In 1977 a sample of dust found on a roof contained even 72,500 ppm of lead. It steadily became clear that forty years of lead production had resulted in an unacceptable accumulation of toxic metals in the soil. MHO admitted itself that every year some 26 to 30 tons of lead were blown into the air through its chimney. People living nearby started realizing that this could have serious negative repercussions on their health.

At first, provincial and municipal authorities and MHO management tried to minimize the scale and health effects of lead pollution at Hoboken. People living near MHO organized demonstrations, left-wing organizations taking the lead. Several environmental studies were carried out, chemical analyses were made by various laboratories and school children were screened on lead concentration in their blood. The details of results were not made public or were described as 'reassuring' and 'not alarming' by the authorities but some elements leaked out anyhow. Especially, the 1978 report of a medical commission led by Professor Dr Clara of the University of Antwerp caused concern. The commission recommended that in some areas near the factory no children under 12 should live or attend school. Children are much more sensitive to lead intoxication than adults. High lead concentrations hamper the production of haemoglobin which carries oxygen in the blood. In the long run this can cause anaemia, nervous disorder, paralysis of arms and legs, and behavioural disturbances. Chronic lead intoxication also affects organs (mainly kidneys) and muscles (intestines and blood vessels). The American Center for Disease Control (CDC) recommends a maximum acceptable lead concentration of 30 μg (microgram) per 100 ml blood for children. According to the Belgian Fund for Occupational Diseases adult workers with 60 μg or more should be removed temporarily out of the working environment and from 80 μg onwards they are considered incapacitated for work. In the housing estate Moretusburg 97 out of 113 children proved to have lead concentrations above 30 μg in 1977. The blood of children living next-door to MHO contained as much as 80 to 90 μg. Concerning the health of people working at MHO little is known because management was very reluctant to disclose information. It was estimated, however, that each year in the 1970s some 100 workers of MHO were declared incapacitated for work by the Fund for Occupational Diseases.

In 1978 politicians became aware of the scale of the lead pollution. First they considered moving the entire housing estate of Moretusburg. This would cost only 2.5 billion (1978) Belgian francs, far less than the 5 to 10 billion required to move the factory. This proposal was not accepted and a more pragmatic approach was adopted. Emission standards were imposed upon MHO and ore storage facilities had to be covered. A green buffer zone was planned in between the factory and the houses, and all contaminated soil had to be removed. Emissions and concentrations of lead would be monitored intensively and inhabitants were to be screened regularly. It is clear that these measures constitute a compromise. For the authorities, the potential loss of 2,500 jobs at MHO outweighed the health risks of people living at Moretusburg. The situation today at Hoboken has changed very little compared to the 1970s. Only the screening and monitoring has been carried out as planned. MHO installed some smoke-stack scrubbers and dust filters but the average annual atmospheric concentration of lead still exceeds the World Health Organization (WHO) standard of 1 μg/m^3/year. Also daily deposition of cadmium is still above the WHO standard of 20 μg/m^2/day. There is no significant downward trend in these emissions. Last year, MHO was said to be studying the situation and promised to propose fundamental solutions to the problem. Meanwhile informal talks with the city council of Antwerp resulted in nothing. In 1991 the Flemish minister of the environment imposed three additional exploitation requirements for MHO: moving an ore stack to the other side of the factory, planting trees as a green buffer against dust and sprinkling ore storage facilities and roads within the factory. But it is widely felt that the authorities failed to design a comprehensive approach to this lead problem.

The following (Canadian) example is an even better illustration of a conflict between different social values. We can readily assume that the kind of energy used in the economy is of crucial importance for the environment and that no production is possible without the use of energy. Apart from solar and wind energy, which can in the present circumstances only supply a marginal fraction of the energy needed, hydropower is probably the cleanest source of energy. But does this justify the destruction of valuable wildlife areas, vitally important to native peoples? Is it sufficient to pay a monetary compensation to these peoples? And what is the socially correct price of the energy produced by that hydro-electric power station? With, as a related question: how far is one allowed to go with the expansion of the power station?

3.   The case of Hydro-Québec

Western developed economies consume huge amounts of electric power and in most countries there is a lively debate on what technology should be chosen to generate that electricity in the future. Nuclear fission seems to be on its way out since the Chernobyl accident and since the staggering costs to treat and store nuclear waste have become clear. The first commercial nuclear fusion reactor is not expected before the middle of the next century and classic thermal power plants using fossil fuels come under attack because they are producing emissions of carbon dioxide (greenhouse problem) and of sulphur dioxide and nitrous oxides (acid rain). Solar and wind energy are not yet available at a competitive price, so hydropower seems a valid alternative, if the geography of a country is suitable for it. The latter is certainly the case in Québec (Canada) where almost 95 per cent of electricity is generated by means of water. The biggest dam was built by the local electricity company Hydro-Québec on the La Grande river and created an artificial lake of 10,000 square kilometres. It generates electricity at relatively low cost. The consumer price of electricity in Québec is only one-third of the price in New York or Belgium. Hydro-Québec claims its objective is to ensure reliable and cheap electricity supply, while respecting as much as possible the natural beauty of the area and the rights of native people.

But already in the 1970s the projects of Hydro-Québec were contested by the native taiga inhabitants, some 10,000 Cree Indians and 5,000 Inuits, who feared to lose huge parts of their virgin hunting-grounds. Negotiations with the authorities of Québec resulted in a broad agreement on the use of the taiga area. The Indians and Inuits were compensated with exclusive shooting-rights and a financial allowance of 500 million Canadian dollars. The money was used to build houses and hospitals and to set up small enterprises. However, this agreement did not settle all disputes. Some unexpected and severe ecological problems arose when the water of the artificial lakes proved to be contaminated by mercury. The soil in the region is naturally mercury-rich. Hydro-Québec had to inform all Indians and Inuits that the fish in certain parts of the lake was not suitable for consumption. This problem would, however, only be temporary. But the main complaint of the Indians and Inuits was probably the fact that they lost the possibility to enjoy their traditional culture and no amount of money can compensate for that loss.

The environmentalists for their part opposed the hydropower project because some of the last wilderness areas of Québec were sacrificed for cheap electric power. They agree that hydropower is one of the cleanest technologies to generate electricity but they would rather stress the need for energy efficiency. With 6.6 million inhabitants Québec consumes twice as much electricity as Belgium with 10 million inhabitants. This is partly explained by the fact that electric heating of houses and buildings is relatively more important in Canada but the main reason is probably the low electricity price in Québec. Furthermore, much of the planned expansion of capacity would be used to generate electricity for export to New York. The environmentalists do not want to give up one of the last virgin taiga areas in Québec for more export revenue. In the end the planned new projects of Hydro-Québec become a political dilemma. Do the rights and traditions of 15,000 Indians and Inuits and the amenity value of the taiga wilderness prevail over the benefits of cheap electricity and higher export revenues for the other 6.6 million people of Québec?

We consider finally the most extreme example: the greenhouse effect (Example 4). This effect is crucially linked to the industrial development and, hence, to the activity of business firms. But how would it be possible for an environmentally motivated individual business firm to define its correct position concerning this problem? Defining an optimal greenhouse policy requires trading off huge present economic costs versus uncertain benefits, relevant only for future generations and possibly more important in developing countries. This global ethical trade-off is a problem for the world as a whole. If we want to do something about the threat of the greenhouse effect, we will have to cut down our emissions of CO_2, i.e. reduce our use of fossil fuels. This simple (but expensive) policy can be monitored rather easily, but at the same time will lead to a considerable restructuring of the economy. There will be a strong decrease in the activities of the energy-producing and energy-intensive industries. Moreover, co-ordination at an international level is crucial.

4.   The greenhouse problem

In recent years, global warming has received top priority among all international environmental issues. Increasing atmospheric concentrations of greenhouse gases like carbon dioxide (CO_2), methane, CFCs, nitrous oxide and ozone are believed to enhance the natural greenhouse effect. These gases reflect part of the heat emitted by the Earth back to the surface and act as a blanket, trapping heat in the lower parts of the atmosphere. Attention has been focused mainly on emissions of carbon dioxide which result from burning fossil fuels and deforestation. The Intergovernmental Panel on Climate Change (IPCC) predicts that as a result of the enhanced greenhouse effect mean global temperature will rise by approximately 3°C by the end of the next century, causing major shifts in ocean currents and weather patterns. Besides temperature changes IPCC expects the sea level to rise by 60 cm and storms and flooding to become more severe and frequent. At present there exists a general consensus among climatologists about the process of global warming but it remains unclear what time lags are involved, how the effects will be spread over the globe and how agriculture will be affected. It is believed that most countries will face negative effects from global warming although some countries might benefit, at least for moderate changes, because previously cold areas may become available for agriculture (Siberia or Canada). Some evidence from climate simulation models seems to indicate that developing countries are bound to experience more negative effects from global warming than OECD countries.

Should anything be done to slow down or prevent the greenhouse effect? Some countries like the USA chose to wait and see and to do nothing until more scientific evidence becomes available. If the greenhouse effect does indeed materialize they will try to adapt to new climatic conditions. It is obviously easier for Western industrialized countries than for poor countries like Bangladesh, Egypt or the Maldive Islands to adapt to climate change (building higher dikes, agricultural research). Because of the potentially severe ecological consequences and unfavourable distributional effects, many scientists plead for preventive policies. An improvement of energy efficiency would be useful anyway, whether the greenhouse effect materializes or not. In this way the world community would buy insurance against the risk of an unprecedented fast rate of warming. But for many scientists the threat of possible climate change justifies more stringent measures than no-regret policies.

Politicians are starting to realize that global CO_2 emission trends need to be curbed in order to decrease the risk of potential environmental catastrophes. The rich countries of the North are responsible for the bulk of past and present emissions of greenhouse gases but, given demographic evolutions and their endowments of fossil fuels, countries like China, India, Brazil or Nigeria are expected to become the main emitters of CO_2 in the future. Therefore, any climate change agreement will have to include commitments of the major developing countries. But for these developing countries environmental concern is a lower priority than education, health care and economic growth. For the countries of the South it is obvious that, if something is to be done about global warming, the industrialized countries should bear most of the burden.

Assume that scientists would agree upon a critical load for carbon dioxide concentrations in the atmosphere and that a corresponding world emission reduction target and timing are determined. Economists will call for cost-efficient abatement schemes. Minimizing the total cost of achieving a target requires individual emission reduction percentages that equalize marginal abatement costs. It has been stressed over and over by economists that for this reason an equal percentage reduction agreement can never be optimal. At first sight equal percentage abatement agreements look very equitable but they do not take into account the important cost differences among countries and industries. Because abatement costs are rising more than proportionally with the reduction percentage, countries with high marginal costs (Japan, Scandinavian countries) should have to abate less in percentage terms than countries with low marginal costs (China, former Soviet Union) in order to achieve the world emission target at lowest possible global cost.

But at the international level there does not exist a world government or authority which can impose such a cost-efficient reduction scheme. Hence all international environmental co-operation depends upon voluntary multilateral negotiations and agreements. Evidently, countries like India, China and Brazil will never accept to bear the highest efforts. The countries of the South will only accept to join an international carbon treaty if they are compensated sufficiently by industrialized nations. Theoretically compensation could be organized in different ways, such as an international carbon tax system with redistribution of the receipts or a system of tradable carbon emission permits which are initially distributed in function of, e.g., population. The transfers involved would amount to a multiple of current development aid and it is highly questionable whether the time is ripe for such a far-reaching and drastic international carbon agreement. Negotiations at the United Nations Conference on Environment and Development (UNCED) in June 1992 in Rio de Janeiro gave a first indication. Some vague communiqué was signed but the USA refused to agree upon concrete targets and deadlines to reduce CO_2 emissions.

It is not difficult to give more examples, where the environmental problem basically boils down to a choice between different social values. In these cases it is impossible to confine the ethical problem within the four walls of the firm itself. In the next section we will therefore take a broader outlook and link the environmental problem to the working of the market economy. This will give us the necessary background to answer concrete questions about business behaviour later on.

8.3 Ethical dilemmas for society: the environment in a market economy

8.3.1 Private and social costs of business activity

The conflict between different social values is not restricted to the environmental problem. Human beings have many desires, which may conflict in a world of scarce resources. They strive for material welfare and for mobility, for job satisfaction and for social and cultural development. They want to be involved in political life and strongly dislike any intrusion on their own freedom. The basic ethical question in the economic sphere then becomes how to trade off these different desires against each other. Normally, however, firms in a market economy do not consider explicitly these fundamental questions. Why then do they have to face these ethical choices in the environmental context?

To answer this question, let us start from a stylized description of the framework of decision-making in a market economy. In such a market system economic actors try to realize their own objectives within the constraints imposed by their social environment. In a monetized economy prices (following from competition) are the most important constraining force. Firms maximizing their profits in a competitive economy try to produce at the lowest possible cost the commodities for which consumers want to pay. That mechanism may function in a socially desirable way if the input prices reflect the true social costs of the use of these inputs and if the willingness to pay of the consumers is a good indicator of the social desirability of the produced commodities. Under these conditions, simple profit maximization will lead to a socially desirable situation.[1] It is not necessary for firms to face explicitly the ethical trade-offs. The market takes care of that information problem, because market prices give the firms the right signals.

However, these conditions about the working of the market system are not satisfied in the context of the environmental problem. Let us concentrate on the aspect of the input prices. Firms have to pay the cost of all kinds of material inputs, but they are not paid to safeguard the environment, nor do they have to pay for the use of that environment. There is no price to be paid for the use of nature as a waste sink, or to pollute the water and the air, or to kill the last elephant. Nobody is exerting property rights on nature, on the rivers and the sea, on the air and the atmosphere, on the mountain gorillas and the elephants. In such a situation without property rights, the market gives the (socially wrong) signal that nature can be used freely and without cost. It is not difficult to see that the self-interest motive will then lead to overexploitation of nature and to environmental deterioration. Therefore, profit maximization will not lead to a socially desirable result and ethically motivated firms will be directly confronted with the ethical trade-offs.

One can also describe the same phenomenon in slightly different terms. Firms only pay a part of the cost they impose upon society, they do not have to pay the full social cost of their activities. Economists have introduced the notion of 'external cost' to describe the fraction of the (real social) cost, which is not borne by the firms themselves. This fraction may be considerable. This is nicely illustrated by Example 5, describing the case of a Dutch software firm which has calculated its own external costs. Note that software firms are certainly not to be classified among the traditional big polluters.

5.   External costs of a Dutch software firm

Few firms have estimated the damage their activities inflict upon natural ecosystems. An exception to this rule is the Dutch software firm BSO/Origin. As an accounting exercise this software firm calculated the annual environmental damage caused by its office heating system, water use, car and airplane transport and waste production. Environmental damage was defined as the monetary cost to clean up pollution resulting from their activities. Ecological externalities produced by suppliers or clients of BSO/Origin were neglected, except for electricity use (in Holland more than 90 per cent of electricity is produced by coal- and gas-fired power plants). BSO/Origin estimated that it would cost about 2.2 million Dutch guilders every year to compensate for the external costs it imposes upon society. Car transport proved to be the highest cost: 1.5 million guilders. Burning natural gas for heating purposes caused environmental damage amounting to 53,000 guilders and electricity use accounted for 432,000 guilders. Air traffic and waste combustion were responsible for 44,000 and 20,000 guilders respectively. It would cost 43,000 guilders to clean up water pollution caused by BSO/Origin and 71,000 guilders to compensate for the disposal of solid waste.

Every year BSO/Origin pays about 216,000 guilders of environmental taxes and pollution fees. Deducting these taxes from the 2.2 million estimated external cost yields 1.9 million guilders. This amount represents 0.75 per cent of the firm's annual turnover (255 million guilders in 1990) and can be considered to be an approximation of the external cost or environmental loss caused by BSO/Origin. Hence, in a system of 'green' national accounting BSO/Origin contributes 253 instead of 255 million guilders to the green national product. If the software firm were to bear the full social cost of its activities, profits would be diminished by 6 per cent and amount to 29.7 million guilders. This estimate of external costs is remarkably high, given the industry BSO/Origin operates in. It casts some doubt on the widely cited argument that environmental stress is likely to diminish as developed economies move away from traditional heavy industry towards the service industries.

The emphasis on the external costs of economic activity is one way of looking at the causes of the environmental problem. There are many other approaches to that problem, however, and the literature on the environmental crisis is tremendously large and rapidly growing. Different aspects are interrelated and need to be integrated if we want to get at a complete explanation. To mention a few: the social and economic structure, the exploitative attitude towards nature embodied in the Western culture, the direction taken by technological development, the growth of population. An integrated approach shows how silly it is to point to culprits, be they the churches, the scientists, the consumers or business. But such a grand and complete explanation has the disadvantage that it does not help us very much if we look for remedies. Saying that 'attitudes and social structures' matter to explain the existing situation is almost a tautology. If we want to get at solutions, we have to go beyond this tautology and take a more concrete line of approach, in which we try to describe specific mechanisms which seem to be important and which can be influenced (at least in principle).

The slice of reality one chooses to shed light on will be determined mainly by the purpose of the exposition. We have chosen to concentrate on the concrete pricing system in a market economy, because this is the most relevant approach to understand the position of business and the possibilities for businesspeople to react. This approach undoubtedly is a partial one. It can be integrated into a broader framework, however. The market system (with the wrong price signals as described) indeed will guide technical progress in the direction of the satisfaction of material desires of the consumers, to the detriment of other (unpriced) needs. Also, the attitude towards nature probably has been a crucial component in the development of market capitalism itself (and in the way property rights on nature have or have not been defined). While it is very well possible that the latter factors (technology and cultural values) are the more basic ones, it is not obvious what concrete lines of conduct can be derived from this insight. Even if one believes in the need for a completely new world, it will only be possible to reach this world through a sequence of small steps. Concentrating on the defects of the price system immediately suggests a concrete way of handling the problem within the structure of the market economy. Firms should take into account (whether voluntarily or under coercion) the full social cost of their production process and consumers should be confronted with this full price when making their own decisions.

It is important to realize that introducing the notion of 'correct social costs' does not solve the ethical problem. It is only another way of interpreting the trade-offs between different social values, as sketched in the previous section. To determine the social cost of health risks or of the destruction of valuable wildlife areas or of the global warming of the atmosphere, one first has to take an ethical position. The monetary valuation in terms of social costs comes afterwards. In all of these cases, where different values are to be traded off against each other, there does not seem to be an alternative for a careful weighing of the importance of these various values. But how to determine the relevant weighting system? Let us first see whether we can derive any guidance in this respect from the environmental literature. We will discuss two broad ethical themes from this literature (ecocentrism and sustainable development) in the following subsection. We will argue that in both cases the underlying idea is of crucial importance but needs to be elaborated in more detail.

8.3.2   *Themes from the environmental literature*

It is not the purpose of this chapter to go deeply into the philosophical discussions on the relationship between humankind and the environment. We have only chosen two broad themes to illustrate the important contribution and at the same time the limitations of these philosophical approaches.

Ecocentrism or anthropocentrism?

A recurrent theme in the recent literature on environmental philosophy is the antithesis between anthropocentric and ecocentric approaches. Ecocentrists claim that the environmental problem is a consequence of the biased relationship between humankind and nature. In their opinion, humanity has always used and abused nature to satisfy its own needs without having respect for the needs (some would say rights) of the natural environment. Human beings have treated nature as an object, about which they can decide autonomously. This is especially striking in our treatment of animals, battery cages and vivisection in laboratory experiments being revolting examples. According to ecocentrists, the only way out of the environmental deterioration is a complete shift in our attitude: we have to realize that nature has an intrinsic value, independent of its potential for satisfaction of human needs. Humankind has to be positioned in a wider ecological or cosmic whole, that is valuable in and for itself.

At a basic level, the extreme ecocentric position that nature would have intrinsic value even if there were no human beings is absurd. After all, the whole idea of 'valuation' is an anthropocentric idea. As human beings we have no other possibility but to start from our own frame of reference, our own emotions, our own ideas when we have to value nature. Even if we claim that nature has intrinsic value, the latter can only be understood in human terms.

There is a less extreme position, however, which admits that values necessarily are defined by human beings, but emphasizes that the intrinsic value of nature must get an important position in that (human-made) value system. Humankind should not abuse nature for its own needs but take an attitude of respect and consideration. The basic inspiration of this criticism is extremely valuable. But can this (rather vague) inspiration be sufficient as a guideline for our actions? Does the fundamental decision to take an ecocentric position help us very much when we are confronted with the kind of situations described in the previous section? It certainly implies that we use energy in an economical way, but how far do we have to go? It seems impossible to state that all ecosystems have the same value. Do we have to protect the AIDS virus? But on what basis can we define a hierarchy of values in an ecocentric system? Is ecocentrism an acceptable alternative for a careful weighing of costs and benefits of specific actions, where costs and benefits will have to be defined in anthropocentric terms?

Despite these questions, it is important to underline the importance of the ecocentric critique. We do believe that there is indeed a fundamental ethical problem associated with the present exploitative attitude of humankind versus nature. Although respect for nature cannot be the only factor determining concrete decisions and must be traded off against other ethical considerations, it must in any case be integrated into our broader ethical value system.

The GNP debate and the notion of sustainable development

Since the 1960s the debate on the economic aspects of the environment has been dominated by the question whether economic growth is an acceptable social objective. Two main points have been raised. First, we are living on a finite planet and we cannot grow for ever because the resources at our disposal are limited. This can be called the 'Spaceship Earth idea'. Second, the desire for economic growth is at the origin of the environmental problem because it reflects an overemphasis on material at the expense of spiritual, aesthetic and cultural values. We feel that both these points are valuable and important. But they do not solve the ethical dilemmas sketched before. At best, they may give us some inspiration for determining our set of weights.

Two more concrete points have been formulated within the framework of this discussion on economic growth. The first relates to the use of the GNP concept as a measure of social welfare, the other to the notion of sustainable development.

The GNP (gross national product) measures the market value of the goods and services produced by an economy during a certain period of time (usually one year). It gives a good indication of the level of economic activity and as such is strongly correlated with private consumption, employment and even tax revenues. Yet it has also been seen as a measure of social welfare and this use is more dubious. Since goods which do not have a monetary market value do not appear in the GNP, the value of nature is completely neglected. It is therefore clear that the political emphasis on GNP growth to the neglect of other social objectives is regrettable. Growth of GNP is important as a proxy for short-run macroeconomic variables, such as employment, but should be weighed against other objectives (including environmental ones) in a broader ethical framework.

This said, it must be emphasized that GNP growth is not necessarily bad for the environment. Of course, the historical link between economic growth and environmental deterioration is undeniable. But we have already argued that this is due to the conditions under which this growth has taken place: firms could use nature at a zero — or in any case too low — price. There is no reason why GNP growth necessarily would become zero or negative, if firms had to pay the socially correct price of nature. This surely would affect the composition of production (and the direction of technological development) but not necessarily its level. (Remember that services are also included in GNP.)

The proposition (rather popular within the business community) that GNP growth is good or even necessary to solve the environmental problem must be judged in the same spirit. Formulated as such, it does not make sense: the relationship between the economy and the environment has to do with what is produced and how it is produced and aggregate concepts such as the total market value of this production do not give any relevant insight into these questions. More production of polluting products increases the GNP and may be terrible for the environment. But at the same time the production of windmills and solar panels also has a market value, which is added to arrive at the global GNP figure. And if the chemical sector adopts new production processes which are less harmful to the environment, this may have a positive or negative effect on the market value of chemical production. This latter effect is quite irrelevant to judge the desirability of the technical change.

In recent years (and mainly since the publication of the Brundlandt Report[2]) a new dimension has been added to the GNP debate: the international distribution of material welfare. Of course, many people have always been aware of the ethical importance of the present situation of hunger and underdevelopment in a large part of the world. But the important new insight popularized by the Brundlandt Report is the link between the development problem and the environment. Both objectives are integrated into the notion of sustainable development. According to this idea, the world has to strive for economic development and for a better international distribution of welfare but in a sustainable way, i.e. without harming the social, economic and ecological opportunities of future generations.

There can be no doubt that this is an attractive idea. It has been intuitively appealing for many people and has become a central motivating force in the social debate. The Commission of the European Communities is already using it as the central notion in its recent action programmes.[3] However, from a more analytical perspective, much more remains to be done to give it a clear content (think of the Hydro-Québec and greenhouse cases in Examples 3 and 4).[4] How do we have to define economic development? And more difficult still: when do we harm the opportunities of future generations? Do we harm future generations by using now a part of the available exhaustible resources (since the present use of these resources necessarily leads to a decrease of stocks for future generations)? This would imply that humankind completely stops using these resources, which does seem a rather extreme position. Perhaps the present generation can be allowed to use exhaustible resources, if it compensates future generations, e.g. through a more productive capital stock. But how do we have to determine the just compensation (given that we do not know the needs of future generations)?

The idea of sustainable development is extremely useful because it has allowed us to go beyond the rather meaningless GNP debate and has centred the debate on these crucial questions of international and intergenerational justice. But, like many other general concepts, it remains too vague to be of much guidance in concrete situations of ethical dilemma.

8.4   What to do? Regulation and self-regulation

Let us now return to the ethical position of individual firms. We have argued that many concrete environmental problems boil down to a trade-off between different social values. Ethically motivated firms in a market economy cannot avoid these difficult choices, because simple profit maximization will lead to the overexploitation of natural resources as a consequence of the distorted information provided by the price system. If we want to determine the (ethically) 'optimal' behaviour of the firm, there does not exist an alternative for a careful and explicit weighting of the different values at stake. Ethical behaviour by firms would then (by definition) amount to the implementation of the result of such ethical deliberation. Despite the common misunderstandings around this term, one can call this deliberation an 'ethical cost-benefit analysis',[5] by which one would try to define what is best for 'society'.

Such a global ethical evaluation is an extremely difficult exercise. In a first step one has to describe the ecological (and other) consequences of a given action. Even this first step may already cause much trouble. We do not understand fully all ecological processes. To give an example: most scientists agree about the phenomenon of global warming as a consequence of the greenhouse effect (see Example 4) but there is still much uncertainty about the exact climatological relationships and about the effects to be expected. The past has shown that apparently innocuous decisions may have unpredicted global consequences: the relationship between the use of CFCs and the destruction of the ozone layer, or between the agricultural fertilization and the quality of the groundwater are good examples. Many decisions taken now are irreversible: the most prominent example is the disappearance of species. We do not know the consequences of such changes. All this implies that even ethical observers with the same set of values might reach a different judgement where a concrete decision has to be taken. How then can firms be sure that they collect the correct information?

The second step, which is the evaluation of the consequences, is still more difficult. In actual reality different people have drastically different ethical frames of reference. The grand philosophical concepts introduced in the previous section point to the leading values which are at stake: respect for nature and care in exploiting it, distrust of concentration on material values, solidarity with the fate of the millions of hungry people in the Third World, concern for the opportunities of future generations. But these values are formulated at such a high level of generality that they still can be interpreted in many different ways. Moreover, in a concrete ethical dilemma, we also have to decide what weights should be attached to these different values if they come in conflict with each other. And different people will prefer different sets of weights. The cases of the hydro-electric plant and the health-damaging production process are good examples: the opinions of the Inuit or of the people living in the immediate neighbourhood of the firm may differ considerably from the opinions of the consumers or the workers in the firm. And, more generally, there is no consensus about how to trade off cleaner energy and wildlife areas or about the social acceptability of the health risk.

It would therefore be extremely naïve to expect that this kind of ethical cost-benefit analysis will yield definite answers to all concrete choice problems or that there could ever be absolute consensus over such an answer. But this immediately implies that there is no unambiguous touchstone for ethical behaviour and that it is impossible to formulate a set of concrete environmental guidelines for individual firms. However, although no definite answers are to be expected, it is still useful to think in terms of 'ethical cost-benefit analysis', because the procedure yields a better insight into the different steps to be taken and the different factors involved in the ethical deliberation.

Given that there is no consensus about the ethical valuation, and that important social values are at stake, we have to face a crucial question: who is to perform the ethical calculus? Who has to take the decisions when values differ? In many cases, there is no good alternative to the political process if we want to solve the environmental problem in an ethically acceptable way. To reinterpret the idea of an ethical cost-benefit analysis within this political context, it is necessary to devise democratic procedures of social decision-making by which people can enter into an open and honest ethical debate over these difficult questions. Business can play an important role in that debate. Yet political intervention is not always necessary, or even desirable. In some cases, the ethical deliberation will largely be a private matter for the firm. We will therefore first indicate what factors are important to determine the scope of isolated action by individual firms.

8.4.1   Limits and possibilities of isolated action by business

The factors circumscribing the role of business versus government regulation can usefully be discussed along three dimensions: the complexity of the ethical dilemma, the technico-scientific complexity and the co-ordination problem.

The complexity of the ethical dilemma

We have given already many examples of extremely difficult choice situations, pointing to the limitations of individual decision-making. We have also emphasized the deficiencies of the free market mechanism, if prices do not play their informative role adequately – remember Examples 2, 3 and 4. In these difficult cases, it is obvious that besides the firms there are other economic actors qualified to influence the decisions. The polluting firm is not the only agent that should have a say in the health risks to be borne by the people in its neighbourhood.

However, in many other cases the ethical deliberation is relatively simple. Consider the example of pollution of a river during the production of a socially useful and highly desirable product. At the same time, there are technical possibilities to set up a cleaner production process. Everybody will agree that the cleaner process is to be preferred (if the economic costs are not too large). Or consider the choice between two locations for a new plant: one is in the centre of a wildlife area, the other is in an industrial zone. In these examples, and taking into account the proviso about the economic costs, the 'environmentally' or 'ethically' correct decision is easy to define. Therefore ethical behaviour by firms is easy to define and businesspeople may be supposed to know that correct behaviour. While the political process may be necessary to sanction unethical business behaviour, business does not need the political process to help define the ethically correct decision.

The technico-scientific complexity

Environmental problems differ considerably in their technical complexity. When this complexity grows, the role of business tends to increase. One cannot expect the political representatives or the government administration to have superior knowledge about complicated and rapidly changing production processes. In many cases it is even impossible for an outsider to measure adequately the damages following from production: regulation is then extremely difficult. In general one can say that the ethical responsibility for individual firms tends to increase when the technico-scientific complexity of the problem grows.

The co-ordination problem

Firms have to take their decisions within the framework of a competitive environment. Take the example of a firm which has developed superior knowledge about a new production process leading to a strong decrease in pollution, but at the expense of higher costs. Should that firm introduce the new technology? From an environmental point of view, the answer to that question is obvious. But the firm will be in a difficult situation (a private ethical dilemma) if its competitors stick to the old, cheaper but polluting, technology and if consumers are not willing to pay a higher price for the same product, produced in a less polluting way. In general one can expect both these reactions. Each competitor can increase its profits by using the old technology and, moreover, if there is a sufficient number of firms, each individual firm's pollution may be only a negligible fraction of the total. Each consumer can gain individually by buying the cheaper product and, moreover, his own consumption is only marginal compared to the total market.

The decision space for individual firms to take environmental decisions without co-ordination with other firms will therefore be determined by three factors. First, there is the cost difference. If the clean technology would be cheaper, there is no problem at all. Note that in a dynamic context there is no reason why a good R&D effort could not yield such a result. But in many cases the clean production process will be more expensive and the larger the cost differential, the more difficult it becomes to implement it. Second, there is the reaction of the competitors. This is partly linked to the market power of the firm. If it is the market leader or in any other sense has a large market power, it may be in the position to set an example. Third, the possibilities of the firm depend on the awareness and the willingness to pay of the consumers. If these are willing to pay more for a cleaner product, a good marketing strategy can be helpful in making the new technology profitable.

The previous analysis shows that many firms will experience a decrease in profits if they take the environmentally optimal decisions. This implies that the incentives to take such decisions will be rather poor, the more so because the loss in profits is a price to be paid for the unethical behaviour of competitors and/or consumers. In more extreme cases there may be a decrease in employment or even a threat of bankruptcy. One cannot reasonably expect such decisions to be taken by a firm in isolation. In all these cases where individual firms are not in a position to take the ethically preferable decisions, co-ordination of the efforts by different firms is the only way out. But co-ordination will not happen spontaneously. In many cases political intervention will be indispensable.

The co-ordination problem is especially obvious if we not only consider microdecisions at the level of the firm but also include in our considerations environmental problems at a continental (e.g., acid rain) or even planetary level (e.g., the greenhouse problem). To solve these problems, a huge restructuring of the world economy is necessary. Individual firms are powerless in such a situation.

In Example 6 we describe the 'Responsible Care' programme of the chemical industry. This example illustrates the different factors determining the possibilities for individual firms to do something about the environment. The ethical problem is rather simple and formulated in a way which can be solved by individual firms (the cleaner the process, the better, if consumers are willing to pay the economic cost). Devising and introducing new technologies requires highly specialized knowledge, which is concentrated within the industry itself. There is a co-ordination problem, but it seems that the chemical industry is rather successful in solving it by setting up its own institutions. In these circumstances, the role to be played by the industry can be extremely important.

6.   Responsible Care and the chemical industry

The chemical industry is well aware of the fact that its environmental reputation with the general public is rather low. Many outside observers believe that environmental, health and safety considerations are subordinated to competitiveness and profitability. But one should not forget that people working in chemical companies share the same concerns as people outside the industry. Often they are the first to be confronted with adverse health and environmental effects. There is no reason to believe a priori that the chemical industry is less concerned about the environment than other sectors of the economy. Due to the nature of their activities chemical companies often deal with highly toxic substances which in case of accident may cause catastrophes (see also Example 10). Or their production processes may inflict considerable external costs upon society in terms of water and air pollution. These considerations often motivated authorities to design coercive regulation to ensure safety standards or to safeguard the environment. But it is clear that legislation cannot foresee every eventuality and that in many cases industry itself has an informational advantage over public authorities. Both practical and ethical considerations therefore urge the industry to adopt some kind of voluntary self-regulation.

A good example of self-regulation is given by the *Responsible Care* programme of the Chemical Industries Association. This initiative started in Canada and spread steadily over the USA and Europe. The aim of the programme is to improve performance through a public commitment of its members to observe a set of guiding principles. These include operating to the best practice of the industry, concern for continuous improvement in health, safety and environmental policy, and releasing all relevant information about activities to employees, customers and the public in general. No formal sanctions are included in Responsible Care but it is obvious that members cannot afford to violate one of the principles since comparisons between companies will be published. Programmes have been set up in seven countries and several more are planned.

The Responsible Care programme was motivated mainly by the declining respectability of the sector. The programme mentions explicitly that it wants to enable companies to demonstrate their improvement to the public: *the reputation of the chemical industry is not a good one. We must win back respect and the way forward is to develop trust and confidence. It will be a long, slow haul but the industry is determined to succeed. The public needs to know that all reasonable steps are being taken to reduce risks in safety, health and environmental protection.* Although self-interest is an important motive for Responsible Care, the programme illustrates that an industry itself can play an important role to overcome co-ordination problems in environmental and safety issues.

8.4.2   Coercion and politics

In cases where the ethical dilemma is complicated and involves different economic actors and in cases where there is a problem of co-ordination because of free rider-ship, political intervention will be needed. This does not mean that the part of business and of business ethics is played out. Business must participate in the political debate. So doing, it can influence the decisions on the instruments to be used by government and in some cases reach a voluntary agreement.

The political debate
In business folklore a sharp distinction is often made between, on the one hand, respect for individual freedom and markets and, on the other hand, authoritarian pressure and government intervention. Often these two poles are associated with efficient production and wasteful redistribution respectively. This dichotomy does not make sense. Firms may coerce themselves, for instance if they reach an agreement to ban certain products or production processes. Government may help in negotiating such agreements. Or government intervention may consist of stimulating instead of coercing measures.

At a basic level, the political system has to define the rules of the game within which individuals operate. This has always been the case. The free market system could not work without a legal framework guaranteeing respect for property rights, i.e. without a certain degree of government intervention. Since the environmental problem is closely linked to the rules of the market game, it cannot be solved without a change in these rules. In the business community the fear that the environmental concern will lead to a huge increase in inefficient government regulations is widespread. This fear is easily understandable. However, a conservative defence of the existing system is not the right reaction to this fear. It would be better if businesspeople would actively and constructively participate in the political debate.

In the first place, this debate will be about the ethical trade-offs sketched earlier. Although we argued that solving these dilemmas should not be the monopoly of firms, it is obvious that they often have superior practical or technical knowledge which is crucial to the debate. Popular political discourse is sometimes dominated by utopian visions of a regained Paradise where the destruction as a consequence of the technological and economic development would be repaired. Most citizens have no idea about the real trade-offs involved, and more specifically about the loss in material welfare which would result from a strong environmental policy. Here, the business community has an important role to play. Practical knowledge from within the firms can help formulate a more realistic and less naïve vision of an ecological future. This does not mean that this realistic vision must be necessarily narrow-minded. The debate is about the important values emphasized in the previous sections: how can we trade off material welfare (for all the people in the world), respect for nature, concern for future generations? A good description of a businessperson taking up the challenge appears in Example 7: in this Example we give some excerpts from an interview with a Belgian manager who is in charge of electricity production and clearly formulates the dilemmas involved.

7.   Interview with Philippe Bodson

Philippe Bodson is the director of Electrabel, the newly created Belgian energy holding which produces and distributes almost all electricity in Belgium. In a recent interview with Johan Mortelmans of the newspaper *De Standaard*, Philippe Bodson made some remarkable statements concerning the environmental objectives of Electrabel. Environmentalists are very suspicious of Electrabel and they often claim that the prime objective for the holding is to sell a maximal amount of electricity. According to Bodson this is not true because profits of Electrabel are more or less institutionally fixed. Electrabel receives an allowance of approximately 12.5 per cent of its capital stock. The main objective of the firm is not to maximize profits but to ensure reliable electricity supply at a competitive price in the European market.

Electricity producers are faced with various environmental dilemmas. Whatever technology they choose to generate electric power, they will always inflict considerable damage upon natural ecosystems, even in the case of hydropower (recall the case of Hydro-Québec). Motivated partly by the oil crisis the Belgian government decided in the 1970s that private electricity producers could build (subsidized) nuclear power plants to meet basic electricity demand. Peak demand would be covered by classic thermal power plants burning gas, oil or coal. In the 1980s the share of nuclear energy rose steadily to reach more than 60 per cent in 1986. As a consequence emissions of CO_2 and NOx by power plants in 1990 fell by 30 per cent compared to 1980 and emissions of SO_2 by almost 70 per cent. The reduction of SO_2 was also induced by the introduction of smoke-stack scrubbers and fuel substitution. Since 1986, however, electricity demand has been growing rapidly again and commercial producers were not allowed to build an additional nuclear power plant. According to Philippe Bodson the political decision to build no additional nuclear reactor will inevitably lead to a greater share of thermal power plants and hence to higher emissions, especially of CO_2. Precisely for the latter greenhouse gas strict European measures are to be expected in the near future. There are possibilities to reduce CO_2 emissions by increasing energy efficiency but this will prove insufficient to stabilize CO_2 emissions by the year 2000. Bodson put the political choice to be made very explicitly: *The citizens have to choose: either we opt for more nuclear power, or for higher CO_2 emissions, or for a lower level of social welfare.*

In the second place, the debate will also be about the concrete measures to be taken. Here technical and practical insights play a still more important role and as a consequence the influence of firms on these decisions has been high in the past and will probably remain high in the future. Regulation by government has traditionally taken two broad forms: on the one hand, government can use so-called economic instruments (such as taxes and marketable permits); on the other hand it can impose norms and technical regulations. In the past the business community was in general strongly opposed to the use of the tax instrument. This attitude is short-sighted and inconsistent with the defence of the market mechanism.

Economic instruments or technical regulation?

The economic advantages of taxes and marketable permits are well known[6]. First, they are efficient in a static sense. Those firms who can reduce their pollution only at a high cost will prefer to pay the taxes (or buy the permits), those who can cheaply reduce their pollution will do so (to avoid paying taxes[7]). This leads to an efficient distribution of the efforts over the different firms. Or, in other words: the system implements a least-cost solution to reach a given level of environmental improvement. Second, in a dynamic context, taxes give firms the right incentive to look for less polluting products and production processes. So doing, these firms indeed can diminish their tax payment. In a system of norms this incentive will not exist.

When firms have to pay a higher price for their inputs, an increase in the consumer price is to be expected. Since the tax burden will be higher for the more polluting products, their price increase will be higher. This is exactly as it should be. Consumers must be confronted with the full social cost of the products they buy: this is the best way to change their behaviour and to increase their awareness of the environmental problem. The higher prices will immediately indicate the extent of the trade-off between a better environment and more material welfare.

Thus, the economic arguments for the introduction of pollution taxes or marketable permits are very strong. Indeed, it is difficult to see how an environmentally motivated market adherent can prefer the use of norms and regulations over the use of economic instruments. Not only are the former measures less efficient, they also lead to the imposition of stringent restrictions on the freedom of decision-making by the firms. This is exactly the kind of government interference that business should be afraid of. On the contrary, the imposition of a tax (or the introduction of marketable permits) is only a redefinition of the price of some inputs. After that redefinition, all firms can compete again on an equal basis. No further government interference is needed. Then why are so many businesspeople opposed to the use of economic instruments?

There is an easy explanation based on mere short-run self-interest considerations.

In a system of norms, firms do not have to pay anything if they obey the norms. In a system of taxes, even a firm which has considerably reduced its pollution level will still have to pay for the remaining pollution. At first sight, this will lead to a decrease in profits. However, the latter conclusion is not necessarily true. If taxes are imposed on all polluting firms in all sectors and to a certain extent will be shifted onto the consumers, the final effect on profits will depend on a number of economic parameters and on the behavioural reactions of the firm itself.

At a more basic level, however, ethical valuation may also play a role in the negative reaction of firms. There is indeed a feeling that the imposition of taxes on a firm that has reduced its pollution level in an optimal way is not just. To answer that argument we have to return to the basic structure of the market system. Earnings in the market are a compensation for effort and productivity within a specified set of property rights. The initial distribution of property rights was given before markets developed and has been consolidated by the political system afterwards. Ideas of just and unjust rewards refer to that set of property rights. The whole interpretation of the environmental problem as sketched before rests on the proposition that this given set of property rights is no longer acceptable, because it does not take into account the value of nature. Nature cannot be used freely by everyone, but has a price. Those who are willing to use nature have to pay that price to the owners. If nature belongs to all human beings, the price has to be paid to the community: the tax is exactly that price. In this interpretation, the present (no-tax) situation is unjust, because the (collective) property rights on nature are not respected. The imposition of a tax is just one way of correcting this disequilibrium.

It has been argued by practical businesspeople that, although all these arguments may perhaps be convincing from a theoretical point of view, they do not reflect the way in which society works. At least two problems must be mentioned. The first has to do with the attitude of government itself. Many people feel that it is extremely naïve to expect that governments will take the ethically desirable decisions. Instead, realism leads to the fear that the newly created tax instrument will not be used for allocational and, more especially, environmental purposes but will simply be exploited by government to increase the financial burden on the private sector. Given the development of taxes in the recent past, this fear is not surprising. Therefore it is essential to make explicit that it is not the aim of this environmental tax to increase government revenues. The revenues can be redistributed to compensate those low-income consumers who are hit very hard by the price increases. Or the introduction of pollution taxes has to be coupled to a decrease in other taxes. One then immediately thinks of the tax on labour. The more concern there is about the concrete stipulations of the economic instruments, the more reason for business to try to influence the decisions and to participate actively in the political debate. The new tax system must be set up in a way which minimizes the possibility of misuse by politicians.

The second problem relates to the monitoring and control problem. It is not necessarily true that the imposition of a pollution tax puts all firms on an equal basis: some will have more possibilities than others to evade the tax and by evading they will acquire a competitive advantage. But of course the same control and monitoring problems will occur with all other forms of government intervention (including technical regulations). This brings us to the topic of voluntary agreements and codes.

8.4.3   Voluntary agreements and codes

The information problem is especially acute for environmental issues. Individual firms have private information on their own production processes and very often government does not possess the information to compute the right tax or impose the most efficient regulation. Moreover, if firms really want to undermine environmental policy, neither economic instruments nor quantitative or technical norms can work adequately. In that case government would have to set up a huge control apparatus. This certainly would lead to all kinds of intrusion in the private domain of the firms and even then the environmental results of the policy are uncertain. All this shows that government intervention is not a substitute for ethical behaviour by firms. It can only complement and support such behaviour by co-ordinating the efforts of different firms.

In a situation of asymmetric information self-regulation by business may become an important factor.[8] A sector or industry is often better placed than government to co-ordinate the necessary technological changes or to control the efforts by different firms. One might consider a situation in which government comes to an agreement with the industry or sector about aggregate standards (which can rather easily be monitored) and then leaves that industry or sector free to choose its own policy to attain these standards. In Europe there is already some experience with these so-called 'covenants' and it is expected that their importance will grow in the future. In any case, recent proposals of the European Commission go in that direction. We illustrate this approach in Example 8.

8.   Covenants

In recent years national Belgian and regional Flemish environmental authorities introduced a new environmental policy instrument. They try to establish voluntary agreements (a code of conduct or 'covenant' in Dutch) with representatives of industries or individual firms to achieve some effluent, emission or environmental quality standard. Examples of environmental problems settled by covenants in Belgium are: the production of CFCs (to translate the multilateral Montreal Protocol on CFCs into national policy), mercury concentration in batteries, phosphates in washing-powder, SO_2 and NOx emissions by power plants, aluminium recycling and the export of pesticides to Third World countries.

Mostly the requirements stipulated in a covenant are more stringent than the currently applying national or European legislation. A covenant is not some loose gentlemen's agreement without legal obligations. It is considered by legal experts as a binding contract having the force of law between the parties. Industries commit themselves to comply with the new standards within the timing agreed upon, and the authorities agree (explicitly or implicitly) not to impose more stringent standards unless they are forced to by, for instance, the European Commission. Some legal questions remain meanwhile unsettled. First, what if an individual firm, a member of an industrial federation, refuses to observe the agreed standards? Not all industrial federations have internal sanctions at their disposal to enforce the covenant. Moreover, membership of industrial federations in Belgium is mostly voluntary. It is obvious that a covenant between the state and a federation cannot bind non-members. Second, it is unclear how far the authority of a minister of the environment reaches. Up to now all covenants were signed by the minister without approval of parliament and hence without democratic control. Third, mostly the codes of conduct do not stipulate which sanctions apply if the standards are not met. It is, however, widely accepted that in the most extreme case the authorities can break their commitment and enforce the standards by issuing binding national (or regional) legislation.

Why was this new procedure introduced in Belgium? First, there is a growing tendency to avoid coercive public regulation. It is felt that industries, environmentalists and the public in general should be consulted more intensively before new legislation is issued. Second, there is a strong economic motive for voluntary agreements given the information advantage of, e.g., the chemical industry over the government. The ultimate effluent or emission standard is specified in the covenant but how individual firms meet this standard is not prescribed. Firms can choose the technology that is most suited for their production structure.

Environmentalists agree that covenants can be useful policy instruments, provided they are signed with industries and not with single companies. Covenants should not replace or relax the existing exploitation licence of an individual producer. In this respect, the agreement with BASF Antwerp concerning the phosphate concentration of its effluent water was widely criticized. In exchange for lower effluent taxes (one-tenth of the normally applicable effluent charges) BASF promised to invest 8 billion Belgian francs to reduce phosphate concentrations to zero by 1994. Greenpeace referred to the extremely mild effluent licence of BASF in the past and to the fact that BASF paid only 10,000 francs effluent charge until 1991. It is felt that BASF used the covenant to escape the new Flemish effluent legislation.

Of course, the industry will also be confronted with a control problem, in the sense that it will be profitable for a minority to cheat on the agreement. What makes us believe that self-regulation nevertheless might work? Arrow (1973) mentions different important factors. The overall success of the scheme can be collectively exploited to improve the image of the sector with the government and (perhaps more importantly) with the consumers and the workers. Individual firms may identify with this collective effort (more intensely than when it would be imposed by government). In the presence of a covenant, those firms who are obeying the rules will have better information on the behaviour of their competitors than government would have and they will find it in their interest to complain openly about all forms of cheating. They also will use all possible ethical and social pressures against their cheating rivals. All this is made easier in a sector dominated by large firms, where it is more likely that individual employees or managers will blow the whistle in case of a breach of the environmental rules.

Although there is reason for some optimism, one should not be naïve about the prospects of covenants. Self-regulation cannot work for many environmental problems involving a large number of poorly organized economic agents or situated at the international level. Moreover, even where it is possible in principle, it will only occur in such difficult (and expensive!) matters as environmental policy if there is a supporting social structure. Government stimulation therefore will remain indispensable.

Two remarks must be made in this respect. First, we have emphasized already that business is not the only social force that should have a say in solving the difficult ethical dilemmas concerning the environment. We therefore have been careful in making explicit that the covenants must be situated within the overall standards formulated by society. In actual reality we now sometimes see that social pressure leads firms in an industry or sector to some easy and superficial agreement or (worse still) to a vague formulation of general principles with as their only objective the avoidance of more severe government regulation. Such tactical manoeuvres can easily be understood as a part of the political game: but they are not an adequate answer to the environmental challenge. Second, our analysis applied to agreements between government and a sectoral organization, not to the agreements between government and individual firms. This kind of exceptional treatment can only be accepted in a transition phase and opens up huge possibilities of corruption and of unequal treatment of competitors.

8.4.4   Internal organization of the firm

Growing environmental awareness and increasing government or sectoral regulation will have implications for the internal organization of the firms. Although the ideal solution will depend on the concrete characteristics of each individual firm, some general points can be made. Since all stages in the production process (including the use of natural resources, marketing and distribution, and waste disposal) have environmental consequences, partial approaches will not suffice. A global perspective is needed. In this respect environmental management is closely related to the better-known concept of 'total quality management'.

The role of the top management will therefore be crucial. The environment must become part of the strategy of the firm. The intentions can be summarized in an ethical code or a mission statement. There must be a continuous attention to environmental aspects and this attention must be clear to everybody within and outside the firm. The appointment in the top management of a kind of environmental director, with as his or her main task the co-ordination and monitoring of the environmental efforts, may be a good idea.

Commitment of the top management is necessary but not sufficient. The global nature of the required reorganization implies that each member of the staff, each worker must feel responsible for the environmental objectives. This requires a big effort of information and education. It also requires a set of new rules for promotion: promotion and planning of a career must be made dependent on respect for the environment.

An essential step in the reorganization of the firm is the collection of information about how well it is performing environmentally. One possibility in this respect is environmental auditing. Such audit can be defined as a systematic and objective evaluation of the performance of the firm in meeting the regulatory requirements and, in a broader sense, in safeguarding the environment. It is carried out by an interdisciplinary team, consisting of natural scientists, lawyers and economists. Of course, it is possible to set up such a team within the firm, but to guarantee objectivity and independency it may be preferable to have an external team in charge of the auditing. A growing number of European firms practise environmental auditing, a prominent example being the Dutch Shell group. There is no doubt that it is impossible to reorientate the firm's policy with respect to the environment without introducing an auditing procedure. However, two questions remain.

1.   Should the result of the audit be made public? If these results are rather poor, the incentive to keep them secret may be very big. However, for a firm that really cares about the environment, there are huge advantages in disclosing the results. Such disclosure not only indicates its commitment for the outside world, it may by itself increase that commitment. Moreover, an environmentally motivated firm may expect a steady improvement in its environmental results and the regular publication of these improvements will undoubtedly improve its image with the general public.

2.   Should the obligation for this environmental auditing be imposed legally? The European Commission also wants to play a leading role here. Since it is impossible to set up an environmental policy without a kind of auditing procedure, the imposition of this auditing cannot be much of a problem for the environmentally motivated firms. Disclosure of the information may be a help to them since it would improve their reputation in comparison with their less scrupulous competitors. The political authorities should be careful, however, not to overburden the firms with a plethora of extremely detailed regulations.

8.4.5   *The issue of responsibility and the burden of the past*

The *Amoco Cadiz* case in Example 9 and the Seveso dioxin accident in Example 10 raise the issue of responsibility in two respects. Not only is there a problem of the relationship between the firm and its employees, there is also the problem of the broader social responsibility of firms when things go wrong, i.e. when there is an accident with large environmental costs. Both cases illustrate the difficulties in measuring the monetary value of the damages, especially awkward when there are casualties. More important for our purposes, they also illustrate how difficult it can be to settle the matter of legal responsibility. And last but not least, there is the question: who is ethically responsible in these cases?

9. Amoco Cadiz

The biggest oil spill in history was caused by the accident with the *Amoco Cadiz* tanker on 16 March 1978. The ship belonged to the American shipowner Amoco and was chartered by the Shell oil company. In heavy weather, the tanker broke adrift with rudder damage some miles off the coast of Brittany, France. The Italian captain of the *Amoco Cadiz* asked for assistance and started to negotiate with the towboat *Pacific* lying nearby. The two parties could not agree upon the price and conditions of the contract and after eleven hours of drifting the tanker ran ashore near the island of Ouessant. The next day, the vessel broke into two pieces and lost some 223,000 tonnes of crude oil. The oil spill polluted more than 250 kilometres of coastline causing massive death of sea-birds, fish and crustacea. The accident paralysed for a long time local fishing and oyster industries, and it took several years before tourism recovered from the pollution of the coastline.

A storm of public indignation broke loose because the accident could presumably have been avoided if the captains of the tanker and towboat had reached an agreement. French authorities could not intervene because the *Amoco Cadiz* was initially adrift in international waters and once the tanker entered French territorial waters it was too late. As a result of the 1967 oil spill caused by the *Torrey Canyon* on the south-west coast of England, an international treaty was agreed upon in 1969 concerning third-party liability for oil spill damage. According to the treaty, shipowners can limit their liability to a maximum of $17 million if the accident is not due to negligence. French lawyers managed to avoid the limited liability clause by bringing the case to court in Chicago (Amoco's registered office), because the USA did not sign the international treaty. This implied that Amoco faced full liability for the damage and clean-up costs. French claims for compensation exceeded $1,600 million but in January 1990, the Chicago Federal Court awarded only $300 million against Amoco. The shipowner accepted the verdict in 1992, fourteen years after the accident, but would try to recover part of the costs from its insurance companies and from the Spanish shipyards Astilleros Espanoles (500 years ago Astilleros built the ships Columbus used to successfully cross the Atlantic). The shipyards are likely to have made mistakes installing the rudder mechanism on the *Amoco Cadiz*.

We noted already that society cannot avoid all risk, because this would imply an almost complete stop to all industrial activities. Norms and regulations have to fix the socially acceptable risk level. If society accepts the use of tankers under certain conditions, it accepts at the same time the possibility of accidents. Insurance schemes have to be set up to compensate the victims if such an accident occurs.

10.   The dioxin accident at Seveso, Italy

The ICMESA chemical plant at Meda (Seveso, north of Milan), a subsidiary of the Swiss-based Givaudan SA which in its turn belongs to the Swiss pharmaceutical group Hoffmann-La Roche, specialized in the production of intermediate chemical substances for use in medicine and herbicides. On Friday, 9 July 1976 one of the chemical reactors was loaded to produce trichlorophenol, an ingredient of hexachlorophene which is a strong disinfectant and herbicide component. The chemical reaction was completed normally and the reactor was left to cool down during the weekend. On Saturday, 10 July, however, a sudden increase in temperature and pressure caused a safety valve to open. A reddish cloud escaped from the reactor and spread over the communities of Meda, Seveso, Desio and Cesano Maderno. It took some days before representatives of ICMESA realized that the cloud contained the highly toxic tetrachlorodibenzodioxin (TCDD), or simply dioxin.

Initially, Italian public authorities tried to minimize the possible consequences of the accident but after a week, some 400 people suffered from severe burns caused by the poisonous cloud. By the end of August, the first cases of chloracne, a skin disease which cures slowly and can cause scars, were reported. By that time the serious nature of the situation was recognized by all parties involved, but nobody knew the potential consequences of exposure to dioxin on human health. Animal tests had indicated that dioxin contamination leads to chloracne, possible damage to the nervous and immunity system, malfunctioning of the liver, and could possibly increase the chances of malignant tumours, spontaneous abortion and malformation of babies. It was therefore decided to close down the ICMESA plant, to evacuate 736 inhabitants from the most contaminated areas and to follow up the health condition of some 220,000 people living near Seveso. Pregnant women were allowed to have abortions carried out. All these measures and the contradicting information on the dioxin danger resulted in popular protest.

Meanwhile, Hoffmann-La Roche had promised to compensate victims of the accident, to support all medical screening, to pay for the clean-up, and to help laid-off workers of ICMESA to find another job. After decontamination 511 people could return to their houses; the other buildings including the factory were demolished. The upper layer of the soil in the area was removed and replaced and on the site of the plant a new park with sports facilities was created. After some wanderings through France, 41 drums of toxic waste from the reactor were burned in the high-temperature incinerator of Ciba-Geigy in Basle, Switzerland. In 1986, Hoffmann-La Roche estimated that the Seveso accident had cost more than 600 million Swiss francs. In 1985, two representatives of ICMESA and Givaudan were sentenced by the Milan Court of Appeal to two years of imprisonment. Concerning long-term health effects of dioxin the medical experts now agree that the consequences were less severe than initially feared in 1976. No significant increase in morbidity/mortality rates, cancer occurrences, spontaneous abortions or malformations have been noticed. However, the Seveso accident is seen by public opinion as one of the worst chemical accidents (in industrialized countries) in history.

Against this background, we can now immediately distinguish different cases. There can be no doubt that a firm is fully responsible if it voluntarily breaks the rules set by the political authorities. In that case legal and ethical responsibility go together and the firm has to bear the full burden of compensation. This does not imply that the firm automatically is exempted of all ethical responsibility if it abides by the legal rules. Suppose it has superior information at its disposal about the risks involved in a certain activity and therefore knows that these risks are much higher than judged by the authorities. From an ethical point of view, it must then bring the relevant information into the political debate. If it is negligent in this respect it is ethically responsible for the possible consequences. Very difficult problems arise when one has to settle an ecological deficit built up in the past. In our opinion, it does not make much sense to blame Western firms for the greenhouse effect or the depletion of the ozone layer. A few decades ago nobody was aware of the negative consequences for the environment of emitting CFCs or CO_2. Firms tried to satisfy the consumers in an economic situation with a low energy price (and at the same time an extremely high cost of labour). Under these circumstances it would have been awfully poor management not to use energy- or CFC-intensive technologies. Of course, now that we know more about the effects of these technologies, the question of ethical responsibility gets a quite different answer.

11.   The burden of the past: the case of PRB Balen

In 1990 the Belgian ammunition producer PRB went bankrupt. At that time PRB was owned by the British defence company Astra who had bought it in 1989 from Gechem, a subsidiary of the Belgian private holding Generale Maatschappij. Four out of five production plants of PRB were sold off to other companies but for the plant in Balen no buyers were found. PRB Balen was placed under legal restraint and the plant was managed by the state-owned holding GIMV (Gewestelijke Investeringsmaatschappij voor Vlaanderen – or Regional Investment Company for Flanders). At that time, the soil at this site in Balen proved to be heavily polluted by zinc slag, combustion ashes and ammunition residuals. Moreover, some ammunition was still lying around in the abandoned plant and had to be protected against terrorists. The Belgian Minister of Internal Affairs and the regional Flemish environmental authorities ordered the trustees of PRB to protect and clean up the site. They did indeed demilitarize the place but there was no money left to remove the chemical soil pollution. In the end the Flemish Ministry of the Environment paid for the clean-up costs and it is now trying to recover part of the expenses, estimated at one billion Belgian francs. With this intention top executives of both Gechem and the bankrupt PRB were summoned by the Flemish Ministry of the Environment. The bankrupt company PRB can never pay the claimed 800 million francs and Gechem on the other hand refuses all responsibility because they do not own PRB any more. Gechem claims that as a result of the sale of PRB in 1989 full environmental liability for the site in Balen was transferred to the British group Astra. But at the same time Astra contests the 1989 sales contract for another reason. Astra is trying in court to get the sale invalidated because Gechem would deliberately have provided incorrect information concerning the financial situation of PRB Balen. To get out of this legal mess the Flemish Ministry of the Environment took the case to court and tried to enforce the 'polluter pays' principle. Beside the validity of the sales contract, an important question will be whether Gechem or Astra knew about the soil pollution in Balen. If it can be proven that the legal owner of the site was acquainted with the pollution problem, it seems just that they pay part of the clean-up costs. But even in the latter case legal experts doubt whether Astra or Gechem can be convicted under Belgian criminal law.

Example 11 is therefore another striking example of the burden of the past. This case is not settled with the same ease, because it can be assumed that the decision-makers should have been aware of the risks involved at the time the decisions were taken. If they indeed had sufficient knowledge, then they are ethically (although perhaps not legally) responsible for the consequences. If not, they cannot be blamed. But who then has to bear the ecological deficit? It is difficult to accept that the deficit should be borne completely by the political authorities (i.e. basically by the tax-payers), if the future activities of the firm itself promise to be highly profitable. At least a part of the ecological burden must be at the expense of these future profits.

8.5   The international dimension

In an open economy, the economic costs of an isolated environmental policy (whether based on economic instruments, on regulation or on voluntary agreements) may be high. International competition tends to be extremely stiff and the industries in the environmentally active countries may experience a loss of competitiveness on the international market. Of course, if all or most countries follow the same policy, this effect would disappear. There would still be a considerable shift from polluting to non-polluting activities all over the world but the polluting industries in all countries would face the same challenge. This is an important argument for the international co-ordination of environmental action.

There is a second argument for such co-ordination. Many important environmental problems are situated at a continental (e.g., acid rain) or even planetary level (e.g., the greenhouse problem). More local problems may also involve more than one country: the pollution of rivers (such as the Rhine) and the location of nuclear power plants are obvious examples. Not only are individual firms powerless in solving these problems, but the same is basically true for individual countries. The positive effects of isolated action by one country may be very small. The reduction of CO_2 emissions by, e.g., Denmark or Norway, would have a negligible effect on the stock of greenhouse gases and the same is true for an isolated acid rain or ozone layer policy. The overall effect of these individual efforts may even be counterproductive if other countries adjust their own behaviour and take advantage of the new situation to start emitting more polluting substances[9].

The conclusion is obvious. If we want to do something about these international environmental problems, the co-ordination of the efforts by different countries is indispensable. Such co-ordination is difficult because there does not exist an international government which could set up the adequate policy. The European Community is perhaps an exception to this statement. At the world level, however, we have to rely exclusively on negotiated voluntary agreements. One can hardly be optimistic about the prospects for these agreements in our present world situation, the more so since the environmental problem is closely linked to the issue of the international income distribution.

8.5.1   The environment and the Third World

The problem of international co-ordination of environmental policy is closely linked to the issue of the underdevelopment of a large part of the world. Again, global warming is a good example. A successful policy is not possible without the co-operation of the developing countries. But these countries are not responsible for the present stock of greenhouse gases and are now only trying to catch up with the rich North. It will therefore be extremely difficult for the rich countries to persuade the developing countries to cut down their energy consumption, unless the latter are compensated by other means. This means that an adequate reaction to the huge income differences in the world may be a prerequisite for an international environmental policy.

Many Third World countries do not have the regulatory apparatus to control all business activities. The transport of hazardous waste to these countries has become a profitable business. Moreover, the importance attached to the environment apparently increases with the level of material welfare. Some poor regions or countries are willing to bear a high health risk or to suffer a high pollution level, if this yields them a higher level of material welfare. This raises some awkward problems for business ethics. Is it acceptable that firms move their dangerous and polluting activities to the poorer regions of the world? Some economists have argued that this is indeed the most efficient solution. We give a prominent example below.

12.   The opinion of a chief economist of the World Bank

In February 1992, *The Economist* published some excerpts of an internal memorandum by Lawrence Summers, chief economist of the World Bank. It says: 'Just between you and me, shouldn't the World Bank be encouraging more migration of the dirty industries to the LDCs?' Summers gives three reasons. First, evaluating economic costs of health risks of pollution involves determining the monetary value of human life. In traditional cost-benefit analysis this problem is dealt with by assuming that the value of life equals discounted lifetime earnings of an individual. This concept attaches less value to human life in low-wage (i.e. developing) countries than in industrialized regions. Hence, economic efficiency calls for exporting polluting industries to LDCs (less developed countries) because opportunity costs of increased morbidity and mortality are lowest there.

Secondly, Summers writes: 'I've always thought that under-populated countries in Africa are vastly under-polluted; their air quality is probably vastly inefficiently low compared to Los Angeles or Mexico City.' In his view welfare could theoretically be enhanced by trading air pollution and waste. Unfortunately, unit transport costs are high and much pollution is produced by non-tradable industries like transport and electricity generation.

His third argument concerns the high income elasticity of environmental concern. It is only in high-income countries that the environment becomes a major public concern. Economic growth, sanitation, reducing child mortality, etc. are more important policy objectives for developing countries than, for instance, saving tropical rainforests.

These statements caused some fuss within the World Bank and far beyond. Most economists agree with Summers' third point on high income elasticity of environmental concern but argue that this should not be taken as an argument to export pollution to LDCs. Many people feel that industrialized countries have a moral obligation to treat their own waste instead of exporting it. And this moral obligation should outweigh economic efficiency considerations. The same applies to Summers' second argument.

Concerning his first point about the value of human life, feelings are running high. Some people claim that it is immoral to attach monetary value to unique human beings. However, every policy decision to fund, for instance, medical research implicitly values human lives. In a world of scarce public funds this kind of harsh choice cannot be avoided. So, the problem is not the valuation of human life but the predominant role Summers gives to economic efficiency. In certain domains of decision-making ethical principles or social considerations prevail over economic calculus. Nowhere in the world are allowances for handicapped or elderly people determined as a function of economic efficiency.

Although this position may be efficient, it is a rather cynical reaction to the present unacceptable income distribution at the world level[10]. The ethical questions become still more acute when human rights of personal safety and dignity are at stake. Many would argue that these should be respected at any price and whatever the economic costs involved. But must this respect be so absolute as to overrule the personal choices of the people involved? And is a positive answer to this question not inconsistent with the very dignity one claims to defend? The latter questions relate to the notion of freedom. Did the people living in the surroundings of the firm described in Example 2 really choose to live there? Did they have any other choice? Or, to give a better known example (summarized in Example 13): can one really say that the poorest people in Bhopal had any other real opportunity but to agree to the location of a dangerous chemical plant in their region? Moreover, these people probably were incompletely informed about the health risks involved. While it is not our intention to go deeply into these fundamental questions, it is obvious that one should be cautious in giving too quick and easy answers. Perhaps the problem of the international income distribution goes beyond the traditional domain of business ethics, but it certainly is the most crucial ethical problem of our actual economic system and therefore also important to all ethically motivated businesspeople.

13.   Developing countries and the environment: the Bhopal case

During the night of 2 December 1984 a cloud containing the poisonous gas methylisocyanate escaped from a Union Carbide chemical plant in Bhopal, in the state of Madhya Pradesh, India. This highly toxic gas is used in the production of pesticides. The gas cloud killed 1,300 persons immediately and some 1,700 people died in the weeks after the accident. Between 30,000 and 40,000 people suffered serious injuries or handicaps for life. Bhopal was surely the most devastating chemical disaster that ever occurred. Soon after the catastrophe many critics accused the Western chemical industry of moving its dangerous activities since the Seveso dioxin accident in Italy in 1976 towards Third World countries where wages are lower and safety regulations are less stringent.

The state of India received 525,000 claims for compensation of victims and their relatives amounting to $3.3 billion. A long legal dispute between the American Union Carbide Corporation and the state of India started. India preferred the case to go on trial in the USA because of the higher compensation rules but this was refused by the US District Court of New York. In Bhopal Union Carbide Corporation (UCC) tried to escape liability by arguing that it was only partly (50.9 per cent) owner of Union Carbide India Ltd (UCIL), operators of the Bhopal plant. UCC filed a counterclaim against the state of India for having allowed the existence of illegal settlements in the vicinity of the plant. UCC also argued that the accident was not caused by negligence on its part but by an act of sabotage by a discontented Indian worker. In order to prevent interminable litigation and to guarantee rapid compensation of the victims the parties started direct negotiations to reach a settlement. This was reached in February 1989 when the Indian Supreme Court ordered UCC to pay $470 million to settle all claims. It was agreed that the settlement would dispose of all past and future claims and all civil and criminal prosecutions.

This legal immunity was lifted in 1991 without changing the amount of compensation paid by UCC.

8.5.2   The European decision level

In the past decades the European Community has developed into an integrated market and an economic superpower. This integration and the ensuing industrial growth by themselves have led to an intensification of the environmental problems.[11] Moreover, they have made it more difficult for the different member countries to follow an efficient environmental policy in isolation. The problem of waste transportation is a striking example. As a reaction, the possibilities of Community policy and action in the field of the environment have been broadened considerably. There is a fundamental difference between the European Community and other international organizations such as the OECD or the United Nations: the Community is a legislative body and can go much further in its concrete interventions. We give an overview of some institutional developments in Example 14.

14.   Institutional developments in the EC

The new Treaty on European Union, signed by all member states on 7 February 1992 in Maastricht, mentions explicitly the environmental dimension of EC policy. A lot of good intentions are formulated in the Treaty but some of the guiding principles might conflict with each other. Article 2 of the general Principles of the EC refers to the promotion of *a harmonious and balanced development of economic activities, sustainable and non-inflationary growth respecting the environment*, and article 3k requires the activities of the Community to include an environmental policy. Compared to the old Treaty on European Union these additions constitute the formal recognition of the environment as a policy objective for the EC.

In addition, a separate section of the Treaty is devoted to environmental policy. According to article 130R.1 the following general principles should guide European environmental policy: (1) preservation, protection and amelioration of environmental quality, (2) protection of human health, (3) responsible and rational use of natural resources, and (4) enhancement at the international level of measures to cope with regional or global environmental problems. Article 130R.2 of the Treaty mentions that EC policy should aim at high environmental quality standards, should take into account regional differences in priorities, preferences and spending power, and should be based on the precautionary and 'polluter pays' principle. Environmental considerations should also be integrated in the decision and implementation processes of all other European policies. Finally, the article stipulates that, under specific conditions, individual member states can obtain an exception on (tax) harmonization directives to allow for more stringent individual regulation on non-economic environmental grounds.

The latter exception reflects the concern that different political preferences should be reflected in the ability of individual member countries to go beyond European minimum environmental requirements. This concern was also expressed in the report of the Task Force on the Environment and the Internal Market: *1992, The Environmental Dimension*. This report gives some examples of potential conflicts between the general principles in the Maastricht Treaty and environmental objectives. The Task Force recommends for instance that the guiding principle of subsidiarity, i.e. the requirement that decision-making competence should rest with the lowest possible level of political hierarchy, should be modified to provide for minimum ambient standards. If countries were free to choose their own ambient standards, and if some country adopted an extremely weak standard, the free movement of citizens in the EC would imply that all Europeans are entitled to this weakest standard. Or, on the other hand, if some country would set very high environmental product standards, this could be interpreted as protectionism conflicting with the general principle of free movement of goods in the EC. These examples illustrate that the Commission faces a major task to substantiate the good intentions expressed in the Treaty of Maastricht.

As a consequence of these developments, the environmental activities of the Community have been expanding rapidly. While these activities sometimes do not go sufficiently far for the environmentally most conscious member states (such as Denmark, The Netherlands or Germany), the Community takes a leading role in comparison to the national policy-makers in other countries. Many businesspeople have reacted strongly to this growing intervention and have pointed to the lack of democratic control at the European level. Recent Community programmes therefore tend to emphasize the importance of discussion and agreements with the enterprises. While the danger of inefficient overregulation remains, one must at the same time emphasize the advantages of taking decisions at the European level.

First, the European level is the adequate one to set up a co-ordinated policy for Continental environmental problems, such as acid rain or pollution of rivers. The recent discovery of the environmental disaster in Eastern Europe has made it very clear that these problems cannot be solved without the help of the richer countries in Europe. As the Chernobyl accident has shown, such help may even be in the self-interest of these countries. This is not a matter for the member countries of the European Community alone, but it is obvious that the Community has to play a key role in the whole process. We give some information in Example 15.

15.   The EC and the Central and Eastern European countries

Environmental issues rank high on the agenda of negotiating between the EC and Central and Eastern European countries. After forty years of centrally planned economies with high priority for heavy industries, pollution has reached critical limits in many parts of Central and Eastern Europe (CEE). It is estimated that 75 per cent of Polish forests are affected by acidification and the safety measures in chemical and nuclear installations are largely insufficient. From the very beginning, all economic co-operation and assistance programmes between the EC and CEE include provisions for protection and amelioration of ambient quality standards and public health. In 1990, the so-called PHARE programme, which includes Poland, Hungary, former East Germany and the Czech and Slovak Federal Republic, spent almost 100 million ECU on environmental projects. Also the European Bank for Reconstruction and Development is involved in financing these projects. In the future, however, CEE countries will have to generate more and more funds by themselves to alleviate environmental stress. Structural changes in the pricing policy and production technology or even the complete closure of the most polluting production units will become inevitable to reduce emissions at the source.

Second, the problem of differences in income levels not only arises in relation to the Third World: it also plays a role within the context of negotiations at the European level, where the richest countries (Germany, Denmark, The Netherlands) have a different opinion about environmental policy than the others (Spain, Portugal, Greece). Here also distributional issues must be settled before any consensus on the environment can be reached. However, contrary to the world, Europe has the set of instruments to do something about this situation. The European Regional Development Fund can devote more funds to environmental projects and additional redistributional institutions (e.g., the Cohesion Fund) are currently set up to facilitate environmental co-operation.

Third, since a large part of trade for all European enterprises is concentrated in Europe itself, a co-ordinated policy at the European level would diminish considerably the effects on international competitiveness. At least, it would restrict the problem to some well-circumscribed industries.

Finally, Europe may also contribute to the solution of environmental problems at the planetary scale. Given its economic power, the effects of a European policy might not be completely negligible. Moreover (and perhaps most importantly), one can expect that the economic power of Europe in the medium run will also lead to a larger political influence in international negotiations. Europe therefore might play an important role in enforcing the kind of international agreements that are indispensable to solve the global environmental problems. The construction of an ethically attractive and economically feasible European project for an internationally co-ordinated environmental policy is a prime task. Business must participate in this task in a constructive way.

8.6   Profit maximization and environmental concern are not always contradictory: possibilities in a dynamic context

We have argued that the pressure of competition is an important constraint for ethically oriented firms that want to change their attitude towards nature. At the same time, one could derive from the previous sections the impression that environmental regulation necessarily leads to a downward pressure on profits. However, the possible conclusion that the profit motive can never be helpful to solve the environmental problem is totally unjustified.

As mentioned before, the constraints imposed by competition depend on various factors. There will be more room for ecologically motivated behaviour if the cost differential between clean and polluting products is not too large, and/or if the firm has sufficient market power, and/or if a sufficient number of consumers is aware of the environmental problem. The regulatory framework also plays a role here. Moreover, these factors have to be interpreted in a dynamic context. We will concentrate on three important aspects.

8.6.1   The growth of environmental industries

As a consequence of the growing environmental awareness of firms and, more importantly, the growing regulation and increasing efforts by the political authorities to clean up the atmosphere, there is a rapidly growing demand for the products of the so-called environmental industry. This is not a homogeneous sector and, following the Task Force Report on the Environment and the European Internal Market (published in 1989) we will define it rather loosely as 'the suppliers of technologies and services which monitor, prevent, limit or correct environmental damage and contribute to clean economic growth'. In the European Community this definition covers several thousand firms.

Experience shows that these firms are mostly concentrated in the countries with a very strict environmental legislation, such as Sweden and Germany. Indeed, it only makes sense to invest in this sector if one can expect a more or less stable demand: and this demand depends upon the regulatory framework. If one expects short-run changes in policy, it is cheaper to buy the technology from abroad. The latter possibility will become more relevant in the future, because of the increasing internationalization of the sector, where European firms have to compete with Japanese and American enterprises.

The message is clear. Here is a growing market where environmentally motivated businesspeople with sufficient imagination and courage may reap important rewards for their efforts. To realize this potential, however, it is crucial that the political authorities commit to a stable environmental policy. To realize economies of scale and compete with large firms from abroad, there must be a commitment at the European level. If Europe sets its standards much lower than, e.g., Japan and the United States, there is a huge danger that its environmental industries will lag behind and will never recover from this false start.

8.6.2   The development of a green market

Even without an increase in government regulation, dynamic effects are surely to be expected on the consumer side of the market. In fact, the environmental awareness of European consumers seems to be rapidly growing. This is encouraging insofar as it reflects a real concern for the environment. For many products there are now already subsets of consumers who are willing to pay a higher price for a clean product. Concentrating on these consumers may be profitable. Moreover, in a longer-run perspective it may lead to the growth of a real 'green market'. As soon as green products are no longer restricted to a negligible fraction of the market, diffusion effects are to be expected. The growing volume of sales and the presence of these products in traditional distribution channels will by themselves increase the environmental awareness and the information of the consumers. Example 16 illustrates some of these issues with the experience of a small Belgian firm venturing out quite successfully on the oligopolistic market of washing-powders.

16.   The ECOVER case

That some entrepreneurs take the ecological challenge seriously is illustrated by the success story of ECOVER which produces detergents and washing-powders. The international market for washing-powder is characterized by an oligopolistic structure. Procter & Gamble and Henkel dominate production, marketing and distribution of detergents almost everywhere in the world. Entering this market was considered economic suicide because it would require huge marketing efforts. In 1979 Frans Bogaerts started in Belgium with the production of an ecological washing-powder and ten years later his firm ECOVER holds a market share of 5 per cent in the UK. ECOVER's products contain neither phosphates (substances that stimulate excessive growth of algae in rivers and lakes which causes oxygen shortage and fish death) nor (toxic) petrochemical detergents. Instead ECOVER products consist of natural soaps, aromatics and oils.

ECOVER does not claim that its products are harmless for ecosystems but their basic concept is to produce detergents which cause as little ecological damage as possible during the entire lifetime of the products. Not only the detergent itself and its waste products are considered. ECOVER also tries to set up an ecologically sustainable production and distribution process. A typical illustration of this concept is the new production plant in Oostmalle (Belgium). The plant is equipped with an electricity generator using rapeseed oil and with a reed field as biological water treatment installation. The roof is covered with a lawn acting as natural isolation. Considerable effort is also devoted to introducing less polluting packaging. In the beginning ECOVER products were only sold in specialized small ecoshops in Belgium but gradually they were introduced in neighbouring countries like Holland, France, Germany and Britain. By the end of 1988 ECOVER succeeded in penetrating supermarkets in the UK and in less than two years they conquered a market share of 3 to 5 per cent proving that there exists a considerable marketing potential and sufficiently high consumer willingness to pay for green washing-powders. Meanwhile ECOVER products are sold in every country of the EC, they signed joint ventures with Japanese and Australian retailing firms and they built a production plant in the United States. The Belgian firm was awarded several prizes for its export success and for the ecological qualities of its detergents. Turnover is expected to exceed one billion Belgian francs in 1992. ECOVER employs some thirty people in Oostmalle and is still growing rapidly.

In contrast to traditional producers ECOVER spends little money on marketing and publicity. Their main communication objective is to inform potential buyers of the products and of the effects of phosphate and artificial chemical additives on ecosystems. Therefore ECOVER built on a lorry a scale model of the natural water cycle demonstrating the effects of water pollution by phosphates and petrochemical substances. This lorry is used to visit schools, trade expositions, etc.

Soon after ECOVER's success in the UK Procter & Gamble and Henkel expanded their range of products to include phosphate-free washing-powders because they were pressed by public opinion and by consumer demand. Phosphates were replaced by petrochemical additives and huge marketing efforts were made to brush up their green image. Despite the response of the multi-nationals ECOVER hopes to conquer in the near future a market share of 2 per cent in Europe, corresponding to a turnover of 8 billion Belgian francs.

Although the trend towards the production of green products is remarkable and encouraging, one should be aware of an important danger. Insofar as the trend towards green products is exploited only by marketing tricks where one-sided information is given without a real change in product design, consumers will feel deceived after a while. The profusion of often unreliable information might create a feeling of apathy. A system of ecolabelling can be extremely helpful to ensure that the information given to consumers is adequate and easy to understand. It will also lead to a better protection for the bona fide firms, which really try to produce environmentally acceptable products. The European discussion around this labelling is summarized in Example 17.

17.   Ecomarketing and ecolabelling in Europe

In recent years marketing people have been trying to exploit growing environmental awareness by claiming that their products are 'ozone friendly', 'non-damaging for the environment' or 'do not contain phosphates'. Some of these claims are exaggerated or misleading because they reveal only part of the truth. Consumers are confronted with information which cannot be verified. In response to this problem, some European countries introduced a national ecological quality label. If a product satisfies a list of environmental requirements, it is allowed to bear a special label or symbol. An example is the Blauer Engel in Germany. In December 1991 the European Commission decided to introduce, much like the Blauer Engel, a uniform European ecolabel which would take into account the effects of a product on the environment from the cradle to the grave. Multiple criteria in every phase of the product's lifecycle, ranging from energy use to packaging waste, would play a role. A special commission would set up a list of requirements for different products and would award the labels. Beside the European label national labels can still exist.

Many people in industry are sceptical about the European ecolabel because it is unclear how the environmental impact of products during their entire lifecycle is to be evaluated. The so-called Life Cycle Analysis (LCA) is currently one of the only methodologies used for this purpose but its results are controversial. Some LCA studies defend, for instance, the use of glass bottles to package milk but other studies prefer milk in cartons. The LCA methodology and database has to be standardized before it can be used to award ecolabels.

For environmentalists the proposed European ecolabel does not go far enough. They say first of all that no product can be 'good' for the environment, it can only be less damaging. Therefore a code of conduct for 'green' publicity is needed and firms should refer to ecological arguments only if they can prove their claims with scientific results. Second, environmentalists would favour a gradual label, a system of ecostars like, for instance, the Michelin stars for restaurants. Producers of washing-powder who ban only phosphates (an important problem, but not the only one with washing-powder) would receive one star whereas other producers who replace also all petrochemical detergents by natural soaps would get an additional star. A differentiated label has the advantage that it identifies the ecological producers from the ones who only try to brush up their public image by complying with the weakest requirement. In Germany, for instance, the credibility of the Blauer Engel waters down because more than 3,000 products are currently allowed to bear the symbol.

Economists offer an additional argument in favour of a gradual ecolabel. A system of ecostars is dynamically efficient because it gives a permanent incentive to producers to look for ecologically more sustainable products. A firm would acquire an important competitive advantage if it succeeds selling at a lower (or even the same) price an equivalent product with an additional ecostar. The proposed European label is static, however. Once a firm meets the basic requirement for being awarded the ecolabel it will make no additional research effort to diminish the environmental impact of its product.

8.6.3   Research and development activities

Both for the development of environmental industries and of green markets, the direction of R&D activities will be the crucial element. Most of the industrial research is concentrated in the research branches of the large firms. This implies that they can make a major contribution to finding new innovative solutions for pollution problems. One can even put it more strongly: if they do not do it, there is nobody else who has the means or the expertise to take over that role. Environmentally motivated firms can shape their own future and the future of society through their R&D decisions. The environmental impact will be most positive if the emphasis in R&D goes in two directions. First, it is preferable to concentrate on new products rather than on improvements in the production technology. Newly created (less polluting) products really can change the outlook of our society and have a positive influence on consumer awareness and on the development of green markets. Special attention should be given to the problem of waste disposal. Second, if concentrated on production technology, the effort should not be directed towards end-of-pipe solutions. One should rather aim at an integrated change in the production process from start to end.

An increase in R&D efforts will not only have positive environmental impacts. It may also lead to a decrease in production costs. Moreover, in a dynamic setting it will give the firm a huge comparative advantage on the newly developing green markets and markets for environmental services. An increase in regulation and in consumer awareness is to be expected in the future. Instead of lagging behind this development, environmentally motivated firms can better take the lead. So doing, they may exert an important influence on the direction of future developments. Here also, economic profitability and environmental concern are by no means contradictory.

8.7 Conclusion

There are different ways of interpreting the environmental problems facing our world today. From the point of view of business ethics, it is necessary to build up a better insight into concrete and specific mechanisms within a market economy. We have argued that a basic feature of a free market is the possibility to use nature freely and without cost. In such a situation the self-interest motive will lead immediately to environmental deterioration. The environmental challenge confronts firms with many difficult ethical dilemmas. The broad themes from the philosophical literature (such as the conflict between ecocentrism and anthropocentrism, or the notion of sustainable development) are useful because they highlight the important values which are at stake. But they remain too general to be of much guidance in concrete situations.

In some cases even isolated firms can make an important contribution to solve environmental problems. This will certainly be the case if these firms have superior technico-scientific knowledge at their disposal. However, the potential of isolated action is limited if the ethical dilemmas are difficult and involve many people and/or if there is an important co-ordination problem. There will be less room for ecologically motivated behaviour if the cost differential between clean and polluting products is large, if the firm has only a small market power and if the environmental awareness of the consumers is limited. The environmental concern certainly will require a change in the internal organization of the firm. Environmental auditing may be quite crucial in this respect.

The fear that there will be a huge increase in inefficient government regulations during the following decades is widespread among businesspeople. However, a conservative defence of the existing (polluting) system is not the right reaction to this fear. It would be preferable if businesspeople would actively participate in the political debate. Government intervention is not a substitute but rather a complement for ethical behaviour. Indeed, in a situation where firms have superior information about many crucial aspects of the problem, there is a huge control and monitoring problem. This implies that there is much need for spontaneous ethical behaviour, possibly embodied in voluntary agreements and codes.

In a dynamic setting profit maximization and environmental concern may coincide. The growing number of regulations will lead to a development of markets for environmental services. If consumers are sufficiently motivated to buy green products, a profitable market of green products may develop where diffusion effects are to be expected. A crucial role is played by research and development activities.

Many environmental problems have an international dimension and an increase in environmental regulation may threaten the international competitiveness of the firms. It is therefore not surprising that the importance of the European decision level has been increasing steadily in the recent past. This tendency can be expected to continue. One would hope that Europe also will play a leading role in negotiations to solve the environmental problems at the world level.

Notes

1. This simple statement disregards the problem of income distribution.
2. World Commission on Environment and Development (1987), *Our Common Future* (Oxford).
3. Volume II of the 'European Community Programme of Policy and Action in Relation to the Environment and Sustainable Development' (27 March 1992) has as its main title: 'Towards Sustainability'.
4. An overview of some important questions is given by Pearce, D., and Turner, K. (1990), *Economics of Natural Resources and the Environment* (New York/London: Harvester Wheatsheaf).
5. While the broader philosophical analyses are not sufficiently concrete to be of much help for this ethical cost-benefit analysis, one should not incline to the other extreme and reduce the problem to a traditional economic cost-benefit analysis. Every good economist is aware of the difficulties related to the evaluation of public goods and to the introduction of distributional judgements in cost-benefit analysis. More fundamentally, many moral philosophers question the traditional economic procedure for accepting uncritically the individual preferences, as revealed in actual consumption behaviour. This is not the place to go deeply into this debate, but it is obvious to us that traditional cost-benefit analysis in the present state of the art can only be a poor first approximation to the global ethical judgement which is required. However, we do believe that this poor first approximation may be very helpful if the economic cost-benefit analyst is aware of the limitations of the exercise and does not present their results as the final or (worse still) 'scientifically correct' answer.

6. In the text we emphasize the advantages of taxes and marketable permits. A more detailed analysis would also mention various cases where norms and regulations are to be preferred. To give an example: the use of highly toxic pollutants should be forbidden. A very readable survey of the economic literature on environmental policy instruments can be found in Bohm, P. and Russell, C., 'Comparative analysis of alternative policy instruments', in Kneese, A. and Sweeney, J. (eds.), *Handbook of Natural Resource and Energy Economics*, vol. I, Amsterdam, North-Holland, 1985, pp. 395–460.

7. From now on we will concentrate in the text on the tax instrument, but the reasoning with respect to marketable permits is analogous.

8. See the analysis by K. J. Arrow (1973), 'Social responsibility and economic efficiency', in *Public Policy*, vol. 21, 3.

9. See the theoretical analysis in M. Hoel (1991), 'Global environmental problems: the effects of unilateral actions taken by one country', in *Journal of Environmental Economics and Management* 20, 55–70.

10. Note that here also there is a co-ordination problem, in that firms may gain a competitive advantage by producing cheaply in underdeveloped regions.

11. An overview of the environmental problems following from the European economic integration can be found in *1992: The Environmental Dimension* (Task Force Report on the Environment and the Internal Market, requested by the Commission of the European Communities).

CHAPTER 9

The ethics of capitalism

Peter F. Koslowski

The Hannover Institute of Philosophical Research, Germany

> Who would not be bright enough to see much in his surroundings which is, indeed, not as it should be?
>
> Hegel, *Enzyklopädie der philosophischen Wissenschaften* (1830) § 6

> The world is always only a little short of salvation.
>
> Carl Sternheim, *Aus dem bürgerlichen Heldenleben* (1913)

Moral inquiry into the ethics and morality of capitalism is certainly most delicate and ambiguous. It must find a path between uncritical apology and presumptuous moralism, between precipitate acceptance of the status quo and abstract imperatives.

Capitalism as an economic order is distinguished by three structural characteristics, namely, private disposal of means of production, market and price mechanisms as means of co-ordination, and profit and utility maximization as the basic motivation in economic action. This chapter's thesis is that capitalism constitutes a necessary component of a free society but that a theory of capitalism (as a societal form) which considers the capitalist economic order to be the whole of society falls short of societal reality. All attempts to base society exclusively upon these three structural characteristics fall to the reductionism objection as raised already by neoliberals such as W. Röpke and A. Rüstow.[1] Tendencies of the contemporary positivist economic theory (Becker, 1974; Hirshleifer, 1978) to make the capitalist economy and its paradigm a universal and conclusive theory of human action and society – indeed, beyond sociobiology to even make it a theory of all life forms – present an interesting theory imperialism of economics but are ultimately economic reductions.

In believing that they can dispose with ethics and with the posing of value questions, contemporary positivist economists overlook that as a society of free individuals, capitalism places enormous moral demands on the individuals and requires a moral attitude that the economy alone cannot produce. Against such attempts it is necessary to recall that economics originated from moral philosophy

236

and that its father Adam Smith wrote two treatises: *The Wealth of Nations* and *The Theory of Moral Sentiments*. A social philosophy of capitalism must have the same breadth of perspective as Adam Smith. It must guard against committing the economic fallacy of believing that an economically efficient system already makes for a good or moral society and that the economy is the whole of society.

9.1   What does morality of an economic system mean?

The question of morality cannot contribute an additional moral aspect to the economic, sociological and political aspects of capitalism; rather, it must be understood as the integration and moral evaluation of the totality of arguments. Morality is not one aspect among others, but a way to appreciate the perspectives and arguments of the sciences, to order and evaluate them, and to render them meaningful for human action.[2] The question of the morality of capitalism cannot be: is capitalism moral? The question must be: is capitalism justifiable under the conditions of human nature and the scarcity of resources? The morality of capitalism can be justified only by the nature of the object, that is, the function of the economy and the possibilities it offers for human self-realization. The moral inquiry is not opposed to economic theory but must take up the latter and ask whether all aspects of reality are done justice.

To the understandable objection that this claim to a totality of perspectives in ethics is very extensive, one must answer that people raise the question of the justification of their actions and of the system in this universality and not as an inquiry into single aspects of their existence. In addition, one lives in a totality of social conditions and is determined by them. One would want neither to live in a just society where there is nothing to buy nor in an efficient, rich society that employs its resources for morally reprehensible purposes. In the inquiry into the ethics of capitalism and into the totality of its characteristics, therefore, scientific precision must not be paid for by the renunciation of the entirety of possible aspects. At the same time it is evident that a social order can never be justified once and for all because the number and importance of the viewpoints by which it must be evaluated constantly change with time.

9.2   The morals of capitalism, or Are morals superfluous in a working market?

The problem of the ethics of capitalism arises already within economic theory insofar as there exists in it the possibility of a trade-off between efficiency and economic freedom.[3] According to J. Marshak, 'the sacrifice of liberty is an organizational cost' (1974: 199). However, this does not advance the inquiry as to how this sacrifice of freedom is to be evaluated. This question remains one of a balancing between social values which transcend the purely economic model. One cannot immediately switch to forced allocation at every disturbance of the optimality conditions nor can one, as K. J. Arrow correctly objects, hold non-interference to be the only value (1967: 12). The science of choice – welfare economics – is of no help here either as the discussion of the possibility of a social welfare function has shown.[4] A mechanical solution of the overall optimum is not available.

F. H. Knight has critically examined the mechanistic analogy in economics. The general equilibrium model interprets economic behaviour in accordance with the analogy of force in which the motive causing an act is understood as force (Knight, 1969: 241). Economics must then be concerned with actions arising from preferences that are not further questioned. The Newtonian concept of force in mechanics has been criticized in physics as metaphysical by Mach and Hertz, but it acquires justification insofar as the forces in nature are observable and experimentally reproducible. That is not the case, however, for economic preferences, which are conceived as forces behind the choices of individuals. Preferences have a primarily social character; that is, they are influenced by social status, training, and education, as well as by error. Preferences and choices are not identifiable like force and the effects of force in the natural sciences. Market competition cannot be considered according to the model of force and opposing force which lead to an equilibrium of forces. The mechanistic model takes goals, motives, and the preferences of individuals as given and only accepts considerations as to means. It is a model of adaption in which the individuals' acts of choice are based upon their unquestionably accepted preferences and the force conditions of the market. No value problem arises concerning the choice of goals.

Through the acceptance of given, constant goals, the moral problem is reduced to an economic one, and ethics is replaced by economics.[5] Knight sees this 'displacement of ethics by a sort of higher economics' in classical economics and in utilitarians like Bentham and J. S. Mill, and it also appears in the case of Spencer (1969: 19). Looking at contemporary theoretical discussions one could see sociobiology and bioeconomics as attempts to introduce a universal economics. For utilitarians, who are thoroughgoing hedonists, well-being is the goal of all action. Ethics is then reduced to the optimal allocation of resources for the goal of the greatest pleasure. This goal is empty and formal, and as long as the substance of pleasure is not determined, the maxim of maximization of pleasure means no more than each doing as that person wishes anyway. No help in making selections can be drawn from the concept of the greatest pleasure or utility. On this basis, the individual cannot choose if he or she does not already know what he or she wants.

Among the objections to hedonism that have been raised since Plato are that people do not want pleasure or utility but rather seek concrete goods, and that they do not desire plain pleasure but distinguish and rank various pleasures. Thus, Plato argues in *Gorgias* that a person interested only in satisfaction should best wish himself an itch, so as to be better able to scratch himself.[6] Max Scheler further criticized hedonism by saying that one cannot attain happiness immediately but rather obtain it 'on the back of other activities' (1966: 351). One does not play the piano in order to be happy; rather, one can be happy when one knows how to play the piano.

The two approaches just presented – i.e. the elimination of ethics from capitalism by means of the mechanistic model and the attempt of utilitarianism to make economics into a kind of metaethics – are attempts to avoid the value problem inherent in the selection of goals. Thus, 'economics might almost be defined as the art of reducing incommensurables to common terms. It is the art of heroic simplification' (Shackle, 1972: 10). Both positions amount to the attitude correctly described by K. E. Boulding as 'knowing the value of nothing and the price of everything', which means nothing other than that the economy can show the individual the relative prices and the optimal allocation of his or her resources for certain goals, but cannot relieve him/her of the choice between goals and values (1967: 67).

9.2.1 Formation and co-ordination of preferences: the coherence of ethics and economics

Preferences are not rigidly given and invariable, and the social problem is not merely one of economizing the use of means. Preferences are ethically and socially transmitted; they are formed in individual ethical reflection as well as social interaction. Symbolic interactionism, as was presented by G. H. Mead and W. I. Thomas, shows how closely one's view of the world and one's perspective is determined by groups and communities.[7] One sees goods not in themselves but rather in a close weave of perspectives of different reference groups to which one belongs and in the symbolic definitions one gives to the qualities of the goods. According to the Thomas theorem, symbolic definitions of situations that people adopt are real in their consequences. From this point of view, culturally defined needs are as real in their consequences as physiological needs. One can consider needs as constant only in abstraction and in the very short run. De facto, preferences continually change by way of the transformation of institutions and society.

As deliberation upon the correct allocation of resources for given purposes, economics can provide information on the possible extent and opportunity costs of the fulfilment of goals. However, Knight points out that it can 'never get beyond the question of whether one end conflicts with another end and if so which is to be sacrificed' (1969: 37). In the case of a conflict between competing goals one must abandon the level of scientific economics and use preference rules. Ethically speaking, the question as to which goals an individual in a society sets for him/herself is more important than the question of how this goal is to be fulfilled.

It is obvious that the ethical and sociological theory of the formation of preferences is logically prior to economics as the theory of the allocation of resources for these preferences. One must ask about the reasonableness of the goals and about the optimal allocation of resources for these goals. Neither of these questions can be reduced to the other. With a given factor endowment and given preferences, a condition is conceivable in which the complete variability of all quantities and of the anthropological presuppositions for the indifference curves leads to a situation in which no one can improve his or her position without another being hurt. Can this be interpreted as a real optimum? Let us set aside the problem of the initial distribution of endowments for the moment. It is still apparent that all adaptations in the system are more or less of a strategic character. Preferences were not examined or transformed for rationality or goodness but merely adapted to variations in the environment. The Pareto-optimum cannot, therefore, define social or ethical optimality beyond the economic viewpoint of allocative optimality.

The ethical postulate must still be raised that individuals should vary their effective demand not only according to their own given preferences and accommodate to those of others in the course of exchange in such a way that a Pareto-optimal position is reached, but that they should transform their preferences in an ethical way respecting the preferences of others. They should not only move on the indifference curve but change their system of indifference curves at times. K. E. Boulding claimed that every movement on the indifference curve to a point on the contract curve presupposes a certain indulgence and the absence of jealousy or envy (1964). If one follows this thesis, the Pareto-optimum implies a moral minimum. Yet such a moral minimum in a Pareto system cannot be an optimum in a moral sense.

The value problem in capitalism arises because it is not centrally predetermined, and individual evaluation of goals, i.e. freedom, is held to be a value. Freedom is both a fact – as non-intervention – and a value category.[8] It can be seen as an instrument for reaching other goods as well as being a value in itself. The understanding of freedom as pure non-interference with market forces eventually leads to a pure mechanism in which everything that occurs without political intervention appears good. This understanding of freedom can be seen in Spencerism and social Darwinism. In Western societies, freedom, understood as the ability to act according to self-chosen goals, is seen as an intrinsic value which has pushed other values, such as stability, calculability, and personal continuity into the background. The concept of freedom is bound up with the dialectic of freedom and self-responsibility, without which a free capitalistic order is unthinkable. This burden of freedom brings about the fact that a free economy cannot be, as it were, derived from efficiency criteria, but rather presupposes a moral will to freedom. Freedom and property must be willed.[9]

Capitalism does not eliminate the problem of value; it rather puts the burden on the individual. Economic individualism, therefore, is necessarily tied to ethical individualism. The problem of economic individualism is the following: what must I do in order to optimally reach my goal under the given constraints, and under the condition that others pursue their goals? The ethical problem is: what should I want? What are reasonable preferences? The answer of ethical individualism is outlined in the *Critique of Practical Reason* by Kant, who must be considered the founder of the philosophical ethics that correspond to a market economy: 'So act that the maxim of your will could at any time serve as a principle of universal legislation.' This ethics corresponds to the structural characteristics of capitalism: individualization, autonomization, and universalization.[10] It attempts to provide a criterion, according to which it can be determined whether or not one's individual goals are compatible with those of all others. If the individual goals pass this test, then at the level of the economy as a whole the question arises: how can these goals coexist with each other?

The same objection to Kantian ethics has been made as was raised against the Pareto criterion. It is not capable of providing an answer to the basic problem of practical philosophy: what should we do? The Categorical Imperative is more a criterion of negative rejection than a procedure for the selection of goals. One cannot live without values as criteria for deliberation between alternative courses of action. But in the selection of alternative forms of action one must treat the situation for action as a whole. It is one of the basic insights of philosophy that the good cannot be expressed in a single principle or value.

The difficulty of making operationable such an ethic of the balancing of the totality of aspects puts quite a burden on the individual; however, the ability to deceive oneself as to possible relevant aspects of an issue to be decided is one of the characteristics of the immoral.

9.2.2   The need for a business ethics

W. J. Baumol asserted that the market cannot sustain a non-economic ethics and that the automatism of competition renders an ethics of business superfluous. Under the conditions of perfect competition, voluntary moral acts of a single entrepreneur – such as ecological measures, training for the handicapped, and so forth – are not desirable for Baumol since the moral entrepreneur will be thrown out of the market within a short time. According to Baumol, 'The merciless market is the consumer's best friend' (Phelps, 1975: 46). Voluntary supererogation only hurts the single businessperson. Baumol asserts that social measures should be enforced by government on all firms.

> Firms should not be all-purpose institutions, but make money for their stockholders. The notion that firms should by themselves pursue the objectives of society is, in fact, a rather frightening proposition . . . Corporate management holds in its hands enormous financial resources. I do not want management to use the capital I have entrusted to it to impose its notions of international morality on the world. (Phelps, 1975: 46–7)

Baumol's dislike of moralism in corporate management derives from an unjustified optimism about the functioning of the mechanism of competition. His position shows the fallacy of the mechanistic model. In reality, the alternatives for actions allowed by the economy are much more complex than the classical minimal cost-profit maximization model suggests. Economic practice always takes place in a social totality in which the consideration of additional aspects of economic action which transcend the model of economic man is not only moral but can be profitable as well. Moral actions can have spillovers in profits.

There is a certain irrational passion for dispassionate rationality in the economic theory of capitalism which bans any kind of moral motivation or thinking in terms of values from social science. But Sauermann and his colleagues have proven that trust reduces bargaining costs.[11] J. M. Buchanan shows that ethics substitute for direct control in large groups where this control would be costly and are designed to solve the large number dilemma (1965: 8; 1978: 364–8). General belief in ethical norms can solve the isolation paradox that each person would do (the) good if he or she knew that the others would do so too, but will not do it if s/he might be the only moral individual in the group (Sen, 1967: 112; 1973: 119). It changes the prisoner's dilemma into an assurance game. Moral codes can be interpreted as reactions of society to the compensation of market failures. Moral codes can lower transaction costs and thus leave everyone better off (Arrow, 1971: 22). So, even the mechanistic model of general market equilibrium shows the need for an ethics of capitalism and for evaluating and choosing between goals. It shows the necessity of bringing mind back in and re-embedding business into ethical and social norms.

9.3   The morality of capitalism and the limits of its justification

According to R. A. Posner, 'in a world of scarce resources, waste should be regarded as immoral' (1977: 23). Posner's statement could be read as a tautology with which everybody agrees: waste is a pejorative notion, and no one would call waste moral. In the context of positivist economics, however, this sentence stands for a tendency to regard the allocation problem as the only ethical-economic problem since ethical judgements concerning goals are considered unscientific. In this perspective, capitalism would be the most moral system since it undoubtedly solves the allocation problem with the least waste as compared to other systems.

Nevertheless, one cannot stop asking questions at the point of the allocation problem as was demonstrated in the discussion of individual ethics. For a justification of capitalism, the distribution resulting from an optimal allocation of resources must be investigated, as well as the question of whether capitalism selects or filters out certain goals in the market process. Apologists for capitalism have continually attempted to evade both questions by representing allocation and distribution as simultaneous processes (marginal productivity theory) and disputing the selectivity of the market in pointing out that everyone, according to his or her willingness to pay, could realize all of his/her goals in the market. Both arguments are correct but do not represent the whole truth. The arguments are connected. It is correct that allocation and distribution must go together, for otherwise there would be no incentives for an optimal allocation. Moreover, the positive contribution of a productive factor to the total product is one criterion of just distribution, and the consumer's willingness to pay for a given good is one measure of the intensity of preference. Goods should go to those who desire them most intensively and – because this can hardly be determined other than through willingness to pay – therefore, to those who are prepared to pay the most.

A competitive market does lead to the employment of every productive factor when it can bring forth the greatest product, measured in prices, and leads to a distribution which reflects productivity and relative scarcity. But this argument from efficiency is not a sufficient ground for the morality of the distribution which results from the remuneration according to a factor's marginal productivity. Even if the problem of economic computation could be solved, the problem of moral computation would remain. All property rights on resources, whether labour (human capital) or capital in general, arise from three sources: effort, inheritance and luck (Knight, 1969: 56). Of these, only the first source can doubtlessly be called just, the second is merely legal, and the third incommensurable with justice. Thus, the distribution which arises from these three factors cannot be considered moral in an emphatic sense, but only be considered not immoral. Scarcity rents stand for the accidental characteristics of the distribution in the market process. Certain factors are scarce, given to their owners only by an accident of nature, yet are in demand. Other factors are just as scarce but not demanded. Is this sufficient reason to justify the enormous difference in distribution between both of the owners? Hayek's (1977) and R. Nozick's (1974) approach that the distribution must be accepted as the result of a game that proceeds according to impartial rules and cannot be manipulated leaves the moralists unsatisfied and cannot even please the players. After a certain time each game requires a new dealing of the cards, a re-creation of the same initial conditions. For the game of life, which we can only play once, this must be even more true. A continual, periodic equalization of the initial positions is for reasons of efficiency not possible and criteria for such a distribution are lacking. Natural differences cannot be redistributed. But one cannot, as Nozick has suggested, disqualify every conception of end state in a theory of justice with reference to the rules of the game. That would be the capitalistic reversal of the dictum, 'let justice be done, though the world perish' (*fiat justitia ut pereat mundus*).

A purely deontological entitlement theory of justice is as abstract as a consequentialist theory of end-state justice that continually shapes society in accord with its image of end-state justice. Hegel's remark in *Philosophy of Right* on ethical principles applies to both: 'The principle of scorning the consequences of action, and the other, of judging actions by their consequences and making them the standard of what is right and good are both abstract understanding.' The unquestioned acceptance of the primary distribution which results from the market in capitalism without giving consideration to the final social effects of the economic process is no more moral than an arbitrary redistribution that is continually reshaping society and economy according to a prefabricated image of social justice.

None the less, there remains a feeling of moral dissatisfaction with the market mechanism that cannot be explained merely by the inequality of the initial distribution and, therefore, by the greater choice possibilities of inherited wealth.

That the market be moral and the point it chooses on the production possibility frontier be reasonable would require that effective demand, i.e. the preferences of consumers were moral and their knowledge perfect. No one could assert that decisions made in the market are on the whole ideal or reasonable. Too much nonsense, bad taste and superfluous luxury wins out over necessary, meaningful and beautiful goods. In addition, not only are given preferences co-ordinated and streams of factors directed through demanded production of goods, but new needs are created through the market as well. As Knight points out, 'The economic system forms, transforms, even creates wants. An examination of the ethics of the economic system must consider the question of the kind of wants which it tends to generate or nourish as well as its treatment of wants as they exist at any given time' (1969: 46). The moral guilt for many nonsensical needs is not to be borne alone by firms, which want to introduce new goods, but rather by the drive to imitation and the needs of consumers for social prestige.

It is thus rather remarkable that the proponents of economic democracy criticize the capitalist system. For if consumers are incapable of asserting their sovereignty as consumers in opposition to commercial advertising, they cannot presuppose that the choice-makers in a democracy would be able to maintain their sovereignty of choice with respect to political advertising. Also, when under certain conditions the individualism of the market leads to fallacies of composition – i.e. the fallacy that what is good for the individual is also good for the whole – then this should be true of the voting process as well. Under these conditions, nothing is to be gained by the transfer of decision-making from the market to a democratic political process. It is much more to be feared that the needs which are not fulfilled in the market (public goods, cultural goods, the environment) would not be properly considered in an ideal democratic process either (Koslowski, 1987; 1993). A good portion of the critique of capitalism is equally a critique of democracy and a critique of the inability of individuals to make reasonable use of their consumer sovereignty.

The strengths of capitalism, that it can admit of many goals and of many values insofar as they can be borne by the market and that it abandons the attempt to finalize social and economic processes, are weaknesses in the eyes of those who hold that the market does not properly deal with certain values. Criteria are not available which would tell in what order at what level values and goals should be realized by the economy. Because freedom in the first place means the ability to set goals for oneself (Kant), one must concede to the economic actors the freedom to set goals for themselves even if one knows better in which order these goals are to be realized.

However, objections must be raised against the *value agnosticism* of capitalism – to the effect that one does not have available any criteria at all. Freedom cannot be the only value which a society can further. One cannot hold an allocation mechanism for a morality which, as Malthus writes, 'denies a man a right to subsistence when his labour will not fairly purchase it'.

Capitalism, despite its successes, has such a bad reputation because it does not deliver complete and simultaneous satisfaction for everyone. Almost every group considers its own goals to be insufficiently provided for by the market system because the goals of the market system cannot be fixed by them. Farmers see their market results as being insufficient, as do artists and philosophers. That the intellectuals are especially active in the critique of capitalism is caused, as Norman (1979) has clearly shown for the English tradition of capitalism critique, by the fact that they view their goals as not being sufficiently encouraged because of the lack of mass demand. This is certainly the case for representatives of the social sciences. Capitalism with its trust in spontaneous, unplanned order offers them little opportunity for the implementation of their knowledge. In this respect capitalism contrasts with planned economies, which by definition must make the social planner the director of the economic process.

It cannot be denied, on the other hand, that capitalism also favours a certain group as far as distributional results are concerned, namely the group that fulfils best the conditions and expectations on which the economic system is based: the group of successful entrepreneurs. Nevertheless, it severely punishes the same group if it does not fulfil the system's expectations: the unsuccessful entrepreneur. Every conceivable system always favours the type that corresponds best to its definition. Planned economies favour the planner, theocratic societies the priest, and belligerent societies the military. Capitalism has here the advantage that the fulfilment of system and role expectations and, therefore, social remuneration are efficiently connected with the interests and needs of the population, i.e. with consumer demand. The consumers' possibility for exit in a competitive market and the control of profits by competition between producers assure to a certain extent that economic success and remuneration is bound to socially desirable and useful performance (Hirschman, 1970).

Against the critique of interest groups of the allocation and distribution effects of a capitalist economy, one must recall one of the oldest views of justice in the European tradition, the idea of balance and measure.[12] The theory of market failure as well as that of government failure indicates that a balance must be found between society and state, market and voting.[13] Both the market mechanism and the state show their failures. The morality of capitalism cannot consist, as Knight has shown, in introducing abstract economics as absolute ethics, i.e. in reducing all question of social and ethical values to the question of the optimal allocation of resources for satisfying given individual preferences (1966). The moral justification of capitalism consists rather in mediating many goals and their pursuit by individuals in such a way as to preserve moral and economic freedom without a war of all against all. That which the individual and society takes to be preferred can only be reached by the market through a compromise between what the individual takes to be important and what all others take to be important. A compromise is all that can be reached when individual pursuit of goals is allowed. Competition in the market is a kind of institutionalized civil war. But the terror of the social determination of goals by one group seems to be the alternative to competition in advanced societies because, as historical experience shows, only through terror can a society which has experienced freedom be sworn to a particular goal. This is shown by the experience of Eastern European planned economies.

9.4   Some social-philosophical conclusions

A purely capitalistic society, built exclusively upon private property, maximization of profit, and co-ordination by way of a market and price system, has yet to become a reality. As a societal model, capitalism is a social utopia. Its utopian character always becomes evident when its defenders seek to immunize opponents' objections with the incompleteness argument, i.e. by pointing out that it has never been realized in its pure form and that its shortcomings can always be traced to exogenous influences. Such a procedure is not justifiable from an ethical standpoint. A social theory must adjust itself to reality.

As a theory of society, capitalism cannot suffice because it is essentially an economic theory of production, exchange and co-ordination. As an economic theory, it must neglect essential aspects of social action and political integration. In this chapter, these omissions have been exhibited above all in the assumption of given preferences in economic theory but also in the limits to the principle of co-ordination by the market. In both cases, the cause is to be found in an exaggerated individualism and subjectivism, which assumes one can neglect the social mediation of one's preferences and the obligation to have reasonable preferences for the sake of individual freedom of choice. By making freedom and efficiency the sole guiding values in its ideal of co-ordination, the theory of capitalism evades the problem of comparing goods and gains its most impressive comprehensiveness in general equilibrium analysis. The problem of weighing goods against one another cannot be avoided. This was already seen with the necessity of weighing efficiency against freedom in the selection of allocation mechanisms.

The necessity of comparing goods also turns up in the preference formation of the individual, which cannot be regarded as a black box from which factual preferences pass into actions of choice. Preference formation gains significance when with increasing social wealth and material satiation the production problem becomes less urgent.[14] This satiation also demonstrates the limitation of a concept of freedom that understands freedom merely as freedom of choice between the greatest number of possibilities. A growing supply of goods shows that one does not feel freer when one has greater possibilities of choice among goods, but rather that the marginal utility of freedom of choice also is decreasing.

Against this conception of economic freedom it must be stressed that freedom primarily means the ability to act according to self-chosen purposes, and that the choice of these purposes or the formation of preferences must be understood as a self-choice, i.e. a decision about one's own being and personality.[15] It follows that the concentration of economic theory upon consumption and consumption decision as the purpose of human and, in particular, economic action is one-sided because the personality forms itself essentially in its action, not in its consumption. This means that an examination of the extent to which the constitution of an economy admits free action and self-realization cannot be based merely on freedom of consumption. The indubitable superiority of the market as a means of co-ordination manifests itself here in that it permits individual pursuit of goals and self-responsible action to a greater extent than all other forms of co-ordination, in that the market permits not only freedom of consumption, but also freedom of action.

It also turns out that maximization of profit and benefits as an economic motive, and free disposition of private property, assume a characteristic abstractness when they lay claim to unlimited social validity. The maximization of profit and benefits can only be admitted as motives under constraints; otherwise they reduce the wealth of human motivation to abstractions of rationality and ignore the social embeddedness of the pursuit of goals. The same is true of rights of disposition over private property. The co-ordination of individual actions in capitalism must occur within a social framework which the conditions of this co-ordination – private property, maximization of profit and utility, and the market system – do not adequately determine, but rather presuppose.[16]

The limits of capitalism as a social theory are that the co-ordination does not comprise the whole, that the medium is not the message, and that the form of economic action does not fully comprise the substance of one's social action. As a social theory, capitalism is *materially underdetermined* and incomplete. It must be complemented by a comprehensive social-philosophical theory concerning the framework within which capitalism can activate its advantage as a method of co-ordination, by a theory of the social genesis and normative justification of preference formation (social psychology and ethics), by a theory of the social institutions of which this framework consists (family, church, state), and by a theory of political compensation for capitalism's failures.

The necessity of such a framework becomes evident in the dialectic proper to the three structural characteristics of capitalism. In all three characteristics a transformation from quantity into quality and from form into a content is observable.

The unlimited accumulation of private property leads, beyond a certain point of control over a market, to a qualitative jump and to a problem of power. Unlimited pursuit of profits and benefits leads to a transformation into greed, miserliness and a loss in the wealth of human purposes. The co-ordination of production and the assignment of social status exclusively by way of market success, i.e. successful anticipation of demand and willingness to pay, leads to an exaggerated subjectivism and the neglect of more substantial purposes.

The form of co-ordination by way of property, maximization of profits, and the market cannot be the content of the social order and individual action, no more so than this form can be abandoned if freedom and efficiency in the economy are to be secured. The theory of capitalism requires a complement from social philosophy and a reminder that reasonable preferences must enter into the co-ordination. It also needs the reminder that capitalism lives from its ethos of freedom and work, which as a form of economic co-ordination it alone cannot bring forth and preserve. An ideal of co-ordination alone cannot do justice to our need for substantial life forms, just as, on the other hand, our need for the recognition of our subjectivity and freedom, in the economy as well, requires the capitalist form of co-ordination.

Notes

This chapter is an edited version of a contribution which appeared in *Economic and Moral Foundations of Capitalism*, edited by Steve Pejovich (1983), Lexington Books, Lexington, MA.

1. Compare from the German neoliberal tradition Röpke (1949) and Rustow (1945); recently Bell (1976). The crisis of capitalism is not caused, as Bell shows, by economic

inefficiency or the superiority of other systems but by the crisis of cultural and ethical integration in the Western world.

2. This chapter's concept of morality follows the reinterpretation of natural right which has been suggested by Robert Spaemann (1980: 39–40) most recently.

3. Compare Rowley and Peacock (1975) and Dupuy (1978).

4. See Buchanan (1969: 62–4).

5. Knight asserts: 'The assumption that wants or ends are data reduces life to economics and raises again the question with which we started out: Is life all economics or does this view require supplementing by an ethical view of value?' (1935b: 34–5). Similarly, decision theory does not tell the decision-maker what to prefer but what to choose under given preferences. According to Stegmüller, 'Normative decision theory is not an ethics' (1973: 325). Thus, decision theory cannot give, in general, effective advice for the selection between alternatives but mostly tells the decision-maker only more precisely what he or she already knew.

6. Plato, *Gorgias* 464c.

7. According to Knight, symbolic interactionism 'offers much greater possibilities for throwing light on behavior than does the science of behaviorism' (1969: 129).

8. See Knight (1947: 4, 372).

9. See W. Röpke (1949: 280).

10. Kant had a thorough knowledge of Adam Smith's work and a high esteem for his theory (Koslowski, 1981: ch. 5). The structural similarities between Kant's and Smith's theories were stressed and criticized by the German conservative Friedrich Julius Stahl (1802–1861), *Die Philosophie des Rechts*, 5 vols., 1878 (reprint Darmstadt 1963). In vol. 2, p. 100 he sees in Smithsonian economics the 'analogon of Kantian social philosophy'.

11. See review article by Albach (1980: 3).

12. See K. v. Fritz, *The Theory of the Mixed Constitution in Antiquity* (New York: Columbia University Press, 1954), p. 490.

13. The dualism of state and society is a structural constant of European societies since the Greek *polis*. Compare Koslowski (1982).

14. The excellent books by Hirsch (1976) and Scitovsky (1976) demonstrate the insufficiency of traditional microeconomic theory upon the analysis of preference formation and the satisfaction of needs and, thereby, show the limits of its suitability for policy recommendations, especially for those concerning economic growth policy.

15. See F. W. J. Schelling, *Philosophische Untersuchungen über das Wesen der menschlichen Freiheit* (1809), ed. W. Schulz (Frankfurt, 1975), p. 77; Krings (1980: 15–39).

16. Nell-Breuning aptly criticizes the theory of the market economy in that 'more and more, problems are pushed into the so-called data wreath, the framework, and consequently the data wreath ultimately becomes that which is most interesting' (1955: 111).

References

Albach, H. (1980). 'Vertrauen in der ökonomischen Theorie', *Zeitschrift fur die gesamte Staatswissenschaft* 136, no. 1; 3.

Alchian, A. A., (ed.) (1977). *Economic Forces at Work*, pp. 15–36. Indianapolis: Liberty Press.

Alchian, A. A., and Demsetz, H. (1977). 'Production, information costs and economic organization', in *Economic Forces at Work*, edited by A. A. Alchian, pp. 73–110. Indianapolis: Liberty Press.

Arrow, K. J. (1967). 'Public and Private Values', in *Human Values and Economic Policy*, edited by S. Hook. New York: New York University Press.

Arrow, K. J. (1971). 'Political and economic evaluation of social effects and externalities,' in *Frontiers of Quantitative Economics*, edited by M. D. Intriligator. Amsterdam: North-Holland.

Banfield, E. C. (1958). *The Moral Basis of a Backward Society*. Glencoe, Ill.: The Free Press.

Baumol, W. J. (1975). 'Business responsibility and economic behavior', in *Altruism, Morality and Economic Theory*, edited by E. S. Phelps. New York: Sage Foundation.

Becker, Gary (1974). 'A theory of social interactions', *Journal of Political Economy* 82.

Bell, D. (1976). *The Cultural Contradictions of Capitalism*. New York: Basic Books.

Böhm-Bawerk, E. v. (1884). *Kapital and Kapitalzins*. Vol. 1., *Geschichte und Kritik der Kapitalzinstheorien*. Innsbruck.

Bonar, J. (1909). *Philosophy and Political Economy in Some of Their Historical Relations*. 1893. Reprint. London: S. Sonnenschein.

Boulding, K. E. (1967). 'The basis of value judgements in economics', in *Human Values and Economic Policy*, edited by S. Hook, pp. 55–72. New York: New York University Press.

Boulding, K. E. (1969). 'Economics as a moral science', *American Economic Review* 59.

Brunner, Otto. (1950). 'Die alteuropäische Ökonomik', *Zeitschrift für Nationalökonomie* 13.

Buchanan, James M. (1954a). 'Social choice, democracy, and free markets', *Journal of Political Economy* 62: 114–23.

Buchanan, James M. (1954b). 'Individual choice in voting and the market', *Journal of Political Economy* 62: 334–43.

Buchanan, James M. (1964). 'What should economists do?' *Southern Economic Journal* 30: 213–22.

Buchanan, James M. (1965). 'Ethical rules, expected values, and large numbers'. *Ethics* 76: 1–13.

Buchanan, James M. (1969). 'Is economics the science of choice?', in *Roads to Freedom: Essays in Honour of Friedrich A. von Hayek*, edited by E. Streissler. New York: A. M. Kelly.

Buchanan, James M. (1978). 'Markets, states, and the extent of morals', *American Economic Review* 68: 364–8.

Buchanan, James M., and Tullock, G. (1974). *The Calculus of Consent*. 5th edn. Ann Arbor: University of Michigan Press.

Churchman, C. W. (1961). *Prediction and Optimal Decision, Philosophical Issues of a Science of Values*. Englewood Cliffs, N.J.: Prentice-Hall.

Coase, R. H. (1960). 'The problem of social cost', *Journal of Law & Economics* 3: 1–44.

Döllinger, I. v., and Reusch, Fr. H. (1889). *Geschichte der Moralstreitigkeiten in der römisch-katholischen Kirche*. Nördlingen: C. H. Beck.

Dumont, L. (1977). *From Mandeville to Marx: The Genesis and Triumph of Economic Ideology*. Chicago: University of Chicago Press.

Dupuy, J. P. (1978). 'L'economie de la morale, ou la morale de l'economie', *Revue d'Economie Politique* 88: 404–39.

Foster, G. M. (1965). 'Peasant society and the image of limited good', *American Anthropologist* 67: 293.

Freyer, H. (1966). *Die Bewertung der Wirtschaft im philosophischen Denken des 19. Jahrhunderts*. 1921. Reprint. Hildescheim: Olms.

Hayek, F. A. von (1968). *Der Wettbewerb als Entdeckungsverfahren*. Kiel: Institut für Weltwirtschaft.

Hayek, F. A. von (1969). *Freiburger Studien*. Walter Eucken Institut (Hrsg.), Wirtschafts-wissenschaftliche und wirtschaftsrechtliche Untersuchungen 5. Tübingen: J. C. B. Mohr (Paul Siebeck).

Hayek, F. A. von (1977). *Drei Vorlesungen über Demokratie, Gerechtigkeit und Sozialismus*. Walter Eucken Institut (Hrsg.), Vorträge and Aufstäze 63, Tübingen: J. C. B. Mohr (Paul Siebeck).

Hegel, Georg Wilhelm Friedrich. *Philosophy of Right*, translated with notes by T. M. Knox. Chicago, Ill.: Encyclopedia Britannica.

Hirsch F. (1976). *Social Limits to Growth*. Cambridge, MA: Harvard University Press.

Hirschman, A. O. (1970). *Exit, Voice, and Loyalty: Responses to Decline in Firms, Organizations, and States*. Cambridge, MA: Harvard University Press.

Hirschman, A. O. (1977). *The Passions and the Interests: Political Arguments for Capitalism before its Triumph*. Princeton, N.J.: Princeton University Press.

Hirshleifer, J. (1978). 'Competition, cooperation, and conflict in economics and biology', *American Economic Review* 68: 238.

Hook, S., (ed.) (1967). *Human Values and Economic Policy*. New York: New York University Press.

Hutchison, T. W. (1979). 'Notes on the effects of economic ideas on policy: the example of the German social market economy', *ZgG* 135: 433.

Johnson, P. (1979). 'Is there a moral basis for capitalism? Dissenting thoughts in a collectivist age', *Encounter* (October): 15–25.

Junger, E. (1952). *Der Waldgang*. Frankfurt: Klostermann

Kant, I. (1898). *Critique of Practical Reason*, p. 368. London: Longmans, Green & Co.

Knight, F. H. (1947). *Freedom and Reform*. New York: Harper.

Knight, F. H. (1966). 'Abstract economics as absolute ethics', *Ethics* 76: 163–77.

Knight, F. H. (1969). *The Ethics of Competition and Other Essays*. 1935. Reprint. Freeport, N.Y.: Books for Libraries Press.

Knoll, A. M. (1967). *Zins und Gnade. Zur Zins-und Gnadenkontroverse der Dominikaner und Jesuiten, Lutheraner und Calvinisten*. Neuwied: Luchterhand.

Koslowski, Peter I. (1979a). 'Haus und Geld, zur aristotelischen Unterscheidung von Politik, ökonomik and Chrematistik', *Philosophisches Jahrbuch* 86: 60–83.

Koslowski, Peter I. (1979b). *Zum Verhältnis von Polis and Oikos bei Aristoteles, Politik und Ökonomie bei Aristoteles*. 2nd ed. Straubing: Donau. 3rd ed. Tübingen: J. C. B. Mohr (Paul Siebeck) 1993.

Koslowski, Peter I. (1982). *Gesellschaft und Staat. Ein unvermeidlicher Dualismus*. Stuttgart: Klett-Cotta.

Koslowski, Peter I. (1987). 'Market and democracy as discourses. Limits to discoursive social coordination', in *Individual Liberty and Democratic Decision-Making. The ethics, economics and politics of democracy*. Tübingen: J. C. B. Mohr (Paul Siebeck).

Koslowski, Peter I. (1989). *Prinzipien der ethischen Ökonomie. Grundlegung der Ethik und der auf die Ökonomie bezogenen Ethik*. Tübingen: J. C. B. Mohr (Paul Siebeck).

Koslowski, Peter I. (1991). *Gesellschaftliche Koordination. Eine ontologische und kultur-wissenschaftliche Theorie der Marktwirtschaft*. Tübingen: J. C. B. Mohr (Paul Siebeck).

Koslowski, Peter I. (1993). *Die Ordnung der Wirtschaft. Studien fur Praktischen Philosophie und Politischen Ökonomie*. Tübingen: J. C. B. Mohr (Paul Siebeck).

Koslowski, Peter I. (ed.): *Ethics in Economics, Business, and Economic Policy*, Berlin, New York, Tokyo: Springer 1992 (= Studies in Economic Ethics and Philosophy; Vol. 1).

Koslowski, Peter I., Yuichi Shionoya (eds.): *The Good and the Economical*. New York, Berlin, Tokyo: Springer 1992 (= Studies in Economic Ethics and Philosophy; Vol. 4).

Krings, H. (1980). *System und Freiheit. Gesammelte Aufsätze*. Freiburg: Alber.

Kromphardt, J. (1980). *Konzeptionen und Analysen des Kapitalismus*. Göttingen: Vandenhoeck.

Luhmann, N. (1977). *Zweckbegriff und Systemrationalität. Über die Funktion von Zwecken in sozialen Systemen*. 2nd edn. Frankfurt: Suhrkamp.

MacPherson, C. B. (1962). *The Political Theory of Possessive Individualism: Hobbes to Locke*. London: Oxford University Press.

Macrae, N. (1981). 'Für eine Welt individueller Lebensstile', in *Fortschritt ohne Maß? Eine Ortsbestimmung der wissenschaftlich-technischen Zivilization*, edited by R. Löw, P. Koslowski, and P. Kreuzer, pp. 213–33. Munich: Piper.

Marshak, J. (1974). *Economic Information, Decision and Prediction*, vol. 2, pp. 193–9. Dordrecht: Reidel.

Mises, L. von (1949). *Human Action*. New Haven: Yale University Press.

Nell-Breuning, O. v. (1955). 'Neoliberalismus und Katholische Soziallehre', in *Der Christ und die soziale Marktwirtschaft*, edited by P. M. Boarmann. Stuttgart: Kohlhammer.

Nell-Breuning, O. v. (1974). *Kapitalismus-kritisch betrachtet*. Freiburg: Herder

Norman, Edward R. (1979). 'Denigration of Capitalism', in *The Denigration of Capitalism: Six Points of View*, edited by M. Novack, pp. 7–23. Washington, D.C.: American Enterprise Institute.

Novack, M., ed. (1979). The Denigration of Capitalism: Six Points of View. Washington, D.C.: American Enterprise Institute.

Nozick, R. (1974). *Anarchy, State, and Utopia*. Oxford: Basil Blackwell.

Passow, R. (1927). *Kapitalismus, Eine begrifflich-terminologische Studie*. Jena: Fisher.

Phelps, E. S., ed. (1975). *Altruism, Morality and Economic Theory*. New York: Sage Foundation.

Polanyi, K. (1971). *Primitive, Archaic and Modern Economies*. Boston: Beacon Press.

Posner, R. A. (1977). *Economic Analysis of Law*. Boston: Little, Brown.

Röpke, J. (1970). *Primitive Wirtschaft, Kulturwandel und die Diffusion von Neuerungen*. Tübingen: J. C. B. Mohr (Paul Siebeck).

Röpke, W. (1949). *Civitas Humana: Grundfragen der Gesellschafts-und Wirtschaftsreform*. Erlenbach-Zürich: Rentsch.

Roscher, W. (1874). *Geschichte der Nationalökonomik in Deutschland*. Munich: Oldenbourg.

Rowley, C. K., and Peacock, A. T. (1975). *Welfare Economics: A Liberal Restatement*. London: Martin Robertson.

Rüstow, A. (1945). *Das Versagen des Wirtschaftsliberalismus als religions-geschichtliches Problem*. Zürich and New York: Europa Verlag.

Sahlins, M. D. (1965). 'Exchange-value and the diplomacy of primitive trade', in *Essays in Economic Anthropology: Dedicated to the Memory of Karl Polanyi*. Seattle: University of Washington Press.

Salin, Edgar. (1967). *Politische Ökonomie*. Tübingen: J. C. B. Mohr (Paul Siebeck).

Sauermann, Heinz, ed. (1978). *Bargaining Behavior*, p. 383. Tübingen: Mohr.

Schall, J. V. (1979). 'Religion and the demise of capitalism', in *The Denigration of Capitalism: Six Points of View*, edited by M. Novack, pp. 32–8. Washington, D.C.: American Enterprise Institute.

Scheler, Max. (1966). *Der Formalismus in der Ethik und die materiale Wertethik*. 5th edn. Bern: Francke.

Schumacher, E. F. (1973). *Small Is Beautiful*. London: Blond and Briggs.

Schumpeter, J. A. (1955). *History of Economic Analysis*. 5th edn. London: Allen & Unwin.

Scitovsky, T. (1976). *The Joyless Economy*. London: Oxford University Press.

Sen, A. (1967). 'Isolation, assurance and the social rate of discount', *Quarterly Journal of Economics* 81: 112–24.

Sen, A. (1973). *On Economic Inequality*. Oxford: Clarendon Press.

Shackle, G. L. S. (1972). *Epistemics and Economics: A Critique of Economic Doctrines*. Cambridge: Cambridge University Press.

Simon, H. A. (1978). 'Rationality as process and as product of thought', *American Economic Review* 68: 1–15.

Singer, K. (1958). 'Oikonomia: an inquiry into beginnings of economic thought and language', *Kyklos* 11: 29–57.

Sombart, W. (1938). *Weltanschauung, Wissenschaft und Wirtschaft*. Berlin: Buchholz and Weisswange.

Spaemann, Robert. (1977). 'Nebenwirkungen als moralisches Problem', in *Zur Kritik der politischen Utopie*, edited by R. Spaemann. Stuttgart: Klett.

Spaemann, Robert. (1980). 'Christentum und Kernkraft. Ethische Aspekte der Energiepolitik', *Die Politische Meinung* 192.

Stegmüller, W. (1973). *Probleme und Resultate der Wissenschaftstheorie und Analytischen Philosophie. Personelle und statistische Wahrscheinlichkeit. I. Halbbd.: Personelle Wahrscheinlichkeit und rationale Entscheidung*. Berlin: Springer.

Strauss, L. (1953). *Natural Right and History*. Chicago: University of Chicago Press.

Tawney, R. H. (1937). *Religion and the Rise of Capitalism*. 2nd edn. London: John Murray.

Troeltschy, E. (1923). *Die Soziallehren der christlichen Kirchen and Gruppen*. Tübingen: J. C. B. Mohr (Paul Siebeck).

Viner, J. (1972). *The Role of Providence in the Social Order: An Essay in Intellectual History*. Philadelphia: American Philosophical Society.

Wagner, F. (1969). *Das Bild der frühen Ökonomik*. Salzburg: Stifterbibliothek.

Weber, Max. (1972). *Wirtschaft und Gesellschaft*. 5th edn. Tübingen: J. C. B. Mohr (Paul Siebeck).

Weber, Max. (1979). *Die protestantische Ethik und der Geist des Kapitalismus*. Gütersloh: Mohn.

Weisskopf, W. A. (1971). *Alienation and Economics*. New York: Dutton.

Williamson, O. E. (1977). 'Firms and markets', in *Modern Economic Thought*, edited by S. Weintraub. Philadelphia: University of Pennsylvania Press.

Williamson, O. E. (1981). 'The modern corporation: origins, evolution, attributes', *Journal of Economic Literature* 19: 1537–70.

Index